CUET-UG

Commerce

15
Solved Papers

5 Accountancy | 5 Business Studies | 5 Economics

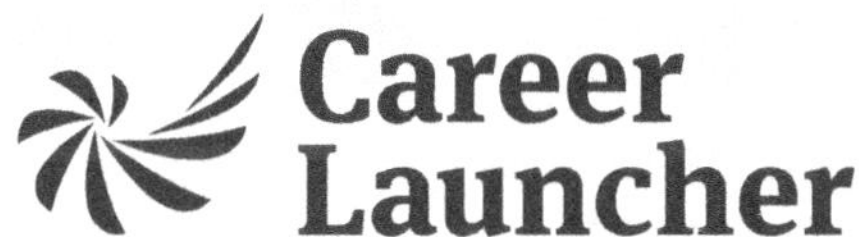

Title   : **CUET - UG :** Commerce - 15 Solved Papers

Language   : English

Editor's Name : AMIT SINGH

Copyright ©   : 2023 CLIP

No part of this book may be reproduced in a retrieval system or transmitted, in any form or by any means, electronics, mechanical, photocopying, recording, scanning and or without the written permission of the Author/Publisher.

Typeset & Published by :

Career Launcher Infrastructure (P) Ltd.

A-45, Mohan Cooperative Industrial Area, Near Mohan Estate Metro Station, New Delhi - 110044

Marketed by :

G.K. Publications (P) Ltd.

Plot No. 9A, Sector-27A, Mathura Road, Faridabad, Haryana-121003

ISBN   : **978-93-5681-124-9**

Printer's Details : Printed in India, New Delhi.

For product information :

Visit **www.gkpublications.com** or email to **gkp@gkpublications.com**

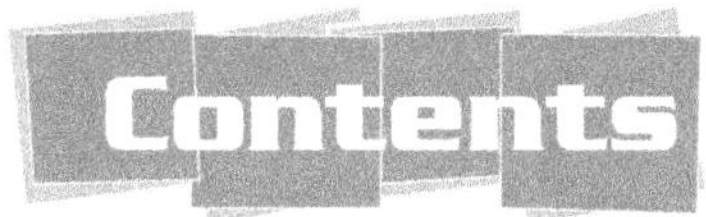

ACCOUNTANCY

BUSINESS STUDIES

ECONOMICS

CUET EXAM PATTERN 2023

Sections	Subjects/ Tests	No. of Questions	To be Attempted	Duration
Section IA	13 Languages	50	40 in each language	45 minutes for each language
Section IB	19 Languages			
Section II	27 Domain-specific Subjects	50	40	45 minutes for each subject
Section III	General Test	75	60	60 minutes

CUET 2023 EXAM STRUCTURE - SLOT 1

Test/Subjects	No. of questions to be attempted	Marks per question	Total marks	Duration of exam
Language (any one of the 13 languages opted in Section IA)	40 out of 50	5	200	45 minutes per language
Domain Specific Subjects (Max. 2 subjects)	40 out of 50	5	200	45 minutes per subject
General Test	60 out of 75	5	300	60 minutes

CUET TEST STRUCTURE 2023 - SLOT 2

Test/Subjects	No. of questions to be attempted	Marks per question	Total marks	Duration of exam
Language (any one of the remaining 12 languages opted in Section IA (if one already taken in slot 1) and 1 from Section IB - as applicable)	40 out of 50	5	200	45 minutes per language
Domain Specific Subjects (Max. 4 subjects)	40 out of 50	5	200	45 minutes per subject

CUET 2023 MARKING SCHEME

Correct Answer	5 marks will be awarded to students
Incorrect Answer	One mark will be deducted
No Answer	0 marks will be awarded

ACCOUNTANCY

CUET

SOLVED PAPER-1
Accountancy

20 July 2022 (Slot-1)

---

1. A firm earns a profit in last three years as follows:

2020 - 21	Rs. 75,000
2019 - 20	Rs. 1,20,000
2018-19	Rs. 50,000

Additional Information:

Closing stock of 2020 - 21 was undervalued by Rs. 10,000.

Calculate the Average Profit.

(a) Rs. 55,000   (b) Rs. 75,000

(c) Rs. 45,000   (d) Rs. 85,000

2. Identify the right combination of type of Account in making Final Accounts of Partnership Firm.

A. Profit and Loss A/c

B. Profit and Loss Suspense A/c

C. Profit and Loss Appropriation A/c

D. Profit and Loss Adjustment A/c

E. Partner's Capital A/c

Choose the correct answer from the options given below:

(a) A, B, D only

(b) A, C, E only

(c) A, D, E only

(d) B, C, D only

3. Interest on drawings of a partner has been calculated Rs. 3,000 @ 8% p.a. who has drawn equal amount in each quarter; commencing from end of the first quarter throughout the year. The amount of drawing of partner per quarter would be:

(a) 25,000   (b) 1,00,000

(c) 60,000   (d) 15,000

4. Match **List - I** with **List - II**.

	List - I		List - II
A.	Building undervalued	I.	Credited to Partner's Capital Account
B.	Building overvalued	II.	Credited to Revaluation Account
C.	Capital withdrawn	III.	Debited to Revaluation Account
D.	Additional capital introduced	IV.	Debited to Partner's Capital Account

Choose the correct answer from the options given below:

(a) A-II, B-III, C-IV, D-I

(b) A-II, B-IV, C-III, D-I

(c) A-I, B-II, C-IV, D-III

(d) A-II, B-I, C-IV, D-III

5. If average capital employed in a firm is Rs. 15,00,000 and fair rate of return in the same industry was 8%. Goodwill was valued at Rs. 90,000 on the basis of three times of super profit. The Average Profit of the firm is?

(a) Rs. 2,50,000

(b) Rs. 50,000

(c) Rs. 90,000

(d) Rs. 1,50,000

6. A and B are partners sharing profits in the ratio of 5 : 4. C is admitted as a partner and he acquires 25% of his share from A. B surrenders 1/4th from his share in favour of C. Calculate C's share in profit.

(a) $\dfrac{3}{16}$ (b) $\dfrac{14}{36}$

(c) $\dfrac{1}{3}$ (d) $\dfrac{1}{12}$

7. From the following information, identify when goodwill is required to be calculated.

A. Admission of a Partner

B. Amalgamation of partnership firms

C. Dissolution of partnership firm

D. Retirement and Death of any partner

E. Preparation of Balance sheet

Choose the correct answer from the options given below:

(a) A, C, D only

(b) A, D, E only

(c) A, B, D only

(d) B, C, D only

8. At the time of admission of a partner, if nothing is specified then new partner acquires his share from old partners.

(a) In New Profit Sharing Ratio

(b) In Old Profit Sharing Ratio

(c) In Gaining Ratio

(d) In Sacrificing Ratio

9. Identify the statement that is/are not true from the following.

A. Shares can be forfeited for non payment of call money.

B. The profit on forfeited shares is transferred to capital reserve.

C. Balance of share forfeiture account is shown is the balance sheet under reserves and surplus.

D. Application money should be at least 10% of the face value of the share.

Choose the correct answer from the options given below:

(a) A only   (b) C only

(c) C, D only   (d) B, D only

10. PQR Ltd. issued 40,000 Equity shares of Rs. 10 each at par payable Rs. 3 on application, Rs. 4 on allotment and balance on first and final call. Application were received for 1,10,000 shares. Applications for 20,000 shares were refused and allotment was made prorate to remaining applicants. Amount received on allotment is:

(a) Rs. 1,00,000   (b) Nil

(c) Rs. 10,000   (d) Rs. 80,000

11. Arrange the following steps as per the procedure of issue of shares:

A. Receipt of applications

B. Allotment of shares

C. Reissue of forfeited shares

D. Issue of prospectus

E. Forfeiture of shares

Choose the correct answer from the options given below:

(a) A, B, C, D, E

(b) B, A, D, C, E

(c) D, A, B, E, C

(d) A, B, E, D, C

12. Match **List - I** with **List - II**.

List - I		List - II
A.	The portion of authorised capital of a company which can be called during winding up	I.	Other current liabilities
B.	Excess of share forfeited amount over the loss on reissue	II.	Reserve Capital

C. Calls-in-advance   III. Capital Reserve
is shown in Balance
sheet under the head __

D. Equity shares   IV. Discount
cannot be issued to
public at ___

Choose the correct answer from the options given below:

(a) A-I, B-II, C-III, D-IV

(b) A-II, B-IV, C-III, D-I

(c) A-II, B-III, C-I, D-IV

(d) A-III, B-I, C-IV, D-II

13. MNO Ltd. forfeited 1,000 shares of Rs. 10 each on which shareholders had paid only application money of Rs. 3 per share. Out of these, 400 equity shares were reissued as fully paid for Rs. 9 per share. The gain on reissue of shares transferred to Capital reserve is:

(a) Rs. 3,000   (b) Rs. 800

(c) Rs. 1,200   (d) Rs. 1,000

14. Identify the items NOT be shown under Investing Activities while making Cash Flow statement.

A. Proposed Dividend

B. Purchase of non-current Investments

C. Interest paid on long term borrowings

D. Sale of machinery

E. Marketable securities

Choose the most appropriate answer from the options given below:

(a) A, B, C only   (b) A, C, E only

(c) B, D, E only   (d) B, C, E only

15. Match **List- I** with **List- II**.

List - I

A. Working Capital Turnover Ratio

B. Acid Test Ratio

C. Operating Profit Ratio

D. Trade Payables Turnover Ratio

List - II

I. $\dfrac{\text{Quick Assets}}{\text{Current liabilities}}$

II. $\dfrac{\text{Operating Profit}}{\text{Rev. from operations}} \times 100$

III. $\dfrac{\text{Revenue from operation}}{\text{Working capital}}$

IV. $\dfrac{\text{Net Credit Revenue from operation}}{\text{Average Trade payables}}$

Choose the correct answer from the options given below:

(a) A-III, B-I, C-II, D-IV

(b) A-I, B-II, C-III, D-IV

(c) A-IV, B-III, C-II, D-I

(d) A-I, B-III, C-IV, D-II

16. Calculate Current Ratio from the following given information.

Liquid Ratio 0.75 : 1

Current Liabilities Rs. 1,80,000

Prepaid Expenses Rs. 20,000

Inventory Rs. 47,250

(a) 2 : 1

(b) 1.25 : 1

(c) 0.38 : 1

(d) 1.12 : 1

17. Payment made for stationary during the year 2021 - 22 is Rs. 46,000.

Stock of stationary as on 1-4-2021 Rs. 8,000

Stock of stationary as on 31-3-2022 Rs. 6,000

Advance for stationary as on 1-4-2021 Rs. 18,000

Advance for stationary as on 31-3-2022 Rs. 5,000

What will be the amount of stationary consumed during the year 2021-22?

(a) Rs. 61,000

(b) Rs. 59,000

(c) Rs. 48,000

(d) Rs. 33,000

18. The closing balance of Receipts and Payments Account depicts _______.

(a) Loss

(b) Profit

(c) Balance of Cash and Bank

(d) Capital fund

19. Income and Expenditure Account is prepared on (A) _______ basis, while Receipts and Payments Account is prepared on (B) _______ basis.

(a) (A) Cash (B) Accrual

(b) (A) Cash (B) Credit

(c) (A) Accrual (B) Cash

(d) (A) Permanent (B) Temporary

20. Match **List - I** with **List - II**.

List - I	**List - II**
A. Honorarium	I. Asset side of balance sheet
B. Life Membership Fees	II. Credited to Income and Expenditure Account
C. General Donations	III. Debited to Income and Expenditure Account
D. Outstanding subscription	IV. Credited to Capital Fund

Choose the correct answer from the options given below:

(a) A-III, B-IV, C-II, D-I

(b) A-III, B-I, C-II, D-IV

(c) A-II, B-IV, C-III, D-I

(d) A-IV, B-I, C-II, D-III

21. The Receipts and Payments Account of Lead Sports Club showed payment for sports materials as Rs. 46,000 for the year ended 31ˢᵗ March 2022.

Additional Information provided is as follows:

Details	31ˢᵗ March 2021	31ˢᵗ March 2022
Stock of sports Materials	Rs. 8,000	Rs. 6,000
Creditors	Rs. 18,000	Rs. 5,000

Calculate the amount of Sports Materials consumed during the year ended 31ˢᵗ March 2022.

(a) Rs. 48,000

(b) Rs. 35,000

(c) Rs. 57,000

(d) Rs. 46,000

22. A, B and C were partners sharing profits and losses in the ratio of 3 : 2 : 1. C died on 1ˢᵗ August, 2022 and his share of profit from the beginning of the accounting year upto the date of death amounted to Rs. 70,000. C's share of profit will be debited to:

(a) Profit and Loss Account

(b) Profit and Loss Adjustment Account

(c) Profit and Loss Appropriation Account

(d) Profit and Loss Suspense Account

23. At the time of retirement of a Partner if retiring Partner's whole amount is treated as loan, then the total amount is Debited is:

(a) Retiring Partner's loan A/c

(b) Retiring Partner's capital A/c

(c) Retiring Partner's current A/c

(d) Bank A/c

24. Monu, Sonu and Golu are partners in a firm sharing profits in the ratio of 2 : 2 : 1. Golu died on 5th November 2021. Under the partnership deed, the executors of the deceased partner are entitled to his share of profit to the date of death, calculated on the basis of last year's profit. Profit for the year ended 31st March 2022 was Rs. 3,00,000. Golu's share of profit will be:

(a) Rs. 1,80,000   (b) Rs. 60,000

(c) Rs. 36,000   (d) Rs. 3,00,000

25. On the death of a partner, his share in the loss of the firm till the date of his death is transferred to:

(a) Debit side of P and L A/c

(b) Credit side of P and L Suspense A/c

(c) Debit side of P and L Suspense A/c

(d) Credit side of P and L A/c

26. In the balance sheet Total Debtors appear at Rs. 1,50,000 and provision for doubtful debts appear at Rs. 1,500. How much amount will be realised from debtors, if bad debts amounted to Rs. 20,000 and remaining debtors realised at a discount of 15%?

(a) Rs. 1,27,500

(b) Rs. 1,10,500

(c) Rs. 1,20,075

(d) Rs. 19,500

27. A firm may not be dissolved by court in the following condition:

(a) When a partner becomes permanently incapable of performing his duties as a partner.

(b) When a partner is guilty of misconduct which is likely to adversely affect the business of the firm.

(c) When a partner persistently commits breach of partnership agreement.

(d) When all the partner give their consent for dissolution.

28. On the dissolution of the partnership firm the amount realised from sale of assets shall be applied in following order.

A. Distributing the amount left among the partners in their profit sharing ratio

B. Paying amount due to partner on account of loan advanced by him

C. Paying amount due to the creditors

D. Paying partner's capital account balances

Choose the correct answer from the options given below:

(a) B, D, A, C   (b) C, B, D, A

(c) A, B, C, D   (d) B, A, D, C

29. The following journal entry is recorded in the books of RST Ltd. on issue of debentures:

Bank a/c Dr	18,00,000	
Loss on issue of	6,00,000	
Debentures a/c Dr		
To 14% Debentures		20,00,000
To Premium on		
Redemption of Debentures		40,000

Debentures have been issued at a discount of:

(a) 5%   (b) 10%

(c) 15%   (d) 30%

30. If a share of Rs. 100 on which Rs. 45 has been paid is forfeited at what minimum price can it be reissued:

(a) Rs. 75   (b) Rs. 45

(c) Rs. 55   (d) Rs. 100

31. Make the right combination of the ratios that enables to find the short term liquidity.

A. Return on Equity

B. Acid Test Ratio

C. Current Ratio

D. Sacrificing Ratio

E. Inventory Turnover Ratio

Choose the most appropriate answer from the options given below:

(a) A and B only

(b) B and D only

(c) C and D only

(d) B and C only

32. On 1st April 2020, the balance of furniture of ABC Ltd. was Rs. 20,000. During the year furniture costing Rs. 4,000 was sold at a gain of Rs. 3,000. Depreciation was charged on it Rs. 5,000. The balance of furniture on 31.3.21 was Rs. 28,000. The amount of furniture purchased was:

(a) Rs. 8,000

(b) Rs. 17,000

(c) Rs. 12,000

(d) Rs. 13,000

33. X Ltd. sold machinery having a book value of Rs. 25,000 (on which accumulated depreciation of Rs. 5,000 had been charged) at a profit of Rs. 3,000. The cash flow from investing activities will be:

(a) Rs. 30,000

(b) Rs. 23,000

(c) Rs. 25,000

(d) Rs. 28,000

34. Arrange the following items to be in order while making Cash Flow Statement as per AS.3

A. Income Tax paid

B. Purchase of Furniture

C. Goodwill written off

D. Debentures issued

E. Shares purchased

Choose the correct answer from the options given below:

(a) C, A, B, E, D

(b) C, B, A, D, E

(c) A, B, C, D, E

(d) C, A, B, D, E

35. Calculate the amount of cash generated from operations from the following information:

Particulars	(Rs.)
Profit before change	
in working capital	2,00,000
Depreciation on plant	
and Machinery	20,000
Gain on sale of Building	10,000
Increase in trade Payables	4,500
Increase in trade Receivables	3,500
Interest paid	2,225
Decrease in Inventories	3,750
Redemption of 10% Debentures	80,000

(a) Rs. 2,04,750

(b) Rs. 2,14,750

(c) Rs. 2,16,975

(d) Rs. 2,36,975

36. Arrange the following into correct sequence while computing cash flow from operating actives.

A. Compute Net Profit before tax after making necessary adjustments.

B. Compute operating profit before working capital changes by making adjustment for non-cash and non-operating activities.

C. Calculate the difference between opening and closing balance in statement of profit and loss.

D. Compute operating profit by making adjustment for working capital changes.

E. Calculate cash generated/cash used from operating activities by deducting tax paid from operating profit.

Choose the correct answer from the options given below:

(a) A, C, D, B, E

(b) C, A, D, B, E

(c) A, B, D, C, E

(d) C, A, B, D, E

37. Identify the chart element that details the data values and categories below the chart.

(a) Data marker

(b) Data table

(c) Data point

(d) Data labels

38. The best way to get started in Excel 2007 was to click the:

(a) Microsoft office button

(b) View toolbar

(c) Home tab

(d) Press enter

39. Which key combination collapses the ribbon?

(a) [Ctrl] + [F_3]

(b) [Ctrl] + [F_1]

(c) [Ctrl] + [F_7]

(d) [Ctrl] + [F_5]

40. 'DBMS' stands for:

(a) Drawing Board Management Software.

(b) Dividend Based Marking Systems.

(c) Data Base Management System.

(d) Data Base Marketing Software.

Direction for questions 41 to 45 : Read the following information to answer.

Rathi Udyog, made a profit of 72,000 after changing depreciation of Rs. 17,000 on fixed assets and paid Rs. 10,000 as interim dividend. The goodwill amortized was Rs. 12,000 and profit (Gain) on sale of furniture was Rs. 2,500.

The other informations were:

Trade Payable showed an increase of Rs. 7,000.

Outstanding expenses showed a decrease of Rs. 5,000.

Accrued Income showed an increase of Rs. 8,000.

Trade payable showed a decrease of Rs. 10,000.

Inventories showed a decrease of Rs. 3,000.

On the basis of above information answer the following questions.

41. If from the above informations, cash flow from operating activity is ascertained, then it is ascertained according to Accounting standard:

(a) AS - 4

(b) AS - 26

(c) AS - 16

(d) AS - 3

42. In the above case study if amount of Goodwill is increasing in current year, then if will be classified in:

(a) Operating Activity

(b) Investing Activity

(c) Financing Activity

(d) Cash and Cash Equivalents

43. Find out Net Profit before tax from the above informations:

(a) Rs. 72,000

(b) Rs. 82,000

(c) Rs. 99,000

(d) Rs. 89,000

44. We add depreciation in order to find out operating profit before working capital changes:

(a) because it is an income

(b) because depreciation is a cash expense

(c) because depreciation being a non-cash expense

(d) because it is given in operating activity proforma

45. Apart from showing interim dividend in Net Profit before tax, where else it will be shown?

(a) Operating Activity

(b) Investing Activity

(c) Financing Activity

(d) Cash and Cash Equivalent

Direction for questions 46 to 50 : Read the following information to answer.

A and B are two partners, dealing in manufacturing steel, sharing profits in the ratio of 2 : 1. They enjoying a buoyant demand of its products as economic growth is about 7% – 8% and the demand for steel is growing. It is planned to set up a new steel plant to encash on the increasing demand. It is estimated that they will require about Rs. 1,00,000. So they admitted, C as a partner. On the date of admission Balance sheet is as follows.

Balance Sheet of A and B

Liabilities	Rs.	Assets	Rs.
Bills Payble	10,000	Cash in hand	10,000
Sundry creditors	58,000	Cash at bank	40,000
Outstanding Expenses	2,000	Sundry Debtors	60,000
Capital	3,30,000	Stock	40,000
A - 1,80,000		Plant and Machinery	1,00,000
B - 1,50,000		Building	1,50,000
	4,00,000		4,00,000

Other information:

1. C will bring in Rs. 1,00,000 as capital and Rs. 60,000 as his share of goodwill for 1/4 share in profit.

2. Plant is to be appreciated to Rs. 1,20,000 and the value of building is to be appreciated by 10%.

3. Stock is found overvalued by Rs. 4,000.

4. A provision for doubtful debts is to be created at 5% of debtors.

5. Creditors were unrecorded to the extant of Rs. 1,000.

On the basis of above cash study, answer the following:

46. Value of stock to be shown in Balance sheet after admission will be:

(a) Rs. 48,000   (b) Rs. 32,000

(c) Rs. 36,000   (d) Rs. 40,000

47. Provision for Doubtful debts to be shown in Revaluation Account:

(a) Rs. 1,000   (b) Rs. 2,000

(c) Rs. 3,000   (d) Rs. 1,500

48. A's share of goodwill brought in by C will be:

(a) Rs. 20,000   (b) Rs. 40,000

(c) Rs. 60,000   (d) Rs. 30,000

49. Plant and Machinery to be shown in Revaluation Account:

(a) Rs. 1,00,000   (b) Rs. 20,000

(c) Rs. 1,20,000   (d) Rs. 2,20,000

50. Creditors to be shown in Balance sheet after admission of partner will be:

(a) Rs. 60,000   (b) Rs. 59,000

(c) Rs. 58,000   (d) Rs. 62,000

Answer Keys

1. (d)	**2.** (b)	**3.** (a)	**4.** (a)	**5.** (d)	**6.** (c)	**7.** (c)	**8.** (b)	**9.** (c)	**10.** (c)
11. (c)	**12.** (c)	**13.** (b)	**14.** (b)	**15.** (a)	**16.** (d)	**17.** (a)	**18.** (c)	**19.** (c)	**20.** (a)
21. (b)	**22.** (d)	**23.** (b)	**24.** (c)	**25.** (b)	**26.** (b)	**27.** (d)	**28.** (b)	**29.** (b)	**30.** (c)
31. (d)	**32.** (b)	**33.** (d)	**34.** (d)	**35.** (a)	**36.** (d)	**37.** (d)	**38.** (a)	**39.** (b)	**40.** (c)
41. (d)	**42.** (b)	**43.** (c)	**44.** (c)	**45.** (c)	**46.** (c)	**47.** (c)	**48.** (b)	**49.** (b)	**50.** (b)

Explanations

1. (d) T.P = 50000 + 120000 + (75000 + 10000)

= 255000

Average profit = 255000 ÷ 3 = Rs.85000.

2. (b) Profit and Loss A/c, P & L Appropriation A/c, partner's capital A/cs.

3. (a) Total drawings of the year = Rs. 100000

Drawings per quarter = 100000 ÷ 4 = Rs. 25000.

4. (a) Match the column.

5. (d) Goodwill = S.P. × P.Y, 90000

= SP × 3, SP = Rs. 30000

S.P = Average profit – Net profit, 30000 = Average profit – 120000

Average profit = 120000 + 30000 = Rs. 150000

6. (c) Let C's share = x

C gets 25% of his share from A, means 75% from B

$\dfrac{75x}{100} = \dfrac{1}{4}$, 300x = 100, x = $\dfrac{100}{300} = \dfrac{1}{3}$

7. (c) Goodwill is calculated at Admission; Amalgamation, Retirement and Death.

8. (b) If nothing is specified than old ratio.

9. (c) (C) and (D) are not true statements.

10. (c) Advance on application　50000 × 3 = 150000

Required on Allotments　40000 × 4 = 160000

____

Difference　　　　　　　　　　= Rs. 10000

11. (c) Correct sequence issue of prospectus. Receipt of application.

Allotment of shares, Forfeiture, Reissue.

12. (c) Match the column.

13. (b) Share forfeited amount on 1000 shares = Rs. 3000 Cr.

Share forfeited amount 400 × 3　= Rs. 1200 Cr.

Share forfeited on reissue 400 × 1 = Rs. –400 Cr.

Transfer to Capital reserve difference = Rs. 800

14. (b) (A) and (C) are in financing activity while (E) is cash equivalent.

15. (a) Match the column.

16. (d) Liquid assets = 180000 × 0.75 = 135000

Current assets = 135000 + 20000 + 47250

= 202250

CR = 202250/180000 = 1.12 : 1

17. (a) = pay + (Opn. Stock + Op. Advance) – (C/o Stock + C/o Adv.)

= 46000 + (8000 + 18000) – (6000 + 5000)

= Rs. 61000

18. (c) C/o Bal of R & P A/c is bal. of cash and bank.

19. (c) I & E = Accrual, R & P = Cash bases

20. (a) Match

21. (b) = pay + (Op. Stock + C/o Creditors) – (C/o stock and Op Creditors)

= 46000 + (8000 + 5000) – (6000 + 18000)

= 46000 + 13000 – 24000 = Rs. 35000

22. (d) Profit and Loss suspense A/c be opened on death.

23. (b) Retiring partner's capital a/c will be debited.

24. (c) 1 April to 5 November = 219 days

$300000 \times \dfrac{1}{5} \times \dfrac{219}{365} = $ Rs. 36000

25. (b) On credit side of P and C suspense A/c.

26. (b) 150000 – 20000 = 130000

15% discount = 19500

Realised Rs. 110500

27. (d) Partner's consent not required by court.

28. (b) First pay to creditors, second loan, third capital and at the end to partners if remaining.

29. (b) Total discount amount = Rs. 200000

$$\% = \frac{200000}{2000000} \times 100 = 10\%$$

30. (c) Maximum permissible limit of discount is paid amount so here minimum price of reissue is $100 - 45 = $ Rs. 55.

31. (d) Liquidity ratios are current ratio and Acid test ratio.

32. (b)

Furniture A/c			
To Bal b/d (Op)	20000	By Dep	5000
To SOPL (Gain)	3000	By Bank (sale)	7000
To Bank (Pur.)	17000	By Bal. c/d (c/o)	28000
	40000		40000

33. (d) $25000 + 3000 = $ Rs. 28000.

34. (d) Sequence operating, Investing, Financing Activity.

35. (a) OPBWCC $= 200000 + (20000) - (10000) - (8000)$
$= 202000$

OP $= 202000 + (3500 + 3750) - 4500$

$= 202000 + 7250 - 4500.$

36. (d) Sequence

37. (d) Computer Accounting

Data Labels are chart elements.

38. (a) Computer Accounting

For Excel 2007 Microsoft office button is click.

39. (b) Computer Accounting

[Ctrl] + [F1] collapse the ribbon.

40. (c) Computer Accounting

DBMS means data base management system.

41. (d) AS – 3 is used for cash flow statement.

42. (b) Goodwill purchase is shown in investing activity.

43. (c) NPBT $= 72000 + 17000 + 10000 = $ Rs. 99000.

44. (c) Depreciation is a non cash item.

45. (c) Dividend paid is a part of financing activity.

46. (c) Stock $= 40000 - 4000 = $ Rs. 36000.

47. (c) Provision for doubtful debts = 5% of 60000
$= $ Rs. 3000.

48. (b) A's share $= 60000 \times \dfrac{2}{3} = $ Rs. 40000 as no information is given about NPR so old ratio is same as sacrifice ratio which is 2 : 1.

49. (b) Value of Plant & Machinery is increase by Rs. 20000 ($120000 - 100000 = $ Rs. 20000)

50. (b) Book value of creditors   = Rs. 58000
Unrecorded creditors   = Rs. 1000
                         ――――
Now value of creditors   = Rs. 59000

1. There are 50 members in a Rotary Club, which provide medical services to people. Each member pays Rs. 1,000 as subscription. During financial year 2021-22, 10 members paid only Rs. 7,000 out of total subscription, 5 members paid subscription, for financial year 2020-21. 2 members left the organisation without any payment. Amount credited to Income and Expenditure Account will be:
   (a) Rs. 50,000 (b) Rs. 48,000
   (c) Rs. 47,000 (d) Rs. 45,000

2. Amount received as per the will of a deceased person is termed as:
   (a) Legacy
   (b) Donation
   (c) Capital Receipt
   (d) Windfall Gain

3. Shikha Ltd. invited application for 30,000 shares of Rs. 10 each and received 50,000 applications. Which of the following alternative can be followed?
   A. Refund the excess money and full allotment to rest of the applicants
   B. Reject few applications, allot full shares to some applicants and allot shares on prorate basis to remaining.
   C. Not all allot shares to some applicants and make prorate allotment to other applicants
   D. Make prorate allotment to all applicants
   Choose the correct answer from the options given below:
   (a) A and B only
   (b) A, B, C only
   (c) A and C only
   (d) A, B, C, D only

4. Devarth withdraws Rs. 5,000 at the end of each quarter for six months. Interest on drawing is charged @10% p.a. Interest on drawings will be:
   (a) Rs. 125 (b) Rs. 375
   (c) Rs. 250 (d) Rs. 675

5. Honorarium paid for guest lecture by a Not for Profit organisation is shown in:
   (a) Cash Book
   (b) Balance Sheet
   (c) Profit and Loss A/c
   (d) Income and Expenditure A/c

6. A company issues 1,000 9% debentures of Rs. 100 each at a premium of 5% and redeemable at a premium of 10%. The amount of loss on issue of Debentures account will be:
   (a) Rs. 15,000
   (b) Rs. 10,000
   (c) Rs. 5,000
   (d) Rs. 20,000

7. Match **List I** with **List II**.

List I Journal Entries	List II Narratives
A. Share Allotment A/c Dr. To Share Capital A/c To securities Premium Reserve A/c	I. (Forfeiture of / Shares for Non-Payment of Second and Final Call)
B. Shares Capital A/c Dr. To Share Second and Final Call A/c To Share Forfeiture A/c	II. (Amount due on allotment of Shares @Rs. _____ per share including premium)
C. Share Forfeiture A/c Dr. To Capital Reserve A/c	III. (First Call amount received on _____ shares)
D. Bank A/c Dr. To Equity Share First Call A/c	IV. (Profit on reissue shares transferred to Capital Reserve)

   Choose the correct answer from the options given below:
   (a) A-I, B-II, C-IV, D-III
   (b) A-II, B-III, C-IV, D-I
   (c) A-II, B-I, C-III, D-IV
   (d) A-II, B-I, C-IV, D-III

8. Funds raised from Not-for-Profit organisation through various sources are credited to:
   (a) Life Membership Fee
   (b) Income and Expenditure A/c
   (c) Specific Fund
   (d) Capital Fund or General Fund

9. P and T partners sharing profits and losses in the ratio of 3 : 2. They admitted R for 1/5th share. General Reserve appeared in the books at Rs. 45,000. New profit sharing ratio among partners is 5 : 3 : 2. General Reserve will be treated follows:

(a) General Reserve will appear in the New Books

(b) General Reserve will be distributed 5 : 3 : 2 among all members.

(c) General Reserve will be distributed in the Ratio of 3 : 2 among old partners

(d) General Reserve will be distributed in the ratio of 5 : 3 among old partners

10. Match **List- I** with **List- II**.

List- I	List- II
A. Long term provisions	I. Current assets
B. Trade payables	II. Non-current assets
C. Cash and Cash equivalent	III. Non-current Liabilities
D. Long-term loans and advances given	IV. Current Liabilities

Choose the correct answer from the options given below:

(a) A-IV, B-III, C-II, D-I

(b) A-III, B-IV, C-I, D-II

(c) A-II, B-III, C-IV, D-I

(d) A-I, B-II, C-III, D-IV

11. Reena Ltd. issued a prospectus inviting applications for 3000 shares of Rs. 100 each at a premium of Rs. 20 payable as follows:

On Application	Rs. 20 per share
On First Call	Rs. 20 per share
On Second Call	Rs. 30 per share

Radha to whom 360 shares were allotted, failed to pay Allotment Money and Call Money and her shares were forfeited. Amount of Securities Premium Reserve in Balance Sheet will be:

(a) Rs. 60,000

(b) Rs. 7,200

(c) Rs. 67,000

(d) Rs. 52,800

12. Out of subscribed Capital of Company, 200 Equity Shares of Rs. 100 each were forfeited for non-payment of the Final Call of Rs. 30 per share. Out of these, 150 shares were reissued at Rs. 60 per share. Amount to be transferred to Capital Reserve will be:

(a) Rs. 6,000   (b) Rs. 4,500

(c) Rs. 3,500   (d) Rs. 10,500

13. Which of the following is correct about Financial Analysis?

(a) It does not consider Price Level Changes

(b) It considers both monetary and non-monetary aspects

(c) It does not include Cash Flow Statement

(d) It can't be used by the lenders

14. TL Ltd. purchased assets of the book value of Rs. 99,000 from another firm. Purchase consideration was to be paid by issuing 11% Debentures of Rs. 100 each, at a discount of 10%. Number of Debentures company needs to issue will be:

(a) 990   (b) 1,000

(c) 900   (d) 1,100

15. Opening Stock (+) Purchase (–) Closing Stock formula applies to the following while calculating consumptions:

A. Machinery

B. Stationery

C. Furniture

D. Sports Equipment

E. Medicine

Choose the correct answer from the options given below:

(a) B, D, C only

(b) B, C, E only

(c) B, D, E only

(d) A, B only

16. Match **List- I** with **List- II**.

List- I	List- II
A. Operating Activities	I. Current Investment
B. Investing Activities	II. Issue of Shares
C. Financing Activities	III. Sale of Goods
D. Cash and Cash Equivalents	IV. Non-Current Investment

Choose the correct answer from the options given below:

(a) A-III, B-IV, C-II, D-I

(b) A-IV, B-III, C-II, D-I

(c) A-III, B-I, C-II, D-IV

(d) A-III, B-IV, C-I, D-II

17. On dissolution of a firm, stock was appearing in the balance sheet Rs. 1,00,000. Part of the stock was taken once by a partner at 10% discount at Rs. 49,500 and balance sold at a profit of 20%. How much amount will be credited to Realisation A/c?

(a) Rs. 49,500   (b) Rs. 1,10,100

(c) Rs. 1,03,500   (d) Rs. 1,04,160

18. W Ltd. has given you the following information:

Machinery as on April 1, 2020 - Rs. 50,000

Machinery as on March 31, 2021 - Rs. 60,000

Accumulated Depreciation on April 01, 2020 -
Rs. 25,000

Accumulated Depreciation on March 31, 2021 -
Rs. 15,000

During the year, a machine, costing Rs. 25,000 with accumulated depreciation of Rs. 15,000 was sold for Rs. 13,000. Cash flow from Investing Activities will be:

(a) Rs. 22,000   (b) Rs. 22,000

(c) Rs. 48,000   (d) Rs. 35,000

19. Which one from the following can be called cash equivalents:

(a) Cash in Hand

(b) Cash at Bank

(c) Short-Term Investment

(d) Short-term loans

20. M, N and R are partners sharing Profit and Losses in the Ratio of 3 : 3 : 2. They decided to change their ratio equally. On that date goodwill appearing in the Balance Sheet was Rs. 2,40,000. Journal Entry will be passed as _______

(a) R's Capital Account   Dr. 20,000

     To M's Capital A/c   10,000

     To N's Capital A/c   10,000

(b) M's Capital Account   Dr. 10,000

     N's Capital A/c   Dr. 10,000

     To R's Capital A/c   20,000

(c) M's Capital A/c   Dr. 90,000

     N's Capital A/c   Dr. 90,000

     R's Capital A/c   Dr. 60,000

     To Goodwill A/c   2,40,000

(d) No entry will be passed for good will

21. On dissolution of a firm, bank overdraft is transferred to:

(a) Cash Account

(b) Bank Account

(c) Realisation Account

(d) Partner's Capital Account

22. Unrecorded liabilities when paid are shown in:

(a) Debit of Realisation Account

(b) Debit of Bank Account

(c) Credit of Realisation Account

(d) Credit of Bank Account

23. On Dissolution of the firm, Partner's Capital accounts are closed through:

(a) Realisation Account

(b) Drawings Account

(c) Bank Account

(d) Loan Account

24. Which of the following options given below are correct?

A. A balancing figure on credit side of Income and Expenditure Account denotes excess of expenses over incomes.

B. Surplus of Income and Expenditure Account is deducted from the Capital/General Fund.

C. Receipts and Payments Account is equivalent to Profit and Loss Account.

D. Receipts and Payments Account records the receipts and payments of revenue nature only

E. Receipts and Payments Account does not differentiate between capital and revenue receipts.

Choose the correct answer from the options given below:

(a) A, E only

(b) A, B, C, E only

(c) A, B, C, D only

(d) B, C, D only

25. Which of the following options given below are correct?

A. If there appears a sports fund, the expenses incurred on sports activities will be shown on the debit side of Income and Expenditure Account.

B. Donations for specific purposes are always capitalized.

C. Scholarships granted to students out of funds provided by Government will be debited to Income and Expenditure Account.

D. Opening balance sheet is prepared when the opening balance of capital fund is not given.

E. If donations received is to be utilised to achieve specified, it is called Specific Donations.

Choose the correct answer from the options given below:

(a) A, B, D only

(b) B, D, E only

(c) B, C, D only

(d) C, D, E only

26. On Dissolution of a firm Investment fluctuation reserve appearing in the balance sheet will be:

(a) debited to Realisation A/c with full value

(b) credited to realisation A/c with full value

(c) debited to all Partner's Capital A/c in their profit sharing ratio

(d) credited to all Partners' Capital A/c in their profit sharing ratio

27. On the admission of a new partner increase in the value of assets is debited to:

(a) Profit and Loss Adjustment Account

(b) Assets Account

(c) Old Partner's Capital Account

(d) Revaluation Account

28. P and Q are partners sharing profit in 2 : 1 ratio. They admitted R into partnership giving him 1/5 share which he acquired from P and Q in 2 : 1 ratio. New Profit Sharing Ratio will be:

(a) 2 : 2 : 1

(b) 4 : 3 : 1

(c) 9 : 3 : 4

(d) 3 : 1 : 1

29. In the absence of any information regarding the acquisition of share in Profit of the retiring/decreased partner by the remaining Partner, it is assumed that they will acquire his/her share in:

(a) Old Profit Sharing Ratio

(b) New Profit Sharing Ratio

(c) Equal Ratio

(d) Capital Ratio

30. The old profit sharing ratio among Rajender, Satish, Tejpal were 2 : 2 : 1. The new Profit Sharing Ratio after Satish's retirement is 3 : 2. The gaining ratio is:

(a) 3 : 2

(b) 2 : 1

(c) 1 : 1

(d) 2 : 3

31. In case of Death of a Partner, Profit till death of deceased partner is debited to which account?

(a) Revaluation Account

(b) Profit and Loss Suspense Account

(c) Deceased Partner's Capital Account

(d) Deceased Partner's Current Account

32. The sequence to develop the Balance Sheet in NPO includes the following steps:

A. Taking all fixed assets with additions and depreciation and show them on the asset side

B. Compare the items of payment of Receipts and Payment A/c with expense of Income and Expenditure A/c to find outstanding and prepaid expenses

C. Taking the capital/General Fund from opening balance sheet

D. Compare items of receipt of Receipts and Payment A/c with Income of Income and Expenditure A/c to find outstanding and Advances etc.

Choose the correct answer from the options given below:

(a) C, A, B, D

(b) C, A, D, B

(c) C, B, A, D

(d) D, A, C, B

33. Arrange the following in appropriate sequence regarding admission of a Partner:

A. Preparation of Revaluation account

B. Partner's Capital Account are completed

C. Preparation of Balance Sheet of New Partnership

D. New Partner brings his share of Capital and good will.

E. Transferring the profit/ loss on Revaluation to old partners.

Choose the correct answer from the options given below:

(a) D, C, B, A, E

(b) A, B, C, E, D

(c) A, E, D, C, B

(d) A, E, D, B, C

34. Give the correct sequence of the following with regard to issue of shares of a Public Ltd. Company:

A. Making the calls due

B. Receiving applications for shares

C. Issue of prospectus

D. Formation of Company

E. Allotment of shares

Choose the correct answer from the options given below:

(a) A, B, D, C, E

(b) B, C, D, A, E

(c) D, C, B, E, A

(d) C, D, B, A, E

35. Arrange the following in correct sequence in regard to Partnership firm:

A. Net Profit transferred to P & L Appropriation account

B. Preparation of Partner's Capital account

C. Division of Profits among partners

D. Interest on Partners Capital accounts

E. Interest on partner's Loan account

Choose the correct answer from the options given below:

(a) D, C, B, E, A

(b) E, D, C, B, A

(c) E, A, D, C, B

(d) E, D, C, A, B

36. Match **List - I** with **List - II**.

List - I		**List - II**	
A.	Investing Activities	I.	Refund of Income Tax Received
B.	Cash & Cash Equivalents	II.	Income Tax Paid
C.	Operating Activities	III.	Under-writing Commission Paid
D.	Financing Activities	IV.	Dividend Received

Choose the correct answer from the options given below:

(a) A-IV, B-I, C-II, D-III

(b) A-IV, B-I, C-III, D-II

(c) A-III, B-II, C-I, D-IV

(d) A-III, B-I, C-II, D-IV

37. Which of these is not an argument of the IF function?

(a) Logical-test

(b) Value-of-false

(c) Value-of-true

(d) Value-when-false

38. SQL stands for:

(a) Simple questions language

(b) Simple query language

(c) Singular quantity loading

(d) Structured query language

39. To expect a well formatted printable data from Access database, we may use

(a) table

(b) Query

(c) Form

(d) Report

40. DBMS stands for:

(a) Drawing Board Management System

(b) Dividend Based Marketing System

(c) Data Base Management System

(d) Data Base Marketing System

Direction for questions 41 to 45:

Passage

Case Study:

Issue of Shares

Superb Limited issued Equity shares of the value Rs. 3,00,000 the face value being Rs. 10 each at a premium of 20%. The amount payable was-

Application - 30%

Allotment - 50% (including premium)

Two calls - Equal amount

Pro-Rata allotment was done to all applicants of 40,000 shares.

Ramit who applied for 80 shares failed to pay both calls and his shares were subsequently forfeited.

41. Ramit was allotted how many shares?

(a) 80 shares

(b) 60 shares

(c) 140 shares

(d) 50 shares

42. The amount received on applications adjusted towards allotment is:

(a) Rs. 90,000

(b) Rs. 3,000

(c) Rs. 30,000

(d) Rs. 12,00,000

43. The value of Second and Final Call is

(a) 2　　　　　　　　(b) 4

(c) 1　　　　　　　　(d) 3

44. The amount of Rs. 120 regarding 1st call is recorded as:

(a) Calls in Advance

(b) Calls in Arearrs

(c) Forfeited Shares

(d) Capital Reserve

45. Forfeited Shares amount on shares, not yet reissued, is a part of:

(a) Reserves & Surplus

(b) Current Liabilities

(c) Current Asset

(d) Share Capital

Direction for questions 46 to 50:

Passage

Following is the Balance Sheet of Titanic Ltd. as at March 31, 2022

Particulars		Rs.
I. Equity and liabilities		
1. Shareholder's Fund		
A. Share Capital		24,00,000
B. Reserves & Surplus		6,00,000
2. Non-current liabilities		
Long-term borrowings	9,00,000	
3. Current liabilities		
A. Short term borrowings	6,00,000	
B. Trade Payables		23,40,000
C. Short-term Provisions	60,000	
Total		**69,00,000**
II. Assets		
Non-Current Assets		
Fixed assets		
Tangible assets		45,00,000
2. Current Assets		
A. Inventories		12,00,000
B. Trade Receivables		9,00,000
C. Cash and Cash equivalent		2,28,000
D. Short-term loans & advances		72,000
Total		**69,00,000**

46. Current Ratio for Titanic Ltd. for the year ended March 31, 2022 will be:
    (a) 0.8 : 1
    (b) 0.4 : 1
    (c) 0.7 : 1
    (d) 0.9 : 1

47. Liquid Ratio for Titanic Ltd. for the year ended 31st March, 2022 will be:
    (a) 0.3 : 1
    (b) 0.8 : 1
    (c) 0.4 : 1
    (d) 0.5 : 1

48. The _______ ratio is are primarily a measure of earning capacity.
    (a) liquidity
    (b) activity
    (c) debt
    (d) profitability

49. The two basic measures of liquidity are:
    (a) Inventory turnover and Current Ratio
    (b) Current Ratio & Liquid Ratio
    (c) Gross Profit Ratio & Operating Ratio
    (d) Current Ratio and average collection period

50. The _______ ratio provides the information critical to the survival of the firm.
    (a) liquidity
    (b) activity
    (c) solvency
    (d) profitability

Answer Keys

1. (b)	**2.** (a)	**3.** (d)	**4.** (a)	**5.** (d)	**6.** (b)	**7.** (d)	**8.** (d)	**9.** (c)	**10.** (b)
11. (d)	**12.** (b)	**13.** (a)	**14.** (d)	**15.** (c)	**16.** (a)	**17.** (c)	**18.** (b)	**19.** (c)	**20.** (c)
21. (c)	**22.** (a)	**23.** (c)	**24.** (a)	**25.** (b)	**26.** (b)	**27.** (b)	**28.** (d)	**29.** (a)	**30.** (c)
31. (b)	**32.** (b)	**33.** (d)	**34.** (c)	**35.** (c)	**36.** (a)	**37.** (d)	**38.** (d)	**39.** (d)	**40.** (c)
41. (b)	**42.** (c)	**43.** (a)	**44.** (b)	**45.** (d)	**46.** (a)	**47.** (c)	**48.** (d)	**49.** (b)	**50.** (c)

Explanations

1. (b) (50 × 1000 = 50000) – (2 × 1000) = 48000

2. (a) Legacy is the amount received as per will of a deceased person.

3. (d) Oversubscription of shares.

4. (a) $\dfrac{10000 \times 10}{100} \times \dfrac{3}{12} \times \dfrac{1}{2} = Rs.125$

5. (d) At expenditure side of income and expenditure account.

6. (b) $\dfrac{100000 \times 10}{100} = Rs.10000$

7. (d) Match the column

8. (d) Funds are credited to capital fund or general fund

9. (c) General reserve will be distributed in old partners in old ratio at the time of admission.

10. (b) Match the column

11. (d) (3000 × 20 = 60000) Less Radha's shares (360 × 20) = Rs.52800

12. (b) Total forfeited amount (200 × 70) = 14000
Amount on 150 shares = Rs. 10500 less
Rs. 6000 = Rs.4500

13. (a) Price level changes are not considered in FSA .

14. (d) Numbers = $\dfrac{99000}{90}$ = 1100 Debentures.

15. (c) This formula apply only on consumable goods.

16. (a) Match the column

17. (c) Taken by partner $\left(\dfrac{49500}{90} \times 100\right)$ = Rs.55000 is
book value in Rs. 49500
Remaining(100000 – 55000 = 45000 + 9000
= Rs.54000
Total amount credited to realisation account
= Rs.103500

18. (b) Purchase of machinery = Rs.35000
Sale of machinery = Rs.13000
Cash outflow from Investing activity = Rs.22000

19. (c) Short term investments are cash equivalent.

20. (c) Old goodwill will be write off in old partners in old ratio.

21. (c) Bank over draft is a liability so transfer to Realisation account.

22. (a) Liabilities paid are shown in Debit side of Realisation account.

23. (c) On dissoulation final payments are to be made by Bank account.

24. (a) Only (A) and (E) are correct.

25. (b) Only (B), (D), (E) are correct.

26. (b) On dissoulation IFR transfer to credit side of Realisation account.

27. (b) Increase in the value of assets is debited to Assets account.

28. (d) Sacrifice of P = $\dfrac{1}{15}$

Sacrifice of Q = $\dfrac{2}{15}$

New of P = $\dfrac{9}{15}$

New of Q = $\dfrac{3}{15}$

NPR = 3 : 1 : 1

29. (a) In the absence of any information old profit sharing ratio.

30. (c) Gaining ratio = 1 : 1

31. (b) Profit and loss suspense account is opened for profit till death.

32. (b) Correct sequence is C, A, D, B

33. (d) Correct sequence is A, E, D, B, C

34. (c) Correct sequence is D, C, B, E, A

35. (c) Correct sequence is E, A, D, C, B

36. (a) Match the column

37. (d) COMPUTER ACCOUNTING
Value when false

38. (d) COMPUTER ACCOUNTING
Structured query language

39. (d) COMPUTER ACCOUNTING
Report is used

40. (c) COMPUTER ACCOUNTING
Data base management system

41. (b) $\dfrac{30000}{40000} \times 80 = 60$ shares

42. (c) No. x Rs.10000 × 3 = Rs.30000

43. (a) (10 + 2) − (3 + 5) = Rs.4 Equally means Rs. 2 Each call

44. (b) Amount not received is call in arrears.

45. (d) Forfeited shares not yet reissued are part of share capital.

46. (a) $\dfrac{CA}{CL}, \dfrac{2400000}{3000000} = 0.8 : 1$

47. (c) $\dfrac{LA}{CL}, \dfrac{1200000}{3000000} = 0.4 : 1$

48. (d) Profitability ratios are measures of earning capacity

49. (b) Current and Liquid ratios are measures of liquidity.

50. (c) Solvency ratios provides the information of long term financial position of survival.

1. On dissolution of a firm, bank overdraft is transferred to:
   (a) Cash Account
   (b) Bank Account
   (c) Realisation Account
   (d) Partner's Capital Account

2. Rearrange the following items in a sequence while preparing common size statement.
   A. Calculate percentage of the total as per common base
   B. Prepare the format of Balance sheet and Profit and Loss A/c
   C. List out absolute figures in rupees at two points of time
   D. Choose a common base
   Choose the correct answer from the options given below:
   (a) B, C, D, A
   (b) A, C, B, D
   (c) B, D, C, A
   (d) B, A, D, C

3. All of them are shown under the sub-heading 'Reserve and Surplus' except:
   (a) Surplus; Balance in Statement of Profit and Loss
   (b) Debenture Redemption Reserve
   (c) Forfeited Shares
   (d) Revaluation Reserve

4. As issue of shares made by the company to the public in general for subscription is called:
   (a) Private placement of shares
   (b) Initial Public Offer
   (c) ESOP
   (d) Sweat Equity Shares

5. Forfeiture of shares results in the reduction of:
   (a) Reserve Capital
   (b) Capital Reserve
   (c) Authorised Capital
   (d) Paid-up Capital

6. Which of the following is not included in Non-current liabilities, while preparing a Balance Sheet of a company:
   (a) Debentures
   (b) Bonds
   (c) Public Deposits
   (d) Cash Credit

7. Which among the following are sources of cash inflow from Investing Activities?
   A. Dividend Received from investment
   B. Cash Receipt from Disposal of shares
   C. Cash Receipt from Disposal of Fixed Assets
   D. Cash proceeds from issuing Shares and Debentures
   Choose the correct answer from the options given below:
   (a) A, B, C and D only
   (b) A, B and C only
   (c) B, C and D only
   (d) B and D only

8. If there is Revenue from Operation Rs. 1,20,000 and gross profit is 20% of cost, then the amount of gross profit will be:
   (a) Rs. 24,000
   (b) Rs. 48,000
   (c) Rs. 20,000
   (d) Rs. 40,000

9. The ideal Debt Equity Ratio is:
   (a) 1 : 1
   (b) 2 : 1
   (c) 4 : 1
   (d) 5 : 1

10. A, B and C are partner's sharing profits and losses in the ratio of $\frac{3}{8} : \frac{1}{2} : \frac{1}{8}$. If A dies, then the new ratio of B and C will be:
    (a) 2 : 1   (b) 4 : 1
    (c) 1 : 1   (d) 3 : 1

11. Which among the following items appear in the Receipt and Payment Account?
    A. Life membership fees
    B. Depreciation of fixed assets
    C. Provision of doubtful debts
    D. Profit/loss on sale of fixed assets
    Choose the correct answer from the options given below:
    (a) B, C and D only
    (b) A, B and C only
    (c) A, C and D only
    (d) A and D only

12. Match **List-I** with **List-II**.

List-I	List-II
A. Operating Activities	I. Issue of equity shares
B. Investing Activities	II. Purchase of Marketable securities
C. Financing Activities	III. Cash sales
D. Cash Equivalent	IV. Purchase of fixed assets

Choose the correct answer from the options given below:

(a) A-III, B-IV, C-II, D-I

(b) A-III, B-IV, C-I, D-II

(c) A-III, B-II, C-IV, D-I

(d) A-III, B-I, C-II, D-IV

13. From the following information of X Ltd, calculate Cash Flow from Financing Activities.

	April 1, 2021	March 31, 2022
Long-term Loan	2,00,000	2,60,000

During the year, the company repaid a loan of Rs. 1,00,000. Long-term loan carried interest rate of 10%. The loan was repaid on 1st April 2021 and a fresh loan was taken on 31st March 2022.

(a) Rs. 50,000 outflow

(b) Rs. 60,000 inflow

(c) Rs. 50,000 inflow

(d) Rs. 1,60,000 inflow

14. Securities Premium Reserve as per section 52(2) of the companies Act 2013 can be used:

A. To write-off preliminary expenses of the company

B. To issue fully paid bonus shares to the extent not exceeding unissued share capital of the company

C. To pay premium on the redemption of preference shares or debentures

D. To write off discount allowed on the goods sold on credit

Choose the correct answer from the options given below:

(a) A, B and D only

(b) B, C and D only

(c) A, C and D only

(d) A, B and C only

15. Uncalled capital that can be called up only in event of winding up of the company is called:

(a) Capital Reserve   (b) Issued Capital

(c) Reserve Capital   (d) Unissued Capital

16. For calculating EPS, the following order will be followed.

A. Calculate number of equity shares

B. Calculate earning available for equity share holders

C. Compute profit after tax

D. Compute EPS

Choose the correct answer from the options given below:

(a) C, B, A, D

(b) A, B, C, D

(c) B, A, C, D

(d) C, A, B, D

17. On 1st April 2022, A, B and C decided to dissolve their firm On the date of dissolution, Sundry debtors appeared in Balance Sheet at Rs. 6,00,000 and Provision for doubtful debt at Rs. 30,000 Debtors to extent of Rs. 60,000 were bad. In journal entry for realisation of debtors.

(a) Bank A/c will be debited with Rs. 6,00,000

(b) Realisation A/c will be credited with Rs. 5,40,000

(c) Bank A/c will be credited with Rs. 5,40,000

(d) Realisation A/c will be credited with Rs. 5,40,000

18. Match **List I** with **List II**.

List I	List II
A. Bank overdraft	I. Non cash item
B. Dividend received	II. Financing activity
C. Provision for doubtful debts	III. Operating activity
D. Cash received from sale of	IV. Investing activity goods

Choose the correct answer from the options given below:

(a) A-I, B-II, C-III, D-IV

(b) A-II, B-IV, C-I, D-III

(c) A-III, B-II, C-I, D-IV

(d) A-IV, B-III, C-II, D-I

19. Nitin Ltd. provides you the following information.

Particulars	1 April 2021	31 March 2022
Machinery	2,40,000	3,50,000
Accumulated Depreciation	50,000	45,000
		Rs. 90,000

During the year, a machine costing Rs. 90,000 with accumulated depreciation of Rs. 31,500 was sold for Rs. 52,000.

Calculate Cash Flow from Investing Activities on the basis of the above information.

(a) 2,00,000　　　　(b) 52,000

(c) 1,48,000　　　　(d) 1,52,000

20. Identify the correct sequence in calculation of Cash Flow from Operating Activities.

A. Addition and subtraction of Non cash/Non operating items

B. Payment of income tax

C. Calculation of operating profit before working capital changes.

D. Calculation of net profit/loss before tax and extraordinary items

Choose the correct answer from the options given below:

(a) D, A, C, B　　　　(b) D, A, B, C

(c) C, D, A, B　　　　(d) C, D, B, A

21. Match **List I** with **List II**.

	List I		List II
A.	Share forfeiture	I.	Cr. share capital
B.	Shares reissued	II.	Dr. share capital
C.	Excess application money refunded	III.	Dr. Bank A/c
D.	Calls money received	IV.	Cr. Bank A/c

Choose the correct answer from the options given below:

(a) A-I, B-II, C-IV, D-III

(b) A-II, B-I, C-IV, D-III

(c) A-II, B-I, C-III, D-IV

(d) A-IV, B-I, C-III, D-II

22. If a share of Rs. 10 on which Rs. 7 has been paid is forfeited, at what minimum price can it be reissued?

(a) Rs. 7　　　　(b) Rs. 10

(c) Rs. 3　　　　(d) Rs. 4

23. Calculate net profit as per P & L A/c for the year ending 31 March, 2022 from the following information:

share of profit transferred to Capital A/c's of partners:

Ram	Rs. 7,000
Shyam	Rs. 3,500

Interest on capital:

Ram	Rs. 1,500
Shyam	Rs. 500

Interest on Drawings:

Ram	Rs. 300
Shyam	Rs. 200

Ram's salary Rs. 1,000

(a) Rs. 13,000

(b) Rs. 13,500

(c) Rs. 12,000

(d) Rs. 11,000

24. M and R are partners sharing profits and losses in the ratio of 3 : 2. Their capital A/c's showed the balance of Rs. 4,00,000 and Rs. 3,00,000 respectively on 1 April, 2021. M introduced additional capital on 1 August, 2021. Interest on capital is allowed @ 6% p.a. Total interest on capital of both the partners is Rs. 50,000.

Calculate additional capital introduced by M on August, 2021 and interest on capital earned on additional capital. Books are closed on 31 March.

(a) Rs. 1,00,000 and Rs. 4,000

(b) Rs. 3,00,000 and Rs. 18,000

(c) Rs. 2,00,000 and Rs. 8,000

(d) Rs. 1,50,000 and Rs. 10,000

25. Match **List - I** with **List - II**.

	List - I		List - II
A.	Receipts and Payment A/c	I.	Special fund
B.	Capital receipt	II.	Life membership fees
C.	Match fund	III.	Accrual basis
D.	Income and Expenditure A/c	IV.	Cash basis

Choose the correct answer from the options given below:

(a) A-III, B-I, C-II, D-IV

(b) A-II, B-III, C-IV, D-I

(c) A-IV, B-II, C-I, D-III

(d) A-I, B-II, C-III, D-IV

26. Value of 12% government securities as at 31 March 2021 was Rs. 85,000 which were purchased at the date at par. Additional 12% securities worth Rs. 50,000 were purchased on 31 March, 2022. Total interest debited to receipts and payment A/c during the year on the above securities is Rs. 9,000 calculate Accrued interest on 31 March, 2022.

(a) Rs. 1,200

(b) Rs. 10,200

(c) Rs. 11,400

(d) Rs. 7,200

27. From the following information calculate how much amount of depreciation will be shown in the Income and Expenditure A/c for the year 2021-22:

	As on 31 March, 2021	As on 31 March, 2022
Furniture	Rs. 1,80,000	Rs. 1,60,250

Furniture worth Rs. 8,000 was sold for Rs. 10,000 on 1 April, 2021.

(a) Rs. 9,750   (b) Rs. 11,750

(c) Rs. 11,250   (d) Rs. 9,250

28. Calculate subscription received during the year 2021-22 from the following information:

Amount of subscription credited to Income and Expenditure

A/c for the year ended 2021-22	Rs. 1,05,000
Subscription received in	Rs. 10,000
advances as on 31 March, 2022	
Subscription received in	Rs. 7000
advances as on 31 March, 2021	
Subscription outstanding	Rs. 10,500
as on 31 March, 2021	
Subscription outstanding	Rs. 20,500
as on 31 March, 2022	

(a) Rs. 95,000   (b) Rs. 92,000

(c) Rs. 98,000   (d) Rs. 1,18,000

29. Calculate prize fund expenses incurred during the year 2021-22 from the following information

Prize funds as on 1 April, 2021	Rs. 80,000
Donation received for Prize Fund	Rs. 15,000
10% Prize Fund Investment	Rs. 80,000
Interest Received	Rs. 5,000
Interest Accrued	Rs. 3,000
Prize fund as on 31 March, 2022	Rs. 70,000

(a) Rs. 33,000   (b) Rs. 23,000

(c) Rs. 28,000   (d) Rs. 25,000

30. Sudhir and Vimal came into partnership with profit sharing ratio of 3 : 2. Due to paucity of time, Sudhir was unable to given time to business so Vimal acted as principle and took all financial and operational decisions.

Due to break down of Covid 19, business suffered a loss of 4,00,000. State the amount of loss to be borne by Sudhir.

(a) Rs. 2,00,000

(b) Rs. 2,40,000

(c) None, as he was not working actively

(d) Rs. 1,60,000

31. Gitansh withdrew Rs. 5000 pm at the end of every month for ten months. Interest on drawing is charged @ 10% p.a. Gitansh's interest on drawings is:

(a) Rs. 1,875   (b) Rs. 2,250

(c) Rs. 2,292   (d) Rs. 2,750

32. Match **List - I** with **List - II**.

List - I	**List - II**
A. Interest on loan	I. Current Account
B. Fixed capital	II. Charge Against Profit
C. Fluctuating capital	III. Capital Account
D. Interest on capital	IV. Appropriation of Profit

Choose the correct answer from the options given below:

(a) A-IV, B-III, C-I, D-II

(b) A-II, B-I, C-III, D-IV

(c) A-IV, B-III, C-II, D-I

(d) A-II, B-I, C-IV, D-III

33. Identify the methods of Redemption of Debenture from the following.

A. By conversion into shares or new debenture

B. Purchase in open market

C. Sinking fund

D. Payment in instalments

E. Payment in lump-sum

Choose the correct answer from the options given below:

(a) A, B and C only

(b) A, B, C and D only

(c) A, B, D and E only

(d) C, D and E only

34. The central government has prescribed the maximum number of partners in a firm to be _______ under Rule 10 of the companies (Miscellaneous) Rules, 2014.

(a) 10   (b) 20

(c) 100   (d) 50

35. Which of the following statement is true?

(a) Decreased partner is not given share in profit if he dies in mid of the year as he has not rendered services for the entire year.

(b) The amount payable to decreased partner is transferred to his Loan A/c.

(c) The balance amount in decreased Partner's Capital is credited to his Executor's A/c.

(d) The decreased partner's share in profit is calculated on the basis of turnover method only.

36. The commonly used Techniques of financial Statements Analysis includes:

A. Common size statements

B. Ratio Analysis

C. Trend Analysis

D. Capital Budgeting Statement

Choose the correct answer from the options given below:

(a) A, B and D only

(b) B, C and D only

(c) A, B and C only

(d) A, C and D only

37. Modern Accounting is based on:

(a) Cash basis

(b) Single entry system

(c) Double entry system

(d) Liabilities

38. "A system of letter or figure with arbitrary meaning for brevity and for machine processing of information".

Above statement refers to the term:

(a) Liabilities   (b) Assets

(c) Code   (d) Debtors

39. A ______ is a special key word which can be entered into a cell in order to perform and process the data which is appended within brackets.

(a) Spreadsheet

(b) Function

(c) Labels

(d) Format

40. The CAS should be:

(a) Able to transform the manual accounting system to computerised accounting system

(b) Simple and integrated transparent, accurate, reliability, scalability

(c) Complex, Accurate, Transparent, Faster to work

(d) Complex, Inaccurate, fixed

Direction for questions 41 to 45:

A, B and C were partner's in a firm sharing profit and losses in the Ratio of 5 : 3 : 2. They admitted D into partnership for 1/5 share of profit which he take equally from A and B. D brought sufficient amount of goodwill in cash Capital brought in by is Rs. 50,000. On the date of admission the Balance Sheet of A, B and C was as follows:

Balance Sheet as on 31ˢᵗ March, 2021					
Liability		**Rs.**	**Assets**		**Rs.**
Capital			Building and Furniture		1,50,000
A	1,00,000		Debtors	55,000	
B	60,000		Provision	5,000	50,000
C	40,000	2,00,000	Cash		20,000
Creditors		50,000	Profit and Loss (2021-21)		30,000
		2,50,000			2,50,000

Goodwill is to be valued at 3 years purchase of average profit of last 4 years which were Rs. 60,000 (2017-18), Rs. 60,000 (18-19), Rs. 30,000 (19-20). On revaluation it was found that all debtors are good.

41. From the above calculate amount of Goodwill:

(a) 1,00,000

(b) 95,500

(c) 1,15,500

(d) 90,000

42. Calculate the total amount brought in by new partner D including Goodwill share:

(a) 50,000

(b) 68,000

(c) 1,40,000

(d) 18,000

43. What would be the new Profit Sharing Ratio:

(a) 2 : 1 : 1 : 1

(b) 5 : 3 : 2 : 1

(c) 4 : 1 : 1 : 1

(d) 20 : 12 : 8 : 4

44. What would be the effect of the line "All Debtors are good."

(a) Provision for Doubtful Debt is Debited to old partner Capital A/c

(b) Provision for Doubtful Debt is Debited to Revaluation Account

(c) Provision for Doubtful Debt is Credited to old partner's Capital A/c

(d) Provision for Doubtful Debt is Credited to Revaluation Account

45. Goodwill brought in by new partners would be_______.

(a) Distributed to A, B and C in old Ratio

(b) Distributed to A, B and C in Sacrificing Ratio

(c) Distribute to only A and B in Sacrificing Ratio

(d) Distribute to A, B and C in new Profit Sharing Ratio

Direction for Questions No. 46 to 50:

Raj Ltd. was registered with 70,000 equity shares. They issued 40,000 equity shares @ 10 each payable as follow:

On Application Rs. 4 per share

On Application Rs. 3 per share

and Balance on 2 calls

The issue was over subscribed by 50,000 shares. The directors decided upon making prorata allotment to 60,000 shares while remaining were returned.

46. Total applications received are for:

(a) 90,000 shares

(b) 50,000 shares

(c) 40,000 shares

(d) 60,000 shares

47. Amount to be returned to the applicants due to non-allotment of shares will be:

(a) Rs. 1,50,000

(b) Rs. 2,40,000

(c) Rs. 1,20,000

(d) Rs. 1,60,000

48. The portion of capital which the company does not issue to the public is known as:

(a) Authorised capital

(b) Paid up capital

(c) Uncalled capital

(d) Unissued Capital

49. The maximum amount that can be called up on the first call by the company is:

(a) 3

(b) 2

(c) 2.5

(d) 1

50. The amount to be adjusted with the call of allotment will be:

(a) Rs. 1,20,000

(b) Rs. 80,000

(c) Rs. 1,60,000

(d) Rs. 2,40,000

Answer Keys

1. (c)	**2.** (a)	**3.** (d)	**4.** (b)	**5.** (d)	**6.** (d)	**7.** (b)	**8.** (c)	**9.** (b)	**10.** (b)
11. (a)	**12.** (b)	**13.** (c)	**14.** (d)	**15.** (c)	**16.** (a)	**17.** (c)	**18.** (b)	**19.** (c)	**20.** (a)
21. (b)	**22.** (c)	**23.** (a)	**24.** (c)	**25.** (c)	**26.** (a)	**27.** (b)	**28.** (c)	**29.** (a)	**30.** (b)
31. (a)	**32.** (b)	**33.** (c)	**34.** (d)	**35.** (c)	**36.** (c)	**37.** (c)	**38.** (c)	**39.** (b)	**40.** (b)
41. (d)	**42.** (b)	**43.** (a)	**44.** (d)	**45.** (c)	**46.** (a)	**47.** (c)	**48.** (d)	**49.** (c)	**50.** (b)

Explanations

1. (c) Bank overdraft is an External liabilities so transfer to realisation A/c.

2. (a) Correct sequence is B, C, D, A.

3. (d) Revaluation Reserve is not shown.

4. (b) I.P.O. is issue for public.

5. (d) Forfeiture reduces the paid up capital.

6. (d) Cash credit is a current liabilities.

7. (b) A, B, C are investing activity.

8. (c) $\dfrac{\text{Rate}}{100 + \text{Rate}} \times \text{RFO}$, $\dfrac{20}{120} \times 120000 = \text{Rs.}20000$

9. (b) Ideal debt equity ratio is 2 : 1.

10. (b) A : B : C, $\dfrac{3}{8} : \dfrac{1}{2} : \dfrac{1}{8}, \dfrac{3 : 4 : 1}{8}$

If A dies than NPR of B & C is 4 : 1.

11. (a) Dropped by NTA.

Correct option is (a) only.

12. (b) Correct match is operating activity with cash sales, investing activity with purchase of fixed asset, financing activity with issue of shares.

13. (c) Loan 260000 – 200000 = 60000

Int. paid 10% of 100000 = 10000

Inflow = Rs. 50,000

14. (d) Securities premium cannot be used for discount on sales.

15. (c) Reserve capital can be called up on wind up.

16. (a) C, B, A, D is the correct sequence.

17. (c) Debtors – Bad debts = Paid by bank

600000 – 60000 = Rs. 5,40,000

18. (b) Match the columns.

19. (c) Machinery purchased = 200000

Machinery sold = –52000

Outflow in Inv. Act. = Rs.1,48,000

20. (a) Correct sequence is D, A, C, B.

21. (b) Match the column.

22. (c) 10 – 7 = Rs.3 is maximum price for reissued.

23. (a) P & L Appropriation A/c

To IOC R	1500	By P & L A/c	
S	500	(Balancing Figure)	13000
To Salary R	1000	By IOD R	300
To P/Cap		S	200
(Profit) R	7000		
S	3500		
	13500		**13500**

24. (c) Total IOC = 50000

(24000 + x) + (18000) = 50000

IOC on Additional x = Rs.8000

Rs.8000 is IOC on capital @ 6% for 8 months so additional capital = Rs.200000

25. (c) Match the columns.

26. (a) Total interest $85000 \times \dfrac{12}{100} = \text{Rs.}10200$

Interest received = Rs. –9000

Accrued Interest = Rs.1200

27. (b) Furniture A/c

To Bal. b/d	180000	By Dep. (B/F)	11750
To P & L (Pro.)	2000	By Bank (sale)	10000
		By Bal. c/d	160250
	182000		**182000**

28. (c) 105000 + (10000 + 10500) – (7000 + 20500)

= 105000 + 20500 – 27500

= Rs.98000

29. (a) (80000 + 15000 + 5000 + 3000) – (70000)

103000 – 70000 = Rs.33000

30. (b) $400000 \times \dfrac{3}{5} = \text{Rs.}240000$ bear by Sudheer.

31. (a) Total drawings = 5000 × 10 = Rs. 50,000

$$\text{IOD} = 50000 \times \frac{10}{100} \times \frac{4.5}{12} = \text{Rs. } 1{,}875$$

32. (b) Match the column.

33. (c) Sinking fund is not a method of redemption of Debentures.

34. (d) Central government has prescribed the maximum number of partners is 50.

35. (c) The balance is transfer to executors A/c.

36. (c) Capital budgeting statement is not a technique of FSA.

37. (c) Computer Accounting

Double Entry system is modern accounting.

38. (c) Computer Accounting

Code is a system of letter or figure.

39. (b) Computer Accounting

Function key is a special key.

40. (b) Computer Accounting

Computer accounting system should be simple & reliable.

41. (d) Total profit = 60000 + 60000 + 30000 – 30000
= 120000

Average profit = 120000 ÷ 4 = Rs. 30,000

Goodwill = 30000 × 3 = Rs. 90,000

42. (b) Capital of D = Rs. 50,000

Share of Goodwill = Rs. 18,000

Total = Rs. 68,000

43. (a) Sac of A $\dfrac{1}{5} \times \dfrac{1}{2} = \dfrac{1}{10}$, Sac of B $\dfrac{1}{5} \times \dfrac{1}{2} = \dfrac{1}{10}$

NPR $\dfrac{4}{10} : \dfrac{2}{10} : \dfrac{2}{10} : \dfrac{1}{5}$ or 4 : 2 : 2 : 2 or 2 : 1 : 1 : 1

44. (d) As all debtors are good means no need of provision for doubtful debts so credited to revaluation A/c.

45. (c) Goodwill brought by new partner will be distributed in sacrifice ratio.

46. (a) Company wants to issue = 40000 shares

Add Shares over subscribed by = 50000

Total application received = 90000 shares.

47. (c) Total application received = 90000 shares

Less Pro rata allotment = 60000 shares

Shares return = 30000

Money return = 30000 × 4 = Rs.120000

48. (d) Unissued capital does not issue to the public.

49. (c) Misprinting in question paper.

If shares issued at 2 Rs. premium than answer will (10 + 2) – (4 + 3) = 12 – 7 = 5 ÷ 2 = 2.5

50. (b) Pro rata = 60000 shares

Less Offered = 40000 shares

Extra = 20000 shares

Advance for allotment = 20000 × 4 = Rs. 80,000

1. Prepaid Expenses is shown in sub-head of the Balance Sheet under:
   (a) Current Assets
   (b) Other Current Assets
   (c) Other Non-current Assets
   (d) Short-term loan and advances

2. Bank overdraft is shown in the liabilities side under the sub-head:
   (a) Current liability
   (b) Short Term Borrowings
   (c) Other Current Liabilities
   (d) Short Term Provision

3. When fixed amount of money is withdrawn quarterly by partners at the beginning of each quarter, for how many months, is interest to be calculated on the total money withdrawn during a year?
   (a) $7\frac{1}{2}$ months
   (b) $6\frac{1}{2}$ months
   (c) $4\frac{1}{2}$ months
   (d) $3\frac{1}{2}$ months

4. Goodwill at 2 years purchase of 3 years average profit is Rs. 1,44,000. If the firm earned a profit of Rs. 33,000 in the previous year and Rs. 46,000 in the year before that, the 3rd year profit would be:
   (a) Rs. 72,000
   (b) Rs. (7,000)
   (c) Rs. 2,16,000
   (d) Rs. 1,37,00

5. Losses are shown in the Balance Sheet under the heading:
   (a) Non current assets
   (b) Cash and Cash equivalents
   (c) Other current assets
   (d) Inventory

6. RK and Company purchased a boiler from No Risk Machine Limited for Rs. 3,80,000. As per purchase agreement, Rs. 20,000 were paid in cash and balance by issue of shares of Rs. 100 each at 20% premium. The number of shares issued will be:
   (a) 3600   (b) 3000
   (c) 3800   (d) 4000

7. Formula for calculating cost of goods sold is:
   (a) Opening stock + Net purchases + Direct Expenses – closing stock.
   (b) Opening stock + total purchases + Direct Expenses – closing stock.
   (c) Opening stock + total purchases – closing stock.
   (d) Opening stock + Net purchases – closing stock.

8. (1) Bank A/C Dr. Rs. 2,91,000

   To Equity Share 2nd and Final call Rs. 2,91,00

   (Being 2nd and final call money received except for 300 share)

   (2) Share Capital A/C. Dr.   Rs. 30,000

   To Equity Share 1st call   Rs. 6,000

   To Equity Share 2nd call   Rs. 9,000

   To Share Forfeiture A/C   Rs. 15,000

   (300 shares being for fecited)

   Based on the above instructions calculate the total number of shares issued by the company were:
   (a) 29,100   (b) 30,000
   (c) 9,700   (d) 10,000

9. Pick the correct statement:
   (a) Goodwill is a real asset.
   (b) Goodwill is a wasting asset.
   (c) Goodwill is an intangible assets.
   (d) Goodwill is a Current assets.

10. In which situation would Profit and Loss Appropriation A/c be credited?
    (a) For Interest on Capital
    (b) For Interest on Drawings
    (c) For Partner's Commission
    (d) For Manager's Commission

11. Proposed dividend is treated as:
    (a) Contingent liability
    (b) Current liability
    (c) Non Current liability
    (d) Tangible assets

12. Ratio's that are calculated for measuring the efficiency of operations is:
    (a) Solvency Ratio
    (b) Turnover Ratio
    (c) Liquidity Ratio
    (d) Profitability Ratio

13. The balance of Shares Forfeited Account is shown under which head till the Forfeited Shares are re-issued.

(a) Non current liabilities

(b) Reserves and Surpluses

(c) Share Capital

(d) Unsecured Loan

14. The Shares of a Public Limited Company are:

(a) Freely Transferable

(b) Transfered with Restriction

(c) Not Transferable

(d) Transferable in the prescribed manner of Articles

15. X and Y are partner's in a firm sharing profits in the ratio of 3 : 2, Z admits in the firm for $\frac{1}{5}$th share in profits. Z brings in Rs. 40,000 capital and required amount of goodwill. The goodwill of the firm was valued at Rs. 6,00,000. The amount of premium brought by Z would be:

(a) Rs. 1,20,000　　　(b) Rs. 6,00,000

(c) Rs. 3,00,000　　　(d) Rs. 2,00,000

16. Write the sequence of treating losses as per section 48 of the Partnership Act 1932.

A. Close Realisation Account

B. Payout of Partners Capital

C. Pay out of Profits

D. Paid by the partners individually in their profits sharing ratio

Choose the most appropriate answer from the options given below:

(a) A, B, C, D　　　(b) A, C, B, D

(c) A, D, C, B　　　(d) A, D, B, C

17. In case of dissolution of a firm, assets of the firm shall be applied in following purposes and order (sequence).

A. Paying to each partner portionately what is due to him on account of capital

B. In paying the debts of the firm to the third party

C. In transferring amount to General Reserves

D. Residue if any to be divided among the partner's in their profit sharing ratio

E. In paying each partner proportionately what is due to him from the firm for advances (Partner's Loan)

Choose the most appropriate answer from the options given below:

(a) B, A, D, E, C　　　(b) C, D, B, D, E

(c) B, E, A, D　　　　(d) E, A, D, C

18. Government Grant received by Not-for-profit organisation will be shown in:

(a) Income of current year

(b) Expenses of current year

(c) Liability of current year

(d) Assets of current year

19. Identify the right sequence of Cash-flow statement as per Accounting Standards 3.

A. Cash Equivalents

B. Cash Flow from Investing Activity

C. Cash Flow from Operating Activity

D. Cash Flow from Financing Activity

Choose the most appropriate answer from the options given below:

(a) C, B, D, A

(b) A, B, C, D

(c) C, A, B, D

(d) C, B, A, D

20. State whether 'Cash withdrawal from Bank' will be classified under which kind of activity?

(a) Cash Flow from Operating Activity

(b) Cash Flow from Financing Activity

(c) No Cash Flow

(d) Cash Flow from Investing Activity

21. Common size Balance Sheet of XYZ Ltd. as at 31st March 2019 and 2020

	Absolute Amounts		Percentage of *	
1. Non-Current Assets (a) Fixed Assets (b) Current Assets	2018-19 (Rs.)	2019-20 (Rs.)	2018-19 (%)	2019-20 (%)
	44,00,000 1,00,000	48,00,000 2,00,000	97.78 2.22	96 4
	45,00,000	50,00,000	100	100

The blank space * in the table row is:

(a) Previous Year　　　(b) Net Revenue from Operation

(c) Total Assets　　　　(d) Fixed Assets

22. Match **List - I** with **List - II** with reference to interest on drawings.

List - I	List - II
(Drawings)	**(Average Period)**
A. When drawings are made in the beginning of every quarter	I. 5.5 Months
B. When drawing are made in the beginning of every month	II. 4.5 Months
C. When drawing are made in the end of every quarter	III. 7.5 Months
D. When drawings are made at the end of every month	IV. 6.5 Months

Choose the correct answer from the options given below:

(a) A-III, B-IV, C-II, D-I

(b) A-II, B-III, C-I, D-IV

(c) A-IV, B-I, C-III, D-II

(d) A-I, B-II, C-IV, D-III

23. P, Q and R are partner's in firm sharing profits in the ratio of 3 : 2 : 1. R retires and the balance in his capital account after making necessary adjustments on accounts of reserve and surplus, revaluation of assets and reassessment of liabilities works out of be Rs. 60,000. P and Q agreed to pay him Rs. 75,000 in full settlement of his claim. It implies that Rs. 15,000 is:

(a) R's salary for the time period

(b) R's loan

(c) R's share of Goodwill

(d) R's share of Profit

24. Match **List - I** with **List - II**.

List - I	List - II
A. Cash and Cash Equivalents	I. Purchase of Equipment
B. Investing Activity	II. Demand Deposits
C. Financing Activity	III. Receipt for Royalties
D. Operating Activity	IV. Payment of Interest

Choose the correct answer from the options given below:

(a) A-II, B-III, C-IV, D-I

(b) A-II, B-I, C-IV, D-III

(c) A-IV, B-I, C-II, D-III

(d) A-III, B-IV, C-I, D-II

25. Abhishek, Rajat and Vivek are partner's sharing profits in the ratio 5 : 3 : 2. If Vivek retires the new profit sharing ratio between Abhishek and Rajat will be:

(a) 3 : 2

(b) 5 : 3

(c) 5 : 2

(d) 2 : 1

26. Comparative statements are also known as:

(a) Dynamic Analysis

(b) Horizontal Analysis

(c) Vertical Analysis

(d) External Analysis

27. Find out the amount of stationery consumed during the year 2021-22.

Payment made for stationery during the year 2021-22.	Rs. 40,000
Stock of stationery on 1st April 2021	Rs. 10,000
Stock of stationery on 31st March 2022	Rs. 20,000
Creditors of stationery on 31st March 2022	Rs. 30,000

(a) Rs. 40,000

(b) Rs. 60,000

(c) Rs. 80,000

(d) Rs 1,00,000

28. From the following information, find out cash flow from investing activities:

Sale of machinery	Rs. 40,000
Purchase of machinery	Rs. 85,000
Rent received	Rs. 5,000
Sale of investment	Rs. 10,000

(a) 55,000

(b) (80,000)

(c) (30,000)

(d) 50,000

29. How will you treat the following items while making cash flow statement

Particulars	2020 - 21	2021 - 22
Provision for Tax	30,000	35,000

  (a) Rs. 35,000 will be added in operating & Rs. 30,000 will be deducted from operating activities

  (b) Rs. 35,000 will be added in operating activities

  (c) Rs. 30,000 will be deducted from operating activities

  (d) Rs. 35,000 will be added in financing activities & Rs. 30,000 will be deducted in operating activities

30. Arrange the below mentioned items/transactions in proper sequence for calculation of Cash Flow from operating activities.

  A. Net profit before taxes & extraordinary items

  B. Income Tax paid

  C. Operating profit before working capital changes

  D. Net profit as per statement of Profit & Loss A/c

  E. Patents Amortised

  Choose the most appropriate answer from the options given below:

  (a) A, D, C, E, B

  (b) D, A, E, C, B

  (c) A, D, B, C, E

  (d) D, A, B, E, C

31. Match **List - I** with **List - II**.

List - I	List - II
A. Permanent Drawings	I. Credit side of Partner's Current A/C
B. Interest on Capital	II. Debit side of Partner's Current A/C
C. Fresh Capital introduced	III. Credit side of Partner's Capital A/C
D. Interest on drawings	IV. Debit side of Partner's Capital A/C

  Choose the correct answer from the options given below:

  (a) A-I, B-II, C-IV, D-III

  (b) A-IV, B-I, C-III, D-II

  (c) A-III, B-IV, C-II, D-I

  (d) A-I, B-IV, C-III, D-II

32. All the following items would be included in company's Operating Activities excepts;

  A. Income Tax Payment

  B. Collection from Customer

  C. Cash Payment to Suppliers

  D. Interest on Current Investment

  E. Dividend paid by Financial Institution

  Choose the most appropriate answer from the options given below:

  (a) C only

  (b) D only

  (c) A only

  (d) E only

33. A, B and C were partner's in a firm. A had advanced a loan of Rs. 20,000 which was settled by paying him Rs. 18,000. The correct treatment would be:

  (a) Bank a/c would be credited by Rs. 20,000

  (b) Realisation a/c would be credited by Rs. 2,000

  (c) Bank a/c would be credited by Rs. 18,000

  (d) Bank a/c & Realisation a/c would be credited by Rs. 18,000 and Rs. 2000 respectively

34. Income and Expenditure Account is:

  (a) Personal Account

  (b) Real Account

  (c) Nominal Account

  (d) Asset Account

35. Compulsory dissolution of a partnership firm takes place in the following circumstances.

  A. Due to death of one of the partners

  B. When all partner's or all but one partner, becomes insolvent rendering them incompetent to sign a contract

  C. When the business becomes illegal

  D. With the consent of all the partners

  E. In accordance with a contract between the partner's

  Choose the most appropriate answer from the options given below:

  (a) A and B only

  (b) B and C only

  (c) C and D only

  (d) D and E only

36. Identify the correct options, not appearing in the 'Receipt and Payment Account but need to be taken into account for determining the surplus/deficit for an accounting year:
    (a) Provision for doubtful debts
    (b) Printing and stationary expenses
    (c) Rates and Taxes
    (d) Wages and Salaries

37. The tern 'Field as applied to Data Base' table means:
    (a) A vertical column of the table
    (b) Name of table
    (c) Size of the table
    (d) Horizontal row of the table

38. Which view show margins and the rulers?
    (a) Page set up
    (b) Page lay out
    (c) Review
    (d) Normal

39. Which formula would result in TRUE if C4 is less than 10 and D4 is less than 100?
    (a) = AND (C4 > 10, D4 < 100)
    (b) = AND (C4 > 10, C4 < 100)
    (c) = AND (C4 < 10, D4 < 100)
    (d) = AND (C4 > 10, D4 < 10)

40. Identify the concept referred to Computerised Accounting System:
    (a) Printing of Balance Sheet and Profit and Loss Accounts using computer
    (b) Processing of accounting transaction through computers and produce records and reports
    (c) Processing of accounts related to data and printing reports
    (d) Creating only Journal entry using computer

Direction for questions 41 to 45: Read the text carefully and answer the questions:

Electronic Follow Pro, a Delhi Based Company dealing the almost all types of electronic products, appointed marketing expert, Mr. Salman Khan as the CEO of the company, with a target to increase their market share from 40% to 50% for the accounting year 2022-23. Mr. Salman discussed the details of target to be achieved with all departmental heads and branch heads of all branches in Delhi. The target is to reach all backward or less developed cities of Delhi NCR, Motto of new Project is "Use More; Save More". Selling, Distribution and Promotional expenses of the firm will increase manifold. The finance manager Mr. Sharukh was asked to prepare the budget accordingly, an additional fund requirement of Rs. 60,00,000 is to be raised. The Finance Manager Mr. Sharukh proposed to (i) issue equity shares of Rs. 100 each for Rs. 20,00,000 (ii) 20,000 10% debentures of Rs. 100 each to the public at a premium of 5%; redeemable after 5 years at Rs. 110 per debenture. (iii) Raise a loan of Rs. 20,00,000 from Bank of India against debenture kept as an additional security.

41. What other name is given to debentures being kept as an additional security?
    (a) Consideration other than cash
    (b) Commitments
    (c) Contingents Liability
    (d) Collateral Security

42. As per section 52, of the companies Act, 2013, Securities Premium Reserve can not be utilised for:
    (a) writing off capital losses
    (b) issue of fully paid bonus shares
    (c) writing off discount on issues of debentures
    (d) writing off preliminary expenses

43. What is the amount of annual fixed obligation?
    (a) Rs. 2,00,000
    (b) Rs. 20,00,000
    (c) Rs. 2,20,000
    (d) Rs. 20,000

44. Under what head sub-head will this annual fixed obligation paid on debentures be shown in companies financial statements?
    (a) Other Current Liabilities in Balance Sheet
    (b) Short term Provisions in Balance Sheet
    (c) Other Expenses in Income Statement
    (d) Finance Cost in Income Statement

45. Choose the correct journal entry to be passed for Redemption of Debentures due after 5 years:
    (a) Debentures ac Dr.   Rs 20,00,000
        Premium on Redemption
        of Debentures A/c   Rs. 2,00,000
        To Debenture holders   Rs. 22,00,000
    (b) Debentures   Rs. 22,00,000
        To Debenture holders   Rs. 20,00,000
        To Premium on Redemption
        of Debentures A/c   Rs. 2,00,000
    (c) No entry
    (d) Debenture holder A/c   Rs. 20,00,000
        To Bank A/c   Rs. 20,00,000

Direction for questions 46 to 50: Read the text carefully and answer the questions:

One step organisation is an NPO established to work in areas of Environment, Health & Education for the sustainable development of the society, for this, they create replicable and scalable models of plantation through an integrated approach. This organisation was started by Mr. Sushant and his 19 other friends. They all paid life membership fee Rs. 20,000 each. A well known industrialist Mr. Modi donated Rs. 2,00,000 for purchase of plants. All 20 members were to pay annual subscription Rs. 500; two member could not pay the subscription during the year, but other 5 members paid their subscription for the next year. Two gardener's were appointed at a salary Rs. 2,500 p.m. They had a session to brief about environment and health whom they paid Rs. 2,000.

46. The donation Rs. 2,00,000 received for Plants will be shown in which A/c statement?

(a) Income and Expenditure A/c (Income side)

(b) Income and Expenditure A/c (Expenditure side)

(c) Balance sheet (Assets side)

(d) Balance sheet (Liabilities side)

47. The money paid to the environment expert, Rs. 2,000 for a session is known as:

(a) honorarium

(b) salary

(c) wages

(d) donation

48. The salaries Rs. 2500 per month being paid to the gardeners will be shown in which A/c statement?

(a) Receipts side of Receipts & Payment A/c

(b) Income side of Income & Expenditure A/c

(c) Expenditure side of Income & Exp. A/c

(d) Assets side of Balance Sheet

49. The subscription not paid by 2 members will be shown where and which side?

(a) Rs. 1000 outstanding subscription liabilities side of Balance Sheet and income side of Income and Expenditure Account.

(b) Receipts and Payment A/c only on Receipts side Rs. 1000

(c) Rs. 1000 on Assets side and Income side of Income and Expenditure A/c

(d) Expenditure side and Liabilities side of Balance Sheet

50. Where will be the advance subscription paid by 5 members shown?

(a) Rs. 2,500 on payment side (R/P A/c) and Assets side of Balance Sheet

(b) Rs. 2,500 on Income side as a deduction and liabilities side of Balance Sheet

(c) Rs. 2,500 on Income side as an additional and Assets side of Balance Sheet

(d) Rs. 2,500 on Expenditure side as a deduction and liabilities side of Balance Sheet

Answer Keys

1. (b)	**2.** (b)	**3.** (a)	**4.** (d)	**5.** (d)	**6.** (b)	**7.** (a)	**8.** (d)	**9.** (c)	**10.** (b)
11. (a)	**12.** (b)	**13.** (c)	**14.** (d)	**15.** (a)	**16.** (b)	**17.** (c)	**18.** (a)	**19.** (a)	**20.** (c)
21. (c)	**22.** (a)	**23.** (c)	**24.** (b)	**25.** (b)	**26.** (b)	**27.** (b)	**28.** (c)	**29.** (a)	**30.** (b)
31. (b)	**32.** (b)	**33.** (d)	**34.** (c)	**35.** (b)	**36.** (a)	**37.** (a)	**38.** (b)	**39.** (c)	**40.** (b)
41. (d)	**42.** (a)	**43.** (a)	**44.** (d)	**45.** (a)	**46.** (d)	**47.** (a)	**48.** (c)	**49.** (c)	**50.** (b)

Explanations

1. (b) Prepaid expenses are shown in sub head of balance sheet under other C.A.

2. (b) Bank overdraft is shown under the sub head of balance sheet under S.T. borrowings

3. (a) 7.5 months as beginning of each quarter.

4. (d) Average profit = $\dfrac{144000}{2}$ = 72000

Total profit = 72000 × 3 = 216000

Remaining profit = 216000 – 33000 – 46000

= Rs.137000

5. (d) Loose tools are shown under heading Inventory.

6. (b) 380000 – 20000 = Rs.360000

Numbers $\dfrac{360000}{120}$ = 3000 shares

7. (a) COGS = OP STOCK + NET PUR + D.E – CLO STOCK

8. (d) Arrears of II call on 300 shares = Rs.9000

Amount of II call = $\dfrac{9000}{300}$ = Rs. 30 each

Money received for $\dfrac{291000}{30}$ = 9700 shares

Total no. of shares issued = 9700 + 300 = 10000

9. (c) Goodwill is an intangible assets.

10. (b) For IOD, P and L App a/c be credited

11. (a) Proposed dividend is treated as contingent liabilities.

12. (b) Turnover ratios are calculated for measuring the efficiency of operations.

13. (c) Forfeited shares are shown under share capital till re issued.

14. (d) Shares of public company are transferable.

15. (a) Goodwill of the firm = 600000

Z's share = 600000 × $\dfrac{1}{5}$ = 120000

16. (b) A, C, B, D is the correct sequence

17. (c) B, E, A, D is the correct sequence

18. (a) Government grant is a source of income of NPO

19. (a) C, B, A, D is the correct sequence

20. (c) Cash withdrawal from bank is no flow of cash

21. (c) In common size balance sheet % is based on T.A or T.L.

22. (a) Match the column

23. (c) Full settlement = 75000

Less balance after adjustments = 60000

Share of goodwill = 15000

24. (b) Match the column

25. (b) NPR of A and R is 5 : 3

26. (b) Comparative statement are also known as Horizontal analysis

27. (b) Pay + op stock + clo creditors – clo stock

40000 + 10000 + 30000 – 20000

= Rs. 60000

28. (c) Outflow = 85000

Inflow = 40000, 5000, 10000 = 55000

Net outflow = Rs.30000

29. (a) C.Y. will be added, P.Y. will be deducted

30. (b) D, A, E, C, B is correct sequence

31. (b) Match rhe column

32. (b) Dividend paid by financing company is not included in operating activity.

33. (d) Bank account by 18000 and Realisation account by 2000 credited

34. (c) Income and expenditure account is a nominal account

35. (b) Compulsory dissolution takes place at the time of insolvency of all partners and illegal business.

36. (a) Provision for doubtful debts taken into account.

37. (a) A vertical column of the table.

38. (b) Page layout shows margins and rulers.

39. (c) Computer accounting

40. (b) CAS refers processing of accounting transactions through computers.

41. (d) Additional security is known as collateral security

42. (a) SPR can not be utilised for writing off capital losses.

43. (a) $\dfrac{20000 \times 100 \times 10}{100}$ = Rs.200000

44. (d) Interest on debentures is a finance cost in the income statement.

45. (a) First entry is correct

46. (d) Specific donation is shown under balance sheet liabilities side.

47. (a) Honorarium is paid to visiting expert for temporary services.

48. (c) Salary is shown on expenditure side of income and expenditure account.

49. (c) Accrued subscription will be shown at income side by adding and assets side of balance sheet.

50. (b) Advance subscription will be shown at income side as deduction in subscription and liabilities side of balance sheet.

1. As per Receipts and Payments Account for the year ended on March 31, 2020, subscriptions received were Rs. 2,50,000 subscriptions outstanding on 1-04-2019 Rs. 50,000. Subscriptions received in advance as on 31-3-2020 are Rs. 30,000. Subscription for the year 2019-20 will be:
   (a) Rs. 2,30,000
   (b) Rs. 1,50,000
   (c) Rs. 2,40,000
   (d) Rs. 1,70,000

2. At the time of admission of a new partner general reserve appearing in the old balance sheet is transferred to __________.
   (a) All Partner's Capital A/C
   (b) New Partner's Capital A/C
   (c) Old Partner's Capital A/C
   (d) Gaining Partner's Capital A/C

3. Match **List - I** with **List - II**.

List - I	List - II
Basis of Debenture	**Types of Debenture**
A. Tenure	I. Zero coupon rate
B. Interest rate point of view	II. Irredeemable
C. Security	III. Registration
D. Bearer	IV. Secured

   Choose the correct answer from the options given below:
   (a) A-I, B-III, C-II, D-IV
   (b) A-IV, B-I, C-III, D-II
   (c) A-II, B-I, C-IV, D-III
   (d) A-III, B-IV, C-I, D-II

4. On retirement of a partner, the retiring partner's capital account will be credited with __________.
   (a) His/her share of Goodwill
   (b) Good will of the firm
   (c) Share of Good will Remaining Partners
   (d) His/her share of Goodwill and share of Goodwill of Remaining Partners

5. Journal entry of be passed for unrecorded assets for preparing Revaluation A/C at the time of Retirement of a partner will be _______.
   (a) Assets A/C Dr. To all Partners capital A/C
   (b) Assets A/C Dr. To Revaluation A/c
   (c) Revaluation A/C Dr. To assets A/C
   (d) Revaluation A/C Dr. To old partner's capital A/C

6. Match **List - I** with **List - II**

List - I	List - II
Major Head	**Sub Head**
A. Fixed assets	I. Short term provisions
B. Current Assets	II. Money received against share warrants
C. Current Liabilities	III. Non current investment
D. Shareholder's Funds	IV. Inventories

   Choose the correct answer from the options given below:
   (a) A-IV, B-I, C-II, D-III
   (b) A-III, B-IV, C-I, D-II
   (c) A-I, B-IV, C-II, D-III
   (d) A-II, B-I, C-IV, D-III

7. Match **List - I** with **List - II**.

List - I	List - II
A. Cash Equivalents	I. Interim Dividend paid
B. Financing Activities	II. Selling & Distribution expenses paid
C. Operating Activities	III. Marketable securities
D. Investing Activities	IV. Dividend received on Shares held as investment

   Choose the correct answer from the options given below:
   (a) A-IV, B-I, C-II, D-III
   (b) A-III, B-I, C-II, D-IV
   (c) A-III, B-IV, C-II, D-I
   (d) A-III, B-IV, C-I, D-II

8. At the time of retirement of a Partner the remaining gaining partners should compensate the __________.
   (a) Remaining Partners only
   (b) Retiring Partners only
   (c) Retiring Partners as well as remaining partners who have sacrificed
   (d) Sacrificing partners only

9. If a partner retires in the middle of the year his/her share of profit from the date of last balance sheet till the date of retirement will be transferred to: __________

(a) Profit & Loss A/C credit side

(b) Profit & Loss suspense A/C debit side

(c) Retiring partners capital A/C debit side

(d) Profit & Loss suspense A/C credit side

10. If debentures are converted into equity shares, it is a/an: ___________

(a) Inflow of cash

(b) No flow of cash

(c) Outflow of cash

(d) Cash and Cash equivalents

11. Match List - I with List - II in context of not having partnership deed.

List - I		**List - II**
A.	Interest on loan	I. Equal
B.	Interest on drawings	II. Will not be charged
C.	Salary	III. @ 6% p.a.
D.	Profit sharing ratio	IV. Will not be allowed/provided

Choose the correct answer from the options given below:

(a) A-IV, B-I, C-III, D-II

(b) A-III, B-IV, C-II, D-I

(c) A-IV, B-III, C-II, D-I

(d) A-III, B-II, C-IV, D-I

12. What is the correct sequence of allotment of shares

A. Allotment money received

B. Inviting applications from investors

C. Allotment Due

D. Application money Received

E. Share Call Money Due

Choose the correct answer from the options given below:

(a) E, C, A, B, D

(b) A, B, C, D, E

(c) B, D, C, A, E

(d) C, A, E, D, B

13. What is the correct sequence of types of capital in company's Balance sheet while preparing notes to accounts.

A. Issued Capital

B. Subscribed and fully paid up capital

C. Share forfeited Balance

D. Authorised Capital

E. Subscribed but not fully paid up capital

Choose the correct answer from the options given below:

(a) C, B, D, E, A

(b) D, A, B, E, C

(c) A, B, C, D, E

(d) B, A, D, E, C

14. Identify the correct sequence to find out profit after tax while preparing comparative income statement

A. Deduct expenses

B. Find out total revenue by adding other incomes to revenue from operations

C. Find out profit after tax

D. Deduct tax

E. Calculate profit before tax

Choose the correct answer from the options given below:

(a) E, B, A, D, C

(b) B, A, E, D, C

(c) B, E, A, C, D

(d) E, C, B, A, D

15. If net profit made during the year are Rs. 50,000 and the bills receivables have decreased by Rs. 10,000 during the year then the cash flow from operating activities will be:

(a) Rs. 40,000

(b) Rs. 60,000

(c) Rs. 30,000

(d) Rs. 20,000

16. The capital accounts of partners will always show a ______ balance under fixed capital account method

(a) Debit

(b) Credit

(c) Zero

(d) Negative

17. Aman and Mohan, partners of a firm decided to dissolve the business on 31-03-22. The firm decided to pay realisation expenses of Rs. 1,000 on behalf of Mohan. Rs. 1,000 will be debited to

(a) Realisation A/C

(b) Mohan's capital A/C

(c) Bank A/C

(d) Aman's capital A/C

18. Common size analysis is also known as

    (a) Horizontal Analysis

    (b) Vertical Analysis

    (c) Cash Flow Analysis

    (d) Ratio Analysis

19. Calculate the amount of yearly interest payable on 9% debentures (10,000 debentures of Rs. 100) issued as collateral security.

    (a) No Interest payable

    (b) Rs. 90,000

    (c) Rs. 9000

    (d) Rs. 99000

20. If the net profit earned during the year is Rs. 1,00,000 and the amount of Bills receivables in the beginning and the end of the year is Rs. 20,000 and Rs. 40,000 respectively, then cash flow from operating activities will be:

    (a) Rs. 60,000

    (b) Rs. 1,00,000

    (c) Rs. 80,000

    (d) Rs. 1,20,000

21. Sale of copy rights are considered as a part of

    (a) Investing Activities

    (b) Financing Activities

    (c) Operating Activities

    (d) Financing & Operating Activities

22. Romi Ltd. purchased building worth Rs. 1,50,000 machinery worth Rs. 1,40,000 and furniture worth Rs. 10,000 from xyz co. and took over its liabilities of Rs. 20,000 for a purchase consideration of Rs. 3,15,000. They paid the purchase consideration by issuing 12% debentures of Rs. 100 each at a premium of 5%. What will be the number of debentures issued by Romi Ltd.

    (a) 4,000

    (b) 3,500

    (c) 3,000

    (d) 2,000

23. Securities premium Reserve can be utilised ______.

    A. to return excess money received on application

    B. to write off preliminary expenses

    C. to issue partly paid bonus shares

    D. for premium paid on Redemption of Debentures or preference shares

    E. for buy back of shares

Choose the correct answer from the options given below:

    (a) A, B, C only

    (b) B, C, E only

    (c) C, D, E only

    (d) B, D, E only

24. What are different types of debentures from the view point of registration

    A. Convertible　　　　B. Bearer

    C. Redeemable　　　　D. Secured

    E. Registered

Choose the correct answer from the options given below:

    (a) A & E only

    (b) B & C only

    (c) B & E only

    (d) C & D only

25. Identify the steps in preparation of final accounts of not for profit organisation (NPO)

    A. Prepare Balance Sheet of NPO

    B. Prepare Income and Expenditure Account from Receipts and payment Account

    C. Prepare Receipts and payment Account

    D. Adjust outstanding/prepaid expenditure/Income and determine surplus/Deficit

    E. Prepare cash book

Choose the correct answer from the options given below:

    (a) E, C, B, D, A

    (b) D, E, A, B, D

    (c) A, B, C, D, E

    (d) E, C, A, B, D

26. Match **List - I** with **List - II** in context g cashflow statement

List - I	List - II
A. Sale of fixed asset	I. Outflow in operating activities
B. Purchase of Goodwill	II. Inflow in Investing Activities
C. Tax Paid	III. Outflow in Investing Activities
D. Dividend Paid	IV. Outflow in Financing Activities

Choose the correct answer from the options given below:

(a) A-II, B-I, C-IV, D-III

(b) A-II, B-III, C-I, D-IV

(c) A-II, B-I, C-III, D-IV

(d) A-III, B-II, C-IV, D-I

27. Identify the limitations of financial statements:

A. Can be biased

B. Report on stewardship function

C. Aggregate information

D. Only interim reports

E. Basis of fiscal policies

Choose the correct answer from the options given below:

(a) A, C, B only

(b) A, C, D only

(c) E, A, D only

(d) B, A, C only

28. What are the different types of liquidity ratios

A. Interest coverage ratio

B. Current ratio

C. Inventory turnover ratio

D. Gross profit ratio

E. Acid test ratio

Choose the correct answer from the options given below:

(a) A & B only	(b) B & E only

(c) B & D only	(d) D & E only

29. Identify the components of equity:

A. Money received against share warrants

B. Working capital

C. Share capital

D. Reserves & surplus

E. Cash Revenue from operations

Choose the correct answer from the options given below:

(a) A, C & E only

(b) B, C & D only

(c) A, B & C only

(d) A, C & D only

30. Identify the correct sequence of current assets in company's Balance sheet?

A. Bills Receivables

B. Cash & cash equivalents

C. Short term loans & advances

D. Inventories

E. Current investments

Choose the correct answer from the options given below:

(a) C, A, B, E, D

(b) D, C, E, A, B

(c) B, D, E, C, A

(d) E, D, A, B, C

31. When debentures are issued at premium with the term of redeeming them at par. The amount of premium received at the time of issue will be:

(a) Debited to premium on Redemption of Debentures A/C

(b) Credited to Premium on Redemption of Debentures A/C

(c) Debited to Securities Premium Reserve A/C

(d) Credited to securities premium Reserve A/C

32. While preparing common-size Balance sheet, each item of Balance sheet is expressed as % of

(a) Non-current assets

(b) Current assets

(c) Non-current liabilities

(d) Total assets or total liability

33. It is the amount-paid to the person who is not the regular employee of the institution.

(a) Wages

(b) Honorarium

(c) Salary

(d) Donation

34. When the total amount withdrawn is given but the date of withdrawal is not given then interest on drawings is charged for a period of:

(a) 3 months

(b) 6 months

(c) 9 months

(d) 12 months

35. At the time of admission of partner if goodwill exist in the books of account it will be written off among:

(a) Old partners in sacrificing ratio

(b) All the partners in new ratio

(c) New partners in gaining ratio

(d) Old partners in old profit sharing ratio

36. Rani, Sandhya and Kangana are partners sharing profit in the ratio of 4 : 3 : 2 Rani retires. Sandhya and Kangana decided to share profits in future in the ratio of 5 : 3. Gaining ratio of Sandhya and Kangana will be

    (a) 11 : 21 (b) 21 : 11

    (c) 31 : 12 (d) 23 : 13

37. What are the internal controls designed to do?

    (a) Only ensure accurate accounting records

    (b) Safeguard assets and optimize use of resource

    (c) Only safeguard assets

    (d) Only achieve maximum revenue

38. How many blank worksheets are shown when a new workbook is created.

    (a) Four (b) Three

    (c) Two (d) One

39. Which of the following arguments in a financial function represents the total number of payments

    (a) FV (b) PV

    (c) NPer (d) Rate

40. the term 'field' as applied to database table means.

    (a) Name of the table

    (b) Horizontal row of the table

    (c) Size of the table

    (d) Vertical column of the table

Direction for Questions No. 41 to 45:

Passage

Case study

A and B were partners in a partnership firm. Due to the ill health of B they decided to dissolve the firm. The position of Assets and Liabilities on the date of dissolution was:

Balance Sheet

Liabilities	Rs.	Assets	Rs.
Loan by B	20,000	Goodwill	30,000
Capitals		Furniture	40,000
A. 1,00,000		Building	90,000
B. 1,40,000	2,40,000	Debtors	50,000
		Cash	50,000
	2,60,000		**2,60,000**

It was agreed that following transactions will take place:

A. A wanted to start the business in sole proprietorship So he took Building and Furniture at 10% less than book value.

B. All the debtors proved good except a person C who did not pay Rs. 10,000.

41. Due to the ill health of B, they decided to dissolve the firm. It comes under _______ form of dissolution.

    (a) Dissolution by Notice

    (b) On the happening of certain contingencies

    (c) Dissolution by court

    (d) Dissolution by Agreement

42. The amount recovered from the debtors is:

    (a) Rs. 1,00,000

    (b) Rs. 40,000

    (c) Rs. 50,000

    (d) Rs. 60,000

43. Following items appear on the Debit side of Realisation A/C except:

    A. Transfer of Assets

    B. Payment of liabilities

    C. Provisions

    D. Realisation expenses

    E. Asset taken over by partner

    Choose the correct answer from the options given below:

    (a) A, C, E only

    (b) C, D, E only

    (c) D, E only

    (d) C, E only

44. The treatment of Goodwill appearing in the balance sheet will be:

    (a) Transferred to Debit of Realisation A/C

    (b) Written off among partners in old ratio

    (c) Transferred to credit of Realisation A/C

    (d) Raised and written off

45. The accumulated profits and reserve are transferred to:

    (a) Revaluation A/C

    (b) Realisation A/C

    (c) Partner's Capital A/C

    (d) Cash/Bank A/C

Direction for questions 46 to 50: Read the passage carefully and answer the following questions.

Passage

XYZ Ltd is registered with an authorised capital of Rs. 20 lakh divided into 2 lakh equity shares of Rs. 10 each.

The company is in manufacturing of pickles and spices. Due to the increase in demand of packed food in the market they decided to diversity its operation. For this purpose they decided to issue 1 lakh equity share of Rs. 10 each. The company issue 20,000 equity shares to a vendor to supply the machinery required to manufacture the packed food. Rest of the equity shares were issued to general public for subscription. The application were received for 46,000 equity shares, Due to undersubscription of equity shares the shares were not issued to public.

46. The company issued 20,000 equity shares of Rs. 10 each to vendor. After issuing them the shares the vendor will be considered as:

   (a) Creditors

   (b) Owners

   (c) Customer

   (d) Lender

47. In order to raise money by issuing the shares in the market the company must get applications for at least ________.

   (a) 1,00,000 shares

   (b) 80,000 shares

   (c) 72,000 shares

   (d) 20,000 shares

48. The process of issuing shares to a vendor in exchange of any asset is known as:

   (a) Issue of share for cash

   (b) Issue of share at discount

   (c) Issue of share at premium

   (d) Issue of share for consideration other than cash

49. If the company is unable to get minimum subscription, the shares cannot be issued and the amount must be refunded within 8 days from the date of closure. If not, company shall be liable to pay ______ % interest p.a.

   (a) 10%

   (b) 15%

   (c) 6%

   (d) 5%

50. The following refer to the maximum amount of share capitals issued by a company in its life times except:

   (a) Subscribed Capital

   (b) Authorised Capital

   (c) Nominal Capital

   (d) Registered Capital

Answer Keys

1. (d)	**2.** (c)	**3.** (c)	**4.** (a)	**5.** (b)	**6.** (b)	**7.** (b)	**8.** (c)	**9.** (b)	**10.** (b)
11. (d)	**12.** (c)	**13.** (b)	**14.** (b)	**15.** (b)	**16.** (b)	**17.** (b)	**18.** (b)	**19.** (a)	**20.** (c)
21. (a)	**22.** (c)	**23.** (d)	**24.** (c)	**25.** (a)	**26.** (b)	**27.** (b)	**28.** (b)	**29.** (d)	**30.** (d)
31. (d)	**32.** (d)	**33.** (b)	**34.** (b)	**35.** (d)	**36.** (b)	**37.** (b)	**38.** (b)	**39.** (c)	**40.** (d)
41. (d)	**42.** (b)	**43.** (d)	**44.** (a)	**45.** (c)	**46.** (b)	**47.** (c)	**48.** (d)	**49.** (b)	**50.** (a)

Explanations

1. (d) 250000 – 50000 – 30000 = Rs.170000

2. (c) Old general reserve distributed in OP/OR.

3. (c) Match

4. (a) Retiring partner will take his share of goodwill.

5. (b) Asset A/c Dr., Revaluation A/c Cr.

6. (b) Match the column.

7. (b) Match the column.

8. (c) Gaining partner will compensate to sacrificing partner.

9. (b) Profit of duration will be entered in P & L suspense A/c.

10. (b) Conversion means no flow of cash.

11. (d) Match the columns.

12. (c) B, D, C, A, E is the correct sequence.

13. (b) D, A, B, E, C is the correct sequence.

14. (b) B, A, E, D, C is the correct sequence.

15. (b) 50000 + 10000 = Rs. 60000

16. (b) Under fixed method capital A/c shows always credit balance.

17. (b) On behalf of Mohan so Mohan's A/c debited.

18. (b) Common size is vertical analysis.

19. (a) On collateral security no interest payable.

20. (c) Increase in B/R = 40000 – 20000 = Rs.20000
Flow from operating activity = 100000 + 20000
= Rs.120000

21. (a) Sale of Intangible asset is a part of investing activity.

22. (c) Purchase consideration = Rs.315000
Issue price of 1 debenture = Rs.105

$$\text{No.} = \frac{315000}{105} = 3000 \text{ Debentures.}$$

23. (d) Sec. pre. can be used for B, D, E only.

24. (c) Bearer and secured are types of debentures.

25. (a) (I) Cash Book, (II) Receipt & Payment A/c, (III) I & E A/c, (IV) Adjustments, (V) Balance sheet of NPO

26. (b) Match the column.

27. (b) A, C, D are the limitations.

28. (b) Current ratio and acid test ratio are liquidity ratios.

29. (d) A, C, D are components of equity.

30. (d) E, D, A, B, C are correct sequence.

31. (d) Amount of premium received at the time of issue will be credited to S.P.R. A/c.

32. (d) Each item is expressed as % of T.A or T.L.

33. (b) Honorarium is paid to temporary employee in NPO.

34. (b) If nothing is mentioned than IOD is charged for average period.

35. (d) Old goodwill write off in OP/OR.

36. (b) Gain = New – Old   21:11

$$S = \frac{5}{9} - \frac{3}{9} = \frac{45-24}{72} = \frac{21}{72}$$

$$K = \frac{3}{8} - \frac{2}{9} = \frac{27-16}{72} = \frac{11}{72}$$

37. (b) Computer Accounting
Internal control designed for safe guard assets.

38. (b) Computer Accounting
Three work sheets are shown.

39. (c) Computer Accounting
NP_{er} Represents the total No. of payments.

40. (d) Computer Accounting
Vertical Column of the table.

41. (d) All partners decided to dissolve by agreement.

42. (b) Amount Rec. from debtors = Total Debtors − Bad debts

= 50000 − 10000

= Rs.40000

43. (d) Provisions and Asset taken by partner not shown at debit side of realisation A/c.

44. (a) On dissolution Goodwill will be transferred to Realisation A/c.

45. (c) Accumulated profits and reserve are transferred to partner's capital A/cs.

46. (b) Now the vendor will be owner of shares as the company taken machinery against it.

47. (c) The company should get minimum subscription which is 90% of (100000 − 20000) 80000 which is 72000 shares.

48. (d) The process of issuing shaves to vendor in exchange of any asset is known as issue of shares for consideration other than cash.

49. (b) The company is liable to pay 15% p.a. interest.

50. (a) Subscribed capital is not the maximum amount of share capitals.

BUSINESS STUDIES

1. It implies a process which coordinates human efforts, assembles resources and integrates both into a unified whole to be utilized for achieving specified objectives. Identify the concept.
   - (a) Organizing
   - (b) Coordination
   - (c) Management
   - (d) Unity of direction

2. An organizational structure requiring high degree of specialization and grouping of jobs into departments like production, purchase, finance, personnel is-
   - (a) Functional foremanship
   - (b) Functional Structure
   - (c) Centralized Structure
   - (d) Divisional Structure

3. Centralization refers to-
   - (a) Retention of decision making authority
   - (b) Dispersal of decision making authority
   - (c) Creating divisions as profit centres
   - (d) Opening new centres or branches

4. A consumer should keep in mind his responsibilities as consumer while purchasing, using and consuming goods and services. Identify the consumer responsibilities from the following:
   - A. Withdrawing the hazardous goods from sale
   - B. Replacing the defective product with a new one
   - C. Choose only legal goods and services
   - D. Remove the defect in goods or deficiency in service
   - E. Form consumer societies which would play an active part in educating consumers

   Choose the correct answer from the options given below:
   - (a) A and D only
   - (b) B and E only
   - (c) A and C only
   - (d) C and E only

5. Match the items in **List - I** with the correct items in **List - II**.

List - I	List - II
A. Right to be heard	I. Providing information on the package and label of the product with regards to price, date of manufacture, quantity, etc.
B. Right to choose	II. Using ISI marked electrical appliances
C. Right to be informed	III. A right to file a complaint in case of dissatisfaction with a good or service
D. Right to safety	IV. Offering wide variety of products

   Choose the correct answer from the options given below:
   - (a) A-I, B-III, C-II, D-IV
   - (b) A-IV, B-II, C-III, D-I
   - (c) A-II, B-I, C-IV, D-III
   - (d) A-III, B-IV, C-I, D-II

6. The composition of National Commission is
   - (a) President and at least four other members
   - (b) President, and not less than two other members
   - (c) President and two other members
   - (d) President and at least 5 other members

7. The quality assurance mark on environment friendly goods is-
   - (a) Agmark
   - (b) FPO
   - (c) Eco-Mark
   - (d) ISI

8. The approach of 'caveat venditor' means-
   - (a) Let the buyer beware
   - (b) Let the seller beware
   - (c) Let the manufacturer beware
   - (d) Let the public beware

9. Arrange the given steps of staffing process in the correct order, considering that a pool of eligible candidates has been created already
   - A. Training and Development
   - B. Placement and Orientation
   - C. Promotion and Career Planning
   - D. Selection
   - E. Performance Appraisal

   Choose the correct answer from the options given below:
   - (a) D, B, A, E, C
   - (b) D, A, B, C, E
   - (c) B, A, D, C, E
   - (d) B, D, A, E, C

10. Arrange the process of selection in correct sequence.

A. Preliminary screening

B. Selection test

C. Selection decision

D. Employment interview

E. Reference and background checks

Choose the correct answer from the options given below:

(a) A, B, D, C, E

(b) A, B, D, E, C

(c) A, E, C, D, B

(d) A, B, C, D, E

11. Staffing ensures the continuous survival and growth of the enterprise-

(a) Through the succession planning for managers

(b) By putting right person on the right job

(c) Discovering and obtaining competent personal for various jobs

(d) Ensure optimum utilization of the human resources.

12. One of the following functions of the management is concerned with appraisal and development of personnel. Identify the function.

(a) Planning

(b) Staffing

(c) Directing

(d) Organizing

13. Arrange the steps in the process of selection in the proper sequence.

A. Reference and background check

B. Job offer

C. Medical examination

D. Selection decision

E. Control of employment

Choose the correct answer from the options given below:

(a) B, D, E, A, C

(b) A, D, C, B, E

(c) A, C, B, D, E

(d) D, A, C, E, B

14. Match the items in **List - I** with the correct items in **List - II**.

List - I	List - II
A. It is very difficult future happenings	I. Complexity
B. Business environment consists of numerous interrelated and dynamic conditions and forces which arise from different sources	II. Relativity
C. Concept differs from to country and region to region	III. Uncertainty
D. It keeps changing in all regards	IV. Dynamic

Choose the correct answer from the options given below:

(a) A-I, B-IV, C-III, D-II

(b) A-III, B-II, C-I, D-IV

(c) A-IV, B-III, C-II, D-I

(d) A-III, B-I, C-II, D-IV

15. To start the business, an e-waste recycling plant in Ghaziabad, the company has obtained a license from UP Pollution Control Board. The Dimension of Business Environment referred here is-

(a) Economic Environment

(b) Legal Environment

(c) Political Environment

(d) Social Environment

16. The Corona Cloud had taken the wind out of the sails of summer products such as ice- creams, soft drinks and frozen deserts with the country-wide lock down and he concerns around the economy bringing sales to a halt. Identify the characteristics of Business Environment.

(a) Relativity   (b) Interrelatedness

(c) Dynamic   (d) Complexity

17. Suhana, after doing MBA got a job in one of the reputed companies in Delhi. She is working as Marketing Manager in the company. She applies various theories of management learnt by her in order to solve managerial problems. Identify the nature of management reflected above, by which Suhana is able to solve managerial problems.

(a) Management as an Art

(b) Management as Science

(c) Management as Profession

(d) Management as Multi-dimensional

18. E-Chaupal created by ITC, is one of the largest consumer product and agri business company. The aim is to enable the farmers in rural India with the opportunity to make use of a direct marketing channel, eliminating multiple intermediation and wasteful handling and unnecessary transaction costs. Identify the importance of management referred above:

    (a) Management helps in achieving group goals

    (b) Management helps in development of society

    (c) Management helps in achieving personal objectives

    (d) Management creates dynamic organisation

19. There is a kind of cost benefit analysis involved and relationship between input and output resources in the term. Identify the concept mentioned here.

    (a) Co-ordination

    (b) Effectiveness

    (c) Planning

    (d) Efficiency

20. One of the decisions in financial management is how much of the profit earned is to be distributed to the shareholders and how much of it should be retained. Identify the decision involved.

    (a) Dividend decision

    (b) Financing decision

    (c) Investment decision

    (d) Capital structure decision

21. An Indian company has entered into Joint Venture with Australian Company in order to set up its new production unit in Australia. Identify the factor affecting fixed capital decision discussed above.

    (a) Technology upgradation

    (b) Financing alternatives

    (c) Scale of operation

    (d) Level of collaboration

22. Match the items in **List - I** with the correct items in **List - II**.

List - I	List - II
A. Capital budgeting decision	I. Choice of technique of production
B. Fixed capital decision	II. Proportion of debt in the total capital
C. Financial	III. Irreversible decision planning
D. Capital structure	IV. Financial blueprint

Choose the correct answer from the options given below:

(a) A-I, B-III, C-IV, D-II

(b) A-III, B-I, C-IV, D-II

(c) A-III, B-IV, C-II, D-I

(d) A-IV, B-I, C-III, D-II

23. Capital structure is affected by many factors. Identify the related factors.

    A. Cash flow position

    B. Scale of operation

    C. Stock market conditions

    D. Level of competition

    E. Cost of equity

    Choose the correct answer from the options given below:

    (a) A and C only

    (b) B, C and E only

    (c) C only

    (d) A, C and E only

24. Toyota Motor Corporations (TMC) follows certain well defined business principles guiding its functioning. One of them was 'Honour the language and spirit of law of every nation and undertake open and fair corporate activities to be a good corporate citizen around the world.

    The principle of management followed by TMC is:

    (a) Equity   (b) Espirit de Corps

    (c) Discipline   (d) Initiative

25. Principles of management are-

    (a) Procedures or methods

    (b) General rules for behaviour in a society

    (c) Broad and general guidelines for decision-making

    (d) Techniques or moral values

26. As per the figures given below, calculate the wages for labour-

    Standard output-20 units per worker per day

    Wage rate for efficient worker-   Rs.50 per unit

    Wage rate for slow worker-   Rs.40 per unit

    Units produced by worker A -   22

    Units produced by worker B -   18

    Units produced by worker C -   20

    Wages earned by workers are:

    (a) A - 900   B - 720   C - 800

    (b) A - 900   B - 720   C - 1000

    (c) A - 1100   B - 720   C - 800

    (d) A - 1100   B - 720   C - 1000

27. "Performing and exercising power under Securities Contracts (Regulation) Act 1956, as may be delegated by the Govt. of India." Which function of SEBI refers to the above statement?

    (a) Development function
    (b) Regulating function
    (c) Protective function
    (d) Role and Purpose of SEBI

28. The Board of NSE does not include-

    (a) Senior executives from promoter institutions
    (b) Eminent Professionals
    (c) Representatives of trading members
    (d) Senior executives from financial institutions

29. In Stock Exchange, the pricing of securities are determined by-

    (a) The forces of demand and supply
    (b) The directors of company
    (c) The stock brokers
    (d) NSE and BSE

30. The money market instrument used by commercial banks only is

    (a) Commercial paper
    (b) Certificate of Deposit
    (c) Treasury Bill
    (d) Call money

31. Match the items in **List - I** with the correct items in **List - II**.

List - I	List - II
A. A market for the creation and exchange of financial assets	I. Financial Intermediation
B. The process by allocation of funds is done	II. Stock Exchange
C. A platform for buying and selling of existing securities	III. Capital market
D. Institutional arrangements through which long-term funds are raised and invested	IV. Financial markets

Choose the correct answer from the options given below:

(a) A-II, B-III, C-IV, D-I
(b) A-IV, B-I, C-III, D-II
(c) A-IV, B-I, C-II, D-III
(d) A-II, B-IV, C-III, D-I

32. Controlling is one of the important functions of a manager. It has a systematic process involving a number of steps. Arrange the following steps of controlling in correct order.

    A. Measurement of Actual performance
    B. Composing actual performance with standard
    C. Taking corrective action
    D. Setting performance standards
    E. Analyzing deviation

    Choose the correct answer from the options given below:

    (a) B, A, D, C, E
    (b) D, A, B, E, C
    (c) A, D, C, B, E
    (d) C, E, A, D, B

33. Which one of the following functions of management is considered as a rescuer of a manager as it may help averting major business shocks by resorting to appropriate corrective measures?

    (a) Planning
    (b) Directing
    (c) Controlling
    (d) Organizing

34. "This technique of managerial control enables the manager to collect first hand information."

    The managerial controlling technique mentioned in the above stated line is:

    (a) Statistical Report
    (b) Personal Observation
    (c) Management Audit
    (d) Budgetary Control

35. An efficient control system helps in reviewing and revising the standards in the light of the changes taking place in the organization and environment.

    Which of the following points of importance best describe the above statement?

    (a) Making efficient use of resources
    (b) Judging accuracy of standards
    (c) Ensuring order and discipline
    (d) Accomplishing organizational goals

36. Only significant deviations which go beyond the permissible limit, should be brought to the notice of management. Name the principle of controlling described in the above lines.

(a) Critical Point Control

(b) Key result area

(c) Management by exception

(d) Critical Path Control

37. Given below is the planning process. Identify the correct sequence.

A. Setting objectives

B. Identifying alternative courses of action

C. Developing premises

D. Evaluating alternative courses of action

E. Selecting an alternative

Choose the correct answer from the options given below:

(a) A, B, C, E, D

(b) A, C, B, D, E

(c) E, D, B, C, A

(d) D, C, E, A, B

38. From the given statements, identify the statement is NOT is limitation of planning.

A. Planning leads to rigidity

B. Planning is futuristic

C. Planning involves huge cost

D. Planning reduces creativity

E. Planning is a mental exercise

Choose the correct answer from the options given below:

(a) A and B only

(b) C, D and E only

(c) A, B and C only

(d) B and E only

39. Identify the statement that is not true about planning.

(a) Planning is an exclusive function of TOP management

(b) All other managerial functions are performed within the framework of planning

(c) Planning is concerned with both ends and means

(d) Planning is what manager at all levels do

40. Out of the following which one is NOT a characteristic of entrepreneurship.

(a) Innovation

(b) Lawful and purposeful activity

(c) Relativity

(d) Systematic activity

Direction for Questions 41 to 45:

Read the following passage and answer the following questions.

Mr. Naidu is an accountant in Silver Bell International School, Tamil Nadu. The school provides free education to a girl child of the staff members. Mr. Naidu is availing such benefit for his only daughter 'Akhila', who is a good sports person. Recently, while participating in an Inter School tournament, she suffered a leg injury. She was advised 2-week rest. Mr. Naidu claimed medical expenses from the school management which they refused asserting that the school provides medical reimbursement policy to its employees and not to the family members. Being disheartened, Naidu become reluctant to work. The Accounts Manager on realizing this, to stimulate Naidu to take up work voluntarily, increased Naidu's scope of authority and responsibility, which he communicated to Mr. Naidu in writing leading to satisfaction of same of his needs. Thereby, Mr. Maidu's work performance improved remarkably.

Based on the case, answer the questions

41. Name the incentive provided by the school to its employees.

(a) free education to all children

(b) medical reimbursement to employee

(c) medical reimbursement to family

(d) free education to male child

42. Name the element of one of the function of management being mentioned in the case.

(a) Motivation

(b) Leadership

(c) Communication

(d) Supervision

43. The incentive used by Account Manager to improve Naidu's performance is-

(a) Promotion

(b) Job security

(c) Status

(d) Employee empowerment and Job enrichment

44. What type of need is not satisfied by the incentive given by the Account Manager to Mr. Naidu to improve his work performance.

(a) Psychological needs

(b) Security needs

(c) Self actualization needs

(d) Esteem needs

45. Identify the type of communication between Account Manager and Mr. Naidu.

(a) Grape Vine Communication

(b) Information Communication

(c) Formal Communication

(d) Inverted 'V' Communication

Direction for Questions 46 to 50:

Answer the following questions based on case study.

Case Study

After completing his graduation in Ayurveda Science, Mohan started his business in the field of Ayurvedic products. He started his venture with full confidence and energy. He wanted to get leading position in the market so he started putting in lot of efforts to achieve it. In this regard, he collected and analyzed the required information from the market. He made the marketing planning for his products through gathered information in which he came to know that consumer compare the prices of the product with its value for them. He reached on this conclusion that the consumers will buy his product if they find that the value of product is at least equal to the value of money which they would pay. Since he started a new setup, he realized that he may not be able to survive in the market in long term. He knew that covering the cost of the product is not easy at the initial stage. So he examined the quality features and prices of his products with other competitors in the market. After this rigorous analysis he decided to add some unique features such as advertising smart packaging, free home delivery, etc. in his Ayurvedic products so that it could be easily sold into the market and achieve the target. In the above passage, the factor of price were discussed.

46. The consumer will be ready to buy a product when find or feel that the value of the product is at least equal to the value of money which they would pay for it. Identify the correct factors of price in the given situation.

(a) Pricing objectives

(b) The utility and demand

(c) Extent of competition in the market

(d) Government and legal regulations

47. He knows that in the long run the business will not be able to survive if he maximizes the profit in early stage. Identify the factor discussed here.

(a) Pricing objective strategy

(b) Product cost

(c) The Utility Demand

(d) Government and legal regulations

48. He also through that competitor's price and their products' features must be considered while declaring the price of his products. Identify the factors.

(a) Level of competition

(b) The utility and demand

(c) Marketing methods used

(d) Pricing objectives

49. After his research work he decided to add some new features due to tough competition in the market such as advertising, free home delivery and smart packaging, etc.

Identify the factors discussed here.

(a) The Utility and Demand

(b) Government and legal regulations

(c) Pricing objectives

(d) Marketing methods

50. Identify the factor affecting the fixation of price of the product which is not highlighted in the above case study.

(a) Pricing objectives

(b) The Utility and Demand

(c) Marketing method used

(d) Government and legal regulations

Answer Keys

1. (a)	**2.** (b)	**3.** (a)	**4.** (d)	**5.** (d)	**6.** (a)	**7.** (c)	**8.** (b)	**9.** (a)	**10.** (b)
11. (a)	**12.** (b)	**13.** (b)	**14.** (d)	**15.** (c)	**16.** (b)	**17.** (a)	**18.** (a)	**19.** (d)	**20.** (a)
21. (d)	**22.** (b)	**23.** (d)	**24.** (a)	**25.** (c)	**26.** (d)	**27.** (b)	**28.** (c)	**29.** (a)	**30.** (a)
31. (c)	**32.** (b)	**33.** (c)	**34.** (b)	**35.** (b)	**36.** (c)	**37.** (b)	**38.** (d)	**39.** (a)	**40.** (c)
41. (b)	**42.** (a)	**43.** (d)	**44.** (a)	**45.** (c)	**46.** (c)	**47.** (a)	**48.** (a)	**49.** (d)	**50.** (d)

Explanations

1. (a) Organising

Organising includes appointing assignments, gathering tasks into offices, designating authority, and distributing assets across the association. During the organising process, administrators coordinate employees, assets, procedures, and policies to work with the objectives distinguished in the plan.

2. (b) Functional structure is roost suitable when the size of the organisation is large, has diversified activities and operations requires a high degree of specialisation.

3. (a) Centralisation refers to the retention of decision making authority. Centralisation implies a situation where the decision making power is retained by the top level management. Under such a system, other levels of management do not have a right to intervene in policy making.

4. (d) C and E

5. (d) A-(III), (B)-(IV), (C)-(I), (D)- (II)

6. (a) Section 20 of the Consumer Protection Act, 1986 deals with the National Commission. It consists of the President and four Members

7. (c) Ecomark or Eco mark is a certification mark issued by the Bureau of Indian Standards (the national standards organization of India) to products conforming to a set of standards aimed at the least impact on the ecosystem.

8. (b) Caveat Venditor is a Latin maxim meaning 'let the seller beware'.

9. (a) (D), (B), (A), (E), (C)

10. (b) (A), (B), (D), (E), (C)

11. (a) Proper staffing ensures continuous survival and growth of an enterprise through succession planning for managers

12. (b) According to Koontz & O'Donell, staffing "involves manning the organisation structure through proper and effective selection, appraisal and development of personnel to fill the roles designed on the structure".

13. (b) (A), (D), (C), (B), (E)

14. (d) (A)-(III), (B)-(I), (C)-(II), (D)-(IV)

15. (c) Legal environment

16. (b) Interrelatedness. Different elements of business environment are closely inter-related and interdependent. A change in one element affects the other elements.

17. (a) Management as an art .

18. (a) It helps in Achieving Group Goals - It arranges the factors of production, assembles and organizes the resources, integrates the resources in effective manner to achieve goals

19. (d) Efficiency is also increased when for the same benefit or outputs, fewer resources are used and less costs are incurred.

20. (a) A financial decision which is concerned with deciding how much of the profit earned by the company should be distributed among shareholders (dividend) and how much should be retained for the future contingencies (retained earnings) is called dividend decision.

21. (d) The companies that prefer collaborations or joint ventures need less fixed capital as these companies can share plants and machinery with the collaborators. However, if a company prefers to operate its business as an independent unit, then it will require more fixed capital.

22. (b) (A)-(III), (B)-(I), (C)-(IV), (D)-(II)

23. (d) (A), (C) and (E) only

24. (a) Equity

Good sense and experience are needed to ensure fairness to all employees, who should be treated as fairly as possible," according to Fayol

25. (c) Broad and general guidelines for decision-making

26. (d) A – 1100 B – 720 C – 1000

    A = 22 × 50

    B = 18 × 40

    C = 20 × 50

27. (b) Performing and exercising such power under Securities Contracts (Regulation) Act 1956, as may be delegated by the Government of India

28. (c) Representatives of trading members:-The Board of NSE comprises senior executives from promoter institutions and eminent professionals, without having any representation from trading members

29. (a) The forces of demand and supply- market conditions

30. (a) Commercial Bills

    Commercial bills, also a money market instrument, works more like the bill of exchange. Businesses issue them to meet their short-term money requirements. These instruments provide much better liquidity

31. (c) (A)-(IV), (B)-(I), (C)-(II), (D)-(III)

32. (b) (D), (A), (B), (E), (C)

33. (c) It implies measurement of accomplishment against the standards and correction of deviation if any to ensure achievement of organizational goals. The purpose of controlling is to ensure that everything occurs in conformities with the standards. An efficient system of control helps to predict deviations before they actually occur.

34. (b) Personal Observation This is the most traditional method of control. Personal observation enables the manager to collect first hand information

35. (b) Judging Accuracy of Standards

    A good control system enables management to verify whether the standards set are accurate & objective. The efficient control system also helps in keeping careful and progress check on the changes which help in taking the major place in the organization & in the environment and also helps to review & revise the standards in light of such changes.

36. (c) 'Management by exception' is an important principle of control, which propagates that only significant deviations which goes beyond the permissible limit should be brought to the notice of management, as an attempt to control everything, results in controlling nothing.

37. (b) (A), (C), (B), (D), (E)

38. (d) (C) and (E) only

39. (a) Planning is required at all levels of management as well as in all departments of the organisation. It is not an exclusive function of top management nor of any particular department

40. (c) Characteristics of entrepreneurship :

    1. Systematic Activity: Entrepreneurship is a systematic, step-by-step and purposeful activity. It has certain temperamental, skill and other knowledge and competency requirements that can be acquired, learnt and developed, both by formal educational and vocational training as well as by observation and work experience.

    2. Lawful and Purposeful Activity: The object of entrepreneurship is lawful business.

    3. Innovation: From the point of view of the firm, innovation may be cost saving or revenue enhancing, Entrepreneurship is creative in the sense that it involves creation of value.

41. (b) Medical reimbursement to employee

42. (a) Motivation

43. (d) Job enrichment is the process of adding motivators to existing roles in order to increase satisfaction and productivity for the employee. This can be done through increasing autonomy, skill and task variety, providing feedback, and so on.

44. (a) Physiological needs - These are biological requirements for human survival.

45. (c) Formal communication refers to the flow of official information through proper, predefined channels and routes

46. (c) Extent of Competition in the Market

47. (a) Pricing Objectives

48. (a) Level of competition

49. (d) Marketing methods used

50. (d) Government and legal Regulations

1. 'The employees in an organisation are happy and satisfied. There is proper orderliness in the organisation and no chaos at all. This statement signifies which feature of the Management?
   (a) Group activity
   (b) Dynamic function
   (c) Intangible force
   (d) Continuous process

2. Kamaljeet is working in Infosys Ltd. His main function is to analyses the business environment and its implication for his company. Name the level of management at which he is working?
   (a) Supervisory level
   (b) Lower level
   (c) Middle level
   (d) Top level

3. 'Co-win-App has helped people in registering for the Covid-19 vaccines, and thus, relived them from the hassle of standing is queues for vaccines in the hospital. 'This is an example of which dimension of business environment? Identify _______.
   (a) Technological environment
   (b) Political environment
   (c) Social environment
   (d) Economic environment

4. 'Demand for Saree' is high in India whereas it is almost non existent in France. Identify the feature of business environment highlighted in the given statement.
   (a) Relativity
   (b) Complexity
   (c) Uncertainty
   (d) Inter relatedness

5. This function of management is futuristic. Identify the function:
   (a) Staffing
   (b) Organising
   (c) Planning
   (d) Directing

6. Owing to Covid 19 Pandemic situation, the owner of Shyam Apparels had to modify its cash budget as it was based on sales target set up before pandemic. He was shocked to find that the business was facing a scarcity of Rs. 20 Lakhs of liquid assets after revised cash budget.

Which limitation of planning is referred to here?
   (a) Planning involves huge cost
   (b) Planning reduces creativity
   (c) Planning reads to rigidity
   (d) Planning may not work in dynamic environment

7. Planning is not an exclusive function of top management but its scope differs at different levels and in different departments. Identify the feature of planning highlighted above:
   (a) Planning is pervasive
   (b) Planning is a mental exercise
   (c) Planning is continuous
   (d) Planning is futuristic

8. In which of the following situation, divisional structure is not appropriate?
   A. Where large variety of products are manufactured using different productive resources.
   B. When an organisation grows and needs to add, more employees, create more departments.
   C. When the organisation is offering only one product.
   D. When operations in the organisation require high degree of specialisation.
   E. When new levels are created in the management hierarchy.

   Choose the correct answer from the options given below:
   (a) C and D only
   (b) A and B only
   (c) A and C only
   (d) D and E only

9. Arrange the steps to complete the process of organising.
   A. Departmentalization
   B. Establishing reporting relationship
   C. Identification & division of work
   D. Assignment of duties

   Choose the correct answer from the options given below:
   (a) B, D, A, C
   (b) D, C, B, A
   (c) A, B, C, D
   (d) C, A, D, B

10. Which of the following is true about Vestibule Training?

    A. It involves shifting the trainee from one department to another or from one job to another.

    B. It stimulates the work environment by programming a computer to imitate some of the realities of job.

    C. Training is conducted away from the actual work floor.

    D. Actual work environments are created in a classroom and employees use the same material and equipment.

    E. It is a joint programme in which educational institutions and business firms cooperate.

Choose the correct answer from the options given below:

    (a) A and B only

    (b) C and D only

    (c) D and E only

    (d) B and C only

11. Name the source of recruitment which is used for training the employees for learning different jobs:

    (a) Promotion

    (b) Casual caller

    (c) Employment Exchange

    (d) Transfer

12. Manu was selected by AB Ltd. as team leader. Identify the sequence which the Human Resource Department will take to complete the staffing process:

    A. Training & Development

    B. Performance Appraisal

    C. Placement & Orientation

    D. Promotion & Career planning

Choose the correct answer from the options given below:

    (a) A, D, C, B

    (b) C, A, B, D

    (c) D, C, A, B

    (d) B, C, D, A

13. Tonu is working as a Software Engineer in an IT firm. Recently, she introduced her friend Manu to her project Manager who is looking for a suitable candidate for the 'Post of Team Leader in the company. After cleaning through the various levels of selection process in the company, Manu is finally selected for the post.

Identify the method of recruitment used by the company to solicit Manu.

    (a) Direct Recruitment

    (b) Management Consultant

    (c) Recommendations of Employees

    (d) Casual Callers

14. Manu is selected for the post of team leader in ABC Ltd. After his selection he went through a process by which his attitudes, skills to perform a specified job is increased.

Identify the improvement process mentioned in the above lines.

    (a) Development

    (b) Recruitment

    (c) Training

    (d) Performance appraisal

15. "Controlling helps to review and revise the targets set in the light of environmental changes and changes taking place in the organisation".

Which importance of controlling is highlighted in the above statement?

    (a) Making efficient use of resource

    (b) Judging accuracy of standards

    (c) Accomplishing organisational goals

    (d) Facilitating coordination in action

16. "Corrective action initiated by control function aims to improve future performance".

Which feature of controlling is highlighted here?

    (a) Controlling is evaluative function

    (b) Controlling is pervasive function

    (c) Controlling is forward-looking function

    (d) Controlling is backward-looking function

17. Mr. Ravi Sachdeva is the marketing manager in Shades Ltd. He regularly prepares performance reports of his subordinates as part of the appraisal. Identify the step of controlling process performed by him:

    (a) Setting Performance standards

    (b) Measurement of actual performance

    (c) Comparison of actual performance with standards

    (d) Analysing deviations

18. Arrange the following steps of controlling process in correct sequence:

A. Comparison of actual performance with standards

B. Establishing the standards

C. Measuring the performance

D. Analysing deviations

E. Taking corrective action

Choose the correct answer from the options given below:

(a) A, D, C, B, E

(b) E, D, C, B, A

(c) B, C, E, D, A

(d) B, C, A, D, E

19. Match the items of **List - I** with the appropriate options of **List - II:**

List - I	List - II
A. Management by Exception	I. Criteria against which actual performance is measured
B. Deviations	II. Controlling significant deviations
C. Critical point control	III. Difference between Actual and standard performance
D. Standards	IV. Control system should focus on key result areas

Choose the correct answer from the options given below:

(a) A-III, B-II, C-IV, D-I

(b) A-II, B-I, C-III, D-IV

(c) A-IV, B-III, C-II, D-I

(d) A-II, B-III, C-IV, D-I

20. Match the items of **List - I** with the appropriate options of **List - II:**

List - I	List - II
A. Business Finance	I. Debt service coverage ratio
B. Financial Planning	II. Different techniques to evaluate investment proposals
C. Capital Budgeting	III. Needed for running, modernising and expansion of business
D. Capital Structure	IV. Smooth operations of fund requirements

Choose the correct answer from the options given below:

(a) A-II, B-IV, C-III, D-I

(b) A-IV, B-II, C-I, D-III

(c) A-III, B-IV, C-II, D-I

(d) A-I, B-IV, C-III, D-II

21. The size of assets, profitability and competitiveness are affected by one of the decisions of financial management. Identify the decision.

(a) Capital budgeting decision

(b) Investment decision

(c) Financing decision

(d) Dividend decision

22. Growth opportunities, Taxation policy, Legal constraints and Stock market reaction are factors of one of financial decisions. Identify the decision:

(a) Financing decision

(b) Investment decision

(c) Dividend decision

(d) Capital budgeting decision

23. "It aims at enabling the company to tackle the uncertainty in respect of the availability and timing of the funds and helps in smooth functioning of an organisation."

This statement is related to one of the concepts of financial management. Identify it:

(a) Capital Structure

(b) Dividend Decision

(c) Investment Decision

(d) Financial Planning

24. Time span between the receipt of raw material and its conversion into finished goods highlights which factor of working capital requirement:

(a) Production cycle

(b) Scale of operation

(c) Business cycle

(d) Seasonal factors

25. Match the items of **List - I** with the appropriate options of **List - II:**

List - I	List - II
A. Interest Coverage Ratio	I. It takes care of deficiencies of Interest coverage ratio
B. ROI	II. Bullish and bearish market
C. Stock market conditions	III. Higher it is, lower is the risk
D. Debt service average ratio	IV. Trading on equity

Choose the correct answer from the options given below:

(a) A-IV, B-III, C-I, D-II

(b) A-III, B-I, C-IV, D-II

(c) A-I, B-IV, C-III, D-II

(d) A-III, B-IV, C-II, D-I

26. Identify the functions of SEBI which helps in regulation of take over bids by companies:

(a) Regulatory functions

(b) Development functions

(c) Protective functions

(d) Advisory functions

27. Name the market in which trading of existing shares is only done:

(a) Primary Market

(b) Secondary Market

(c) Money Market

(d) Capital Market

28. "It gives investors the chance to disinvest and reinvest". This sentence refers to which function of stock exchange?

(a) Pricing of securities

(b) Safety of transactions

(c) Providing liquidity and marketability to existing securities

(d) Contributes to economic growth

29. "The company sells securities enbloc at an agreed price to brokers who, in turn, resell them to the investing public". Name the method of floatation discussed here:

(a) Private placement

(b) Offer for scale

(c) e-IPOs

(d) Offer through prospectus

30. In the financial market, the households are suppliers of funds and business firms represent the demand. Name the function of financial market being referred:

(a) Mobilisation of savings and channeling them into most productive uses.

(b) Facilitating price discovery

(c) Providing liquidity to financial assets

(d) Reducing the cost of transactions

31. ______ is the essence of marketing.

(a) Service motive

(b) Exchange mechanism

(c) Product

(d) Promotion

32. Promotion-mix includes:

(a) Product lines

(b) Product innovation

(c) Product improvement

(d) Advertising and personal selling

33. Under which marketing management philosophy, availability and affordability of the product is considered to be the key to success of a firm?

(a) Production concept

(b) Marketing concept

(c) Product concept

(d) Selling concept

34. Match the items of **List - I** with the appropriate options of **List - II:**

List - I	List - II
A. That part of brand which can be recognised only but can not be spoken	I. Brand Name
B. A name, term, sign, design or some combination of them	II. Trade Mark
C. A brand or part of brand that is given legal protection	III. Brand
D. Verbal component of a brand	IV. Brand Mark

Choose the correct answer from the options given below:

(a) A-IV, B-III, C-II, D-I

(b) A-I, B-III, C-II, D-IV

(c) A-III, B-IV, C-II, D-I

(d) A-III, B-I, C-II, D-IV

35. Match the items of **List - I** with the appropriate options of **List - II:**

List - I	List - II
A. Right to be informed	I. Consumer's choice
B. Right to seek redressal	II. ISI mark
C. Right to be assured	III. Packaging and labelling
D. Right to safety	IV. Replacement of product

Choose the correct answer from the options given below:

(a) A-IV, B-I, C-II, D-III

(b) A-III, B-IV, C-I, D-II

(c) A-III, B-IV, C-I, D-II

(d) A-I, B-III, C-II, D-IV

36. Identify the importance of consumer protection from consumer's point of view.

A. Prevent wide spread exploitation of Consumers.

B. Social Responsibility

C. Govt. Intervention

D. Unorganised Consumers

E. Moral Justification

Choose the correct answer from the options given below:

(a) A and B only

(b) B and C only

(c) C and E only

(d) A and D only

37. Shivani got her birthday gift, a scooty from her father. She happily went for a ride but her scooty stopped after some time. On showing the scooty to the mechanic, she came to know that spark plug was faulty. Complaint can be lodged in consumer forum by:

(a) Shivani's father (b) Shivani's uncle

(c) Shivani's cousin (d) Vendor

38. Ramesh purchased a car worth Rs. 7 Lakhs but found his engine faulty. He filed the case in District Commission but is not satisfied with the order of the District Commission. Within how many days, he can appeal before the State Commission under Consumer Protection Act, 2019:

(a) 15 days (b) 45 days

(c) 20 days (d) 60 days

39. Choose the odd one out from the reliefs available to customer:

(a) To pay punitive damages

(b) To discontinue unfair trade practices

(c) To be honest in dealings

(d) To remove the defect

40. Identify the sequence of steps to complete the process of setting up of Buruness.

A. Project Commission and Launch.

B. Resource Mobilisation

C. Development of Product/Service

D. Scanning the Environment for Entrepreneurial Opportunities

E. Appraisal by the Funding Agencies

Choose the correct answer from the options given below:

(a) D, B, A, C, E

(b) C, B, D, A, E

(c) B, D, C, E, A

(d) C, E, B, A, D

Direction for Questions 41 to 50:

Answer the following questions based on case study.

Case Study

Jagrit, works as a purchase manager in a shoe manufacturing company. As a routine, one day he was in a hurry to board metro train and wanted to reach office in time but while walking fast on escalator, he fell down and got badly hurt. Other co-passengers tried to help him and in no time their was a crowd of nearly 40-50 people.

Jagrit got badly hurt and managed to convey the name of his manager and handed over his phone to the metro worker. He requested that his Boss be informed about the accident.

His boss, Mr. Rohit Jain is a person who when gives instructions does not wish to be contradicted. He gives clear cut instructions to his team and want them to follow without any question. Even after hearing about the tragedy of Jagrit, Rohit Jain was unaffected as he didn't take much interest in providing any help nor bothered to inform his family. Rather, metro worker informed his family and told them to reach to the hospital where he was being treated. Later, Jagrit dropped the mail in his organisation stating about the medical problem. He was then granted medical leave with pay and coverage of his medical bills as he fulfilled the parameters required to be followed by all the staff members.

41. As per Maslow's need hierarchy theory, identify the need of Jagrit not fulfilled:

(a) Safety need

(b) Self Actualisation Need

(c) Belongingness Need

(d) Esteem Need

42. As per Maslow's need hierarchy theory identify the need fulfilled by Jagrit:

(a) Safety need

(b) Self Actualisation Need

(c) Belongingness Need

(d) Esteem Need

43. Identify the leadership style reflected in the behaviour of Mr. Rohit Jain.

(a) Democratic Leader

(b) Paternalistic Leader

(c) Autocratic Leader

(d) Laissez faire Leader

44. Laissez faire leader is effective in one of the following situations. Name that situation:

(a) When employees are illiterate

(b) When employees are capable to work independently and resolve issues on their own

(c) When employees participate in decision making

(d) When employees are reluctant to work

45. "Jagrit dropped the mail in his organisation stating about the medical problem". Name the type of formal communication used by Jagrit.

(a) Horizontal communication

(b) Diagonal communication

(c) Upward communication

(d) Downward communication

46. Jagrit requested metro worker to inform his boss. Identify the principle of Fayol being followed:

(a) Discipline

(b) Unity of Command

(c) Scaler Chain

(d) Equity

47. Jagrit dropped the mail in his organisation stating about the medical problem. Identify the type of plan followed by him.

(a) Strategy

(b) Rule

(c) Procedure

(d) Policy

48. At which level of management is Jagrit working?

(a) Top Level

(b) Middle Level

(c) Lower Level

(d) Supervisory Level

49. Identify the principle of Fayol being followed in the organisation:

(a) Equity

b) Espirit de Corps

(c) Unity of Command

(d) Division of Work

50. Jagrit's medical bills are covered by the company. Identify the incentive provided to him by shoe company.

(a) Retirement benefits

(b) Job security

(c) Perquisites

(d) Bonus

Answer Keys

1. (c)	**2.** (d)	**3.** (a)	**4.** (a)	**5.** (c)	**6.** (d)	**7.** (a)	**8.** (a)	**9.** (d)	**10.** (b)
11. (d)	**12.** (b)	**13.** (c)	**14.** (c)	**15.** (b)	**16.** (c)	**17.** (b)	**18.** (d)	**19.** (d)	**20.** (c)
21. (a)	**22.** (c)	**23.** (d)	**24.** (a)	**25.** (d)	**26.** (a)	**27.** (b)	**28.** (c)	**29.** (b)	**30.** (b)
31. (b)	**32.** (d)	**33.** (a)	**34.** (a)	**35.** (c)	**36.** (d)	**37.** (a)	**38.** (b)	**39.** (c)	**40.** (b)
41. (c)	**42.** (a)	**43.** (c)	**44.** (b)	**45.** (c)	**46.** (c)	**47.** (b)	**48.** (b)	**49.** (c)	**50.** (c)

Explanations

1. (c) Management is an intangible force, as it does not have any physical appearance. It can be felt, by the way an organisation functions.

2. (d) These top level managers are responsible for the welfare and survival of the organisation. They analyse the business environment and its implications for the survival of the firm. They formulate overall organisational goals and strategies for their achievement

3. (a) Technological environment

4. (a) Relativity: Business environment is a relative concept since it differs from country to country and even region to region.

5. (c) Planning is future-oriented and determines an organization's direction.

6. (d) Planning may not work in a dynamic environment: The business environment is dynamic, nothing is constant.

7. (a) Planning is pervasive: Planning is required at all levels of management as well as in all departments of the organisation.

8. (a) C and D only

    Divisional structure is suitable for those business enterprises where a large variety of products are manufactured using different productive resources. When an organisation grows and needs to add more employees, create more departments and introduce new levels of management.

9. (d) (C), (A), (D), (B)

10. (b) (C) and (D) only

11. (d) Transfers can also be used for training of employees for learning different jobs

12. (b) (C), (A), (B), (D)

13. (c) Recommendations of Employees

14. (c) Training

15. (b) **For Evaluating/Judging accuracy of standards:** A good control system enables management to verify whether the standards set are accurate or not by careful check on the changes taking place in the organizational environment.

16. (c) Controlling is forward-looking function

17. (b) Measurement of Actual Performance -There are several techniques for measurement of performance. These include personal observation, sample checking, performance reports, etc

18. (d) (B), (C), (A), (D), (E)

19. (d) (A)-(II), (B)-(III), (C)-(IV), (D)-(I)

20. (c) (A)-(III), (B)-(IV), (C)-(II), (D)-(I)

21. (a) The size of assets, profitability and competitiveness are all affected by capital budgeting decision

22. (c) Dividend decision

23. (d) Financial planning is an important part of overall planning of any business enterprise. It aims at enabling the company to tackle the uncertainty in respect of the availability and timing of the funds and helps in smooth functioning of an organisation.

24. (a) The production cycle time refers to the time required for converting the raw materials into finished goods.

25. (d) (A)-(III), (B)-(IV), (C)-(II), (D)-(I)

26. (a) Regulation of takeover bids by companies is a regulatory function of SEBI. Regulatory functions are performed by SEBI in order to regulate the business in stock exchange. SEBI has framed rules and regulations and code of conduct to regulate the intermediaries. It also regulates the takeover of companies

27. (b) Secondary market is an equity trading avenue in which already existing/pre- issued securities are traded amongst investors.

28. (c) It gives investors the chance to disinvest and reinvest. Providing liquidity and marketability to existing securities

29. (b) Offer for sale

30. (b) Facilitating price discovery

31. (b) Exchange mechanism

32. (d) Advertising and personal selling - A promotional mix is a combination of marketing methods including advertising, sales, public relations and direct marketing to achieve a specific marketing goal.

33. (a) The Production Concept.

    It holds that consumers will prefer products that are widely available and inexpensive.

34. (a) (A)-(IV), (B)-(III), (C)-(II), (D)-(I)

35. (c) (A)-(III), (B)-(IV), (C)-(I), (D)-(II)

36. (d) (A) and (D) only

37. (a) Shivani's father

38. (b) As per the provisions of the Act, any person aggrieved by an order passed by the District Forum may prefer an appeal against such order to the State Commission within a period of 45 days from the date of order.

39. (c) To be honest in dealings

40. (b) (C), (B), (D), (A), (E)

41. (c) Belongingness, refers to a human emotional need for interpersonal relationships, affiliating, connectedness, and being part of a group.

42. (a) A desire for freedom from illness or danger and for a secure, familiar, and predictable environment.

43. (c) Autocratic, or authoritarian leaders, are often described as those with ultimate authority and power over others. These leaders tend to make choices based upon their own ideas alone and do not listen to their team or seek input from others.

44. (b) When employees are capable to work independently and resolve issues on their own

45. (c) Upward communication is the process in which employees directly communicate with upper management to provide feedback, share ideas and raise concerns regarding their day-to-day work

46. (c) Scalar Chain

47. (b) Rules are the plans that provide the required course of action regarding a particular situation. Therefore a rule can also be described as a decision that has to be made by the management regarding what needs to be done in case of a particular situation.

48. (b) Middle level because he manages the purchases and follows the directions of the top level. Also, he is not directly involved with workers

49. (c) The principle of 'Unity of Command' states that employees should receive orders and instructions from one boss only.

50. (c) Perquisites

    Several organizations offer perquisites and fringe benefits such as accommodation, car allowance, medical facilities, education facilities, recreational facilities, etc. in addition to the salary and allowances to its employees. These incentives also motivate the employees to work efficiently.

1. Identify the product with which ISI mark is associated:
   (a) Food products
   (b) Jewellery
   (c) Electrical goods
   (d) Medicines

2. Identify the financial concept which refers to the preparation of financial blueprint of an organisation's future operation.
   (a) Financial Management
   (b) Financial Planning
   (c) Financial Leverage
   (d) Trading on equity

3. Name the primary objective of Financial Management.
   (a) Maximising profits
   (b) Maximising Sales
   (c) Maximising Cost
   (d) Maximising Share holder's Wealth

4. Maslow's Need Hierarchy Theory is based on certain assumptions. Identify the assumption.
   (a) People's behaviour is based on their needs
   (b) People's needs are not in hierarchical order
   (c) Only satisfied need can motivate a person
   (d) Needs are not important to understand the behaviour of people

5. Which of the following statements are incorrect in respect of merits of internal source of recruitment?
   A. It helps in motivating employees which results in improving their performances
   B. It provides a complete solution in filling vacancies in the organisations
   C. It is a cheaper and time saving method of recruitment
   D. It provides a solution of shifting workforce from the surplus departments to understaffed departments
   E. It provides a wider choice
   Choose the correct answer from the options given below:
   (a) B and E Only
   (b) A and C Only
   (c) A and B Only
   (d) B and D Only

6. Match **List - I** with **List - II**:

List - I		List - II
A. Campus recruitment	I.	Government run organization for unskilled and skilled operative jobs
B. Employment Exchange	II.	Applicants introduced by the present employees of the organisation
C. Recommendation of Employees	III.	A notice placed on notice board specifying details of jobs available for unskilled workers
D. Direct Recruitment	IV.	Applicants recruited from colleges and institutions

Choose the correct answer from the options given below:
   (a) A-IV, B-II, C-III, D-I
   (b) A-I, B-IV, C-II, D-III
   (c) A-III, B-I, C-IV, D-II
   (d) A-IV, B-I, C-II, D-III

7. Which of the following statements are true with respect to advantages of functional structure?
   A. It leads to product specialization
   B. It facilitates expansion and growth
   C. It promotes control and coordination within a department
   D. It promotes flexibility and initiatives
   E. It makes training of the employees easier
   Choose the correct answer from the options given below:
   (a) B and E Only
   (b) C and E Only
   (c) D and E Only
   (d) C Only

8. Name the principle of the management under which it is believed that there is only one best way to maximize efficiency and it can be developed through scientific study and analysis.
   (a) Harmony, Not Discord
   (b) Unity of Direction
   (c) Science, not Rule of Thumb
   (d) Development of each and every person to his or her greatest efficiency

9. Identify the correct sequence of steps involved in the process of planning.

   A.　Ideal plan having least negative consequences to be selected

   B.　Specifying quantitative goals to be achieved by the organization

   C.　Weighing the pros and cons of each alternative course

   D.　Forecasting based on assumptions relating to the future

   E.　Identifying all the alternative courses of action available

Choose the correct answer from the options given below:

   (a) B, E, D, A, C

   (b) E, C, D, B, A

   (c) E, B, C, A, D

   (d) B, D, E, C, A

10. X Ltd. has been in steel industry for past 10 years. As per recent survey by a leading financial magazine, it was highlighted that the company's capital investment has increased by 50%, there is increase in sales volume and number of employees as well.

Identify the objective of management achieved by X Ltd.

   (a) Growth

   (b) Profit

   (c) Survival

   (d) Social Objective

11. Put the following points in the correct sequence to complete the staffing process.

   A.　Rajat met a labour contractor and told him to send 30 carpenters the next day

   B.　The 20 carpenters were shown their workplace and the job of making the tables were given them

   C.　Two carpenters were sent for training as they needed some new skills

   D.　Rajat requires 20 carpenters to complete the order of making tables

   E.　Rajat selected 20 carpenters from the 30 candidates sent by the contractor

Choose the correct answer from the options given below:

   (a) D, A, E, B, C

   (b) D, B, C, E, A

   (c) D, C, A, E, B

   (d) A, B, C, D, E

12. Management helps people to adopt the changes so that organization is able to maintain its competitive edge. Identify the importance of management highlighted in the above statement:

   (a) Management helps in development of society

   (b) Management helps in achieving personal objectives

   (c) Management creates a dynamic organisation

   (d) Management helps in achieving group goals

13. 'Business environment differs from country to country and even region to region.' Which feature of business environment is highlighted here?

   (a) Complexity

   (b) Uncertainty

   (c) Relativity

   (d) Dynamic nature

14. Aren has completed his studies and now wants to start his own business. He has undertaken the given steps in the planning process. Rearrange them to create the correct process of planning.

   A.　He has forecasted the demand of his products, interest rate, price of capital goods, tax rate.

   B.　Aren decides to produce in bulk to reduce cost of production.

   C.　Aren found out that increasing price and reducing quality will reduce his customers, but producing in bulk will increase customers.

   D.　Aren sets an objective to earn 20% profit in the first year of business.

   E.　To achieve the target, Aren can reduce price of product or reduce quality of raw material or produce in bulk to reduce cost of production.

Choose the correct answer from the options given below:

   (a) D, A, E, B, C

   (b) D, A, E, C, B

   (c) D, E, A, B, C

   (d) A, E, B, C, D

15. Which concept focuses on increasing the role of the subordinates in the organisation by giving them more autonomy?

   (a) Delegation

   (b) Decentralisation

   (c) Centralisation

   (d) Coordination

16. Which of the following are true of the functional structure?

A. It leads to occupational organisations

B. It leads to minimal duplication of efforts which results in economies of scale

C. Product specialisation helps in development of varied skills in divisional head

D. Easy training of employees as focus is on limited range of skills.

E. New divisions can be added without interrupting the existing operations

Choose the correct answer from the options given below:

(a) A, B, D Only

(b) A, B, D and E Only

(c) B, C, D Only

(d) C, D, E Only

17. Identify the correct sequence of steps involved in the process of selection.

A. Preliminary screening

B. Reference and Background Checks

C. Selection Tests

D. Employment Interview

E. Selection Decision

Choose the correct answer from the options given below:

(a) A, B, C, D, E

(b) B, A, C, D, E

(c) E, B, A, C, D

(d) A, C, D, B, E

18. Which of the following are the functions performed by labelling?

A. Describes the product and specifying its content

B. Provides protection to the content of product

C. Gives generic name to the product

D. Provides information required as per the law

E. Facilitates the introduction of new product

Choose the correct answer from the options given below:

(a) B and D Only

(b) A and D Only

(c) A and B Only

(d) C and E Only

19. Plastic packet for socks, a toothpaste tube, a match box, jar of mixed pickle are the examples of which type of packaging?

(a) Transportation packaging

(b) Secondary packaging

(c) Primary packaging

(d) Tetra packaging

20. Match **List - I** with **List - II**:

List - I	List - II
A. Gathering and analysing market information	I. Sell the product in its 'generic name'
B. Branding	II. Persuading customer to purchase product
C. Promotion	III. Identify needs of customer
D. Transportation	IV. Movement of goods from one place to another

Choose the correct answer from the options given below:

(a) A-III, B-I, C-IV, D-II

(b) A-III, B-I, C-II, D-IV

(c) A-I, B-II, C-III, D-IV

(d) A-I, B-III, C-IV, D-II

21. Which level of Channel is used for consumer goods like soaps, oils, clothes, rice, sugar etc.?

(a) Zero Level

(b) Two Level

(c) Three Level

(d) One Level

22. Obstruction or hindrance to communication is known as __________ .

(a) Noise

(b) Encoding

(c) Decoding

(d) Feedback

23. Aadya joined a new company as Chief Marketing Officer. Although there was not much of monetary benefit, but it was her need for attention and recognition that motivated her to change the job.

Identify the need as per Maslow's need hierarchy theory that made Aadya change her job.

(a) Basic physiological needs

(b) Safety needs

(c) Esteem needs

(d) Affiliation needs

24. Arun, the sales manager ADL Ltd. sent an email to Varun, the marketing manager to share the proposed marketing strategies so that he can plan sale of products accordingly. In response, Varun emailed a detailed marketing schedule for the same.

Identify the type of communication taken place between Arun and Varun.

(a) Vertical - downward communication

(b) Vertical - upward communication

(c) Lateral communication

(d) Informal communication

25. These two functions are inseparable twins of management. One function is considered as forward looking and another is known as backward looking.

Identify the functions of management explained above:

(a) Planning and Organizing

(b) Planning and Staffing

(c) Planning and Controlling

(d) Staffing and Directing

26. In a factory, supervisor follows the technique of sample checking of the units produced. Which step in the process of controlling is being performed by him?

(a) Setting performance standard

(b) Taking corrective action

(c) Analysing deviations

(d) Measurement of actual performance

27. Match **List - I** with **List - II**:

List - I	List - II
A. Investment decisions	I. Source of raising finance
B. Financing decisions	II. Proportion of debt and equity
C. Dividend decisions	III. Long term or short term assets
D. Capital Structure	IV. Amount of money to be retained

Choose the correct answer from the options given below:

(a) A-III, B-IV, C-II, D-I

(b) A-IV, B-I, C-III, D-II

(c) A-III, B-I, C-II, D-IV

(d) A-III, B-I, C-IV, D-II

28. It refers to a position when a company is unable to meet its fixed financial charges namely interest payment, preference dividend and repayment obligations.

Name the concept highlighted in the above lines:

(a) Financial Management

(b) Financial Planning

(c) Financial Risk

(d) Financial Resources

29. From the following source of finance, identify the source that is not related to Owner's fund:

(a) Equity Share Capital

(b) Preference Share Capital

(c) Retained Earning

(d) Debentures

30. The primary aim of financial management is to maximize Shareholder's wealth through proper planning of finance and preparation of a financial blue print of an organisation's future operations. Identify the term being reflected here.

(a) Financial Market

(b) Financial Planning

(c) Financial Resources

(d) Financial Risk

31. Rajat purchased a laptop for Rs.80,000. After one week, the laptop screen stopped working. The company refused to replace the laptop even though it was in guarantee period. In which court should Rajat file a complaint?

(a) State Commission

(b) Supreme Court

(c) District Commission

(d) National Commission

32. Karan bought a luxury, high-end car for Rs.1.5 Crore. It had developed some problem and since the seller did not solve the issue, Karan decided to file a complaint in the consumer court.

Identify the appropriate consumer forum where Karan can file a complaint under the Consumer Protection Act, 2019.

(a) National Commission

(b) Supreme Court

(c) District Commission

(d) State Commission

33. During the period of Diwali, people prefer to keep money at home and hence do not deposit money in the bank. There are also frequent withdrawals from the ATM in the form of cash. Due to this, banks all over the country may face the problem of low liquid cash. Identify the money market instrument that the bank can use to solve their financial problem.

(a) Treasury Bill

(b) Commercial Paper

(c) Certificate of Deposit

(d) Commercial Bill

34. Anek Ltd. Issued a public offer to raise Rs. 70 lakh equity from primary market. In the process of floating the issue, it incurred certain expenses like brokerage, commission, printing of application, advertising etc. Identify the money market instrument that can be used for financing this cost.

(a) Call money

(b) Treasury bill

(c) Commercial paper

(d) Commercial bill

35. Match **List - I** with **List - II:**

	List - I		**List - II**
A.	Right issue	I.	Securities are offered to issuing houses or stock brokers
B.	Offer through Prospectus	II.	Institutional investors
C.	Private placement	III.	Privilege to existing shareholders
D.	Offer for sale	IV.	Most popular method of raising funds

Choose the correct answer from the options given below:

(a) A-IV, B-III, C-II, D-I

(b) A-III, B-IV, C-II, D-I

(c) A-I, B-IV, C-III, D-II

(d) A-II, B-I, C-IV, D-III

36. Identify the example of financial incentive that is used to motivate the individuals at job.

(a) Career Advancement Opportunity

(b) Job Security

(c) Retirement Benefits

(d) Job Enrichment

37. Which of the following is not the characteristics of Entrepreneurship?

(a) Contribution to GDP

(b) Systematic Activity

(c) Innovation

(d) Risk-taking

38. Identify the type of organisation which emerges due to social interaction among employees at job.

(a) Formal Organisation

(b) Divisional Organisation

(c) Informal Organisation

(d) Financial Organisation

39. Even after New Economic Policy 1991, foreign companies found it extremely difficult to cut through the bureaucratic red tape to get permits for doing business in India. Identify the dimension of business environment which posed a hurdle for foreign companies.

(a) Technological environment

(b) Social environment

(c) Political environment

(d) Legal environment

40. One of the economic reforms that was introduced in 1991 led to freedom in deciding the scale of business activities as well as freedom in fixing the prices of goods and services.

Identify the economic reforms.

(a) Privatization (b) Liberalization

(c) Globalization (d) Disinvestment

Direction for Questions 41 to 45:

Answer the following questions based on case study.

Case Study

Matilda is the CEO of Inflorescent Ltd. This year she wants to expand her business and get a growth in profit by 30%. To achieve this target, she has divided the entire work of the organisation into 4 divisions. Each division will be headed by a manager. Each manager will identify 3 workers each who are hardworking and send them for training to increase their efficiency. The Managers also have to decide the best way to do the work. Mr. Aream, who is the manager of the production department has set a chart that all the workers will follow while producing the product. The chart will help in minimising the unnecessary movement. Matilda has also given instructions to all the department managers that they must avoid dual-subordination. To ensure that all the managers are able to achieve their individual targets, Matilda has duly assigned authority to each manager.

41. Matilda has divided the organisation into four different departments to increase the efficiency of her organisation. Identify the principle of Management followed by her.

    (a) Scalar Chain

    (b) Division of work

    (c) Unity of command

    (d) Equity

42. The manager of the production department, Mr. Aream has created the chart to minimize unnecessary movement. Identify the technique of scientific management followed by him.

    (a) Fatigue Study

    (b) Time Study

    (c) Motion Study

    (d) Method Study

43. By assigning each manager authority, Matilda has followed one of the principles of the management. Identify the principles followed by Matilda.

    (a) Scalar Chain

    (b) Unity of command

    (c) Co-operation not individualism

    (d) Authority and Responsibility

44. Identify the principle of management Matilda needs to follow to avoid dual-subordination.

    (a) Unity of command

    (b) Authority and Responsibility

    (c) Unity of Direction

    (d) Scalar Chain

45. Identify the principle of management from the above case study when each manager has to identify and send 3 workers for training.

    (a) Co-operation not individualism

    (b) Harmony not discord

    (c) Science not rule of thumb

    (d) Development of each and every person to his greatest efficiency and prosperity

Direction for Questions 46 to 50:

Read the following passage and answer the question based on it.

Sneha in the HR manager of "Delta Communications Ltd". As a part of her quarterly exercise, she conducted workload and workforce analysis for each department. On the basis of this, she placed an advertisement in a leading newspaper for two junior accountants and after discussion with Finance manager, drafted a letter of vertically shifting Mr. Sharma from lower level to higher level of Internal auditor. However, it took her around one month's time to shortlist candidates for position of junior accountant. As a part of selection process, a written test was conducted for all the candidates in order to judge their level of knowledge and proficiency.

46. Identify internal source of recruitment used by Sneha.

    (a) Transfer   (b) Promotion

    (c) Recommendation   (d) Employment exchange

47. Which step in the process of Staffing did Sneha perform by workload and workforce analysis?

    (a) Selection

    (b) Recruitment

    (c) Estimating manpower requirement

    (d) Performance appraisal

48. Identify external source of recruitment used by Sneha.

    (a) Advertising   (b) Web Publishing

    (c) Casual callers   (d) Direct recruitment

49. Identify the limitations of external source of recruitment highlighted in the above case.

    (a) Dissatisfaction among existing staff

    (b) Lengthy process

    (c) Costly process

    (d) Danger of inbreeding

50. Identify the test conducted by the organisation at the time of selection.

    (a) Aptitude test   (b) Intelligence test

    (c) Personality test   (d) Trade test

Answer Keys

1. (c)	**2.** (b)	**3.** (d)	**4.** (a)	**5.** (a)	**6.** (d)	**7.** (b)	**8.** (c)	**9.** (d)	**10.** (a)
11. (a)	**12.** (c)	**13.** (c)	**14.** (b)	**15.** (b)	**16.** (a)	**17.** (d)	**18.** (b)	**19.** (c)	**20.** (b)
21. (b)	**22.** (a)	**23.** (c)	**24.** (c)	**25.** (c)	**26.** (d)	**27.** (d)	**28.** (c)	**29.** (d)	**30.** (b)
31. (c)	**32.** (d)	**33.** (c)	**34.** (c)	**35.** (b)	**36.** (c)	**37.** (a)	**38.** (c)	**39.** (c)	**40.** (b)
41. (b)	**42.** (c)	**43.** (d)	**44.** (a)	**45.** (d)	**46.** (b)	**47.** (c)	**48.** (a)	**49.** (b)	**50.** (d)

Explanations

1. (c) The ISI mark is mandatory for certain products to be sold in India, such as many of the electrical appliances like switches, electric motors, wiring cables, heaters, kitchen appliances, etc.,

2. (b) 'Financial Planning is a financial blueprint of an organisation's future operations'

3. (d) Wealth maximization (shareholders' value maximization) is also a main objective of financial management. Wealth maximization means to earn maximum wealth for the shareholders. So, the finance manager tries to give maximum dividend to the shareholders. He also tries to increase the market value of the shares.

4. (a) People's behaviour is based on their needs. Satisfaction of such needs influences their behaviour.

5. (a) B and E

6. (d) (A)-(IV), (B)-(I), (C)-(II), (D)-(III)

7. (b) (C) and (E) Only

8. (c) Scientific methods involves investigation of traditional methods through work study.

9. (d) (B), (D), (E), (C), (A)

10. (a) Growth. Can be measured in terms of increase in the number of employees. Increase in the number of products. Increase in the number of branches.

11. (a) (D), (A), (E), (B), (C)

12. (c) Management creates a dynamic organization-Management creates a dynamic organization by motivating employees to accept changes in the organization willingly. Thus creating a dynamic organization.

13. (c) Business environment differs from country to country and region to region, thus it's a relative concept.

14. (b) (D), (A), (E), (C), (B)

15. (b) Facilitates growth as with decentralisation greater autonomy is granted to the lower level managers who then gain more spirit of competition.

16. (a) (A), (B), (D) Only

17. (d) (A), (C), (D), (B), (E)

18. (b) (A) and (D) Only

19. (c) Primary packaging is the packaging in direct contact with the product itself and is sometimes referred to as consumer or retail packaging.

20. (b) (A)-(III), (B)-(I), (C)-(II), (D)-(IV)

21. (b) A marketing channel in which there are two levels of intermediaries (for example, a wholesaler and a retailer) between the manufacturer and the end-user

22. (a) Noise. It refers to any obstruction that is caused by the sender, message or receiver during the process of communication.

23. (c) Esteem needs encompass confidence, strength, self-belief, personal and social acceptance, and respect from others. These needs are represented as one of the key stages in achieving contentedness or self-actualization

24. (c) Horizontal or lateral communication takes place between one division and another.

25. (c) Pre-determined goals can be achieved only through controlling., Planning without control is useless and control without planning is meaningless. Planning, based on facts, makes controlling easier. Thus, planning and controlling are mutually inter-related and interdependent.

26. (d) If performance is not measured, it cannot be ascertained whether standards have been met. Comparing actual performance with standards or goals: Accept or reject the product or outcome.

27. (d) (A)-(III), (B)-(I), (C)-(IV), (D)-(II)

28. (c) Financial risk refers to a situation when a company is not able to meet its fixed financial charges such as interest payment, preference dividend and repayment obligations. In other words, it refers to the probability that the company would not be able to meet its fixed financial obligations

29. (d) Organisations use debentures when they need to borrow cash at a fixed rate of interest for their development. Hence, debentures are not a part of the owner's capital.

30. (b) Financial planning refers to estimating the requirements of a business and determining the sources of funds. Financial planning includes both short-term and long-term planning.

31. (c) jurisdiction for entertaining consumer complaints shall be up to 50 lakh for district commissions.

32. (d) The revised pecuniary jurisdiction for entertaining consumer complaints shall be more than Rs. 50 lakh to Rs. 2 crore for state commissions.

33. (c) Certificates of deposit are short term instruments issued by commercial banks and financial institutions to the individuals, corporations and companies. They are unsecured and negotiable.

34. (c) Commercial paper is an unsecured form of promissory note that pays a fixed rate of interest. It is typically issued by large banks or corporations to cover short-term receivables and meet short-term financial obligations, such as funding for a new project.

35. (b) (A)-(III), (B)-(IV), (C)-(II), (D)-(I)

36. (c) Retirement benefits are incentives that provide employees with long-term retirement funds

37. (a) 5 characteristics of entrepreneurs
- Motivation.
- Passion.
- Vision.
- Confidence.
- Decision making

38. (c) The informal organisation may be defined as "a network of personal and social relationships that arise spontaneously as people associate with one another in a work environment. It is composed of all the informal groupings of people within a formal organisation."

39. (c) Political environment comprises those elements that are related to government affairs in the type of government in power.

40. (b) Liberalisation in economics means minimising the government's restrictions and regulations in an economy, in return for higher involvement of private organisations. In short, liberalisation

means the removal of restrictions in order to promote economic development.

41. (b) In this principle, the work is divided into small tasks/ jobs. A trained and competent specialist is required to perform each job. Thus, division of work leads to specialisation. According to Fayol, division of work intends to produce more and better work for the same effort.

42. (c) In motion study unnecessary movements are sought to be eliminated so that it takes less time to complete the job efficiently.

43. (d) According to this principle, there should be a proper balance between authority and responsibility. Authority is the duty, which a subordinate is expected to perform. Authority and responsibility go hand in hand.

44. (a) The principle of 'Unity of Command' states that employees should receive orders and instructions from one boss only. If two (or more) superiors command a worker at the same time, he will get confused to whose command should he follow.

45. (d) Industrial efficiency depends to a large extent on personnel competencies. As such, scientific management also stood for worker development. Worker training is essential to learn the best method developed as a consequence of the scientific approach.

46. (b) Promotion is when a person is shifted from one job position to another with increase in status and responsibilities.

47. (c) Workload analysis means to find out number and type of employees required to perform various jobs designed in organisational structure. The manpower requirement can find out by equating workload analysis to workforce analysis.

48. (a) Advertising

49. (b) The external system of recruitment is a lengthy process involving advertisement for the posts, wait for the applications' selection, etc. which consumes a lot of time. Since it is a lengthy process, sometimes it is not considered appropriate.

50. (d) Trade Test is conducted to measure the level of skills, knowledge and proficiency of a person in his/her area of profession.

1. Management has three dimensions namely:
   (a) Management of work, Management of people, Management of operations
   (b) Management of work, Management of people, Management of place
   (c) Management of people, Management of product, Management of operations
   (d) Management of work, Management of operations, Management of place

2. "In order to sustain, an organisation must earn enough revenues" which objective of management is being followed here?
   (a) Risk
   (b) Growth
   (c) Profit
   (d) Survival

3. Identify the combination from the following statements which is incorrect about management.
   A. Management is a dynamic function
   B. Management should focus only on efficiency and not effectiveness
   C. Management is a tangible force
   D. Management is a group activity
   E. Management is a continuous process
   Choose the correct answer from the options given below:
   (a) A and B only
   (b) B and C only
   (c) C and D only
   (d) D and E only

4. This technique suggested by Taylor is an extension of Principle of Division of Work and specialization to the shop floor? Identify.
   (a) Differential piece wage system
   (b) Standardisation and simplification
   (c) Functional foremanship
   (d) Motion study

5. Identify the statement which does not indicate the nature of 'Principles of Management'.
   (a) Formed by practice and experimentation
   (b) Flexible
   (c) Mainly behavioural
   (d) Full fledged profession

6. Dhruv and Tara joined Mega textile Pvt. Ltd. as data analysts. Their working hours were 9.00 am to 6 pm.
   Dhruv's salary was Rs. 80,000 per month while Tara got Rs. 85,000 as monthly salary which principle of management is being violated here.
   (a) Order
   (b) Stability of personnel
   (c) Remuneration
   (d) Scalar chain

7. Identify the one from following that is NOT a specific force in context of Business Environment
   (a) Customers   (b) Investors
   (c) Competitors   (d) Stock market indices

8. Match **List - I** with **List - II**.

List - I	List - II
Types of Environment	**Components**
A. Economic Environment	I. Customs, traditions
B. Social Environment	II. Inflation, Interest rate
C. Political Environment	III. Administrative orders, court judgement
D. Legal Environment	IV. Stability and peace in the country

   Choose the correct answer from the options given below:
   (a) A-II, B-I, C-III, D-IV
   (b) A-II, B-I, C-IV, D-III
   (c) A-I, B-II, C-III, D-IV
   (d) A-III, B-IV, C-I, D-II

9. Identify the correct sequence of steps in planning process.
   A. Identifying alternative courses of action
   B. Evaluating alternatives
   C. Setting objectives
   D. Selecting and alternative
   E. Developing premises

Choose the correct answer from the options given below:

(a) C, E, B, A, D

(b) E, C, A, B, D

(c) C, E, A, B, D

(d) A, B, D, C, E

10. Match **List - I** with **List - II**.

List - I		**List- II**
A.	Planning is futuristic	I.	Planning is thinking rather than doing
B.	Planning is a mental exercise	II.	Planning cycle is performed every year
C.	Planning involves decision making	III.	Planning is working ahead
D.	Planning is continuous	IV.	Choosing the best alternative

Choose the correct answer from the options given below:

(a) A-III, B-IV, C-I, D-II

(b) A-III, B-I, C-IV, D-II

(c) A-III, B-II, C-I, D-IV

(d) A-IV, B-I, C-III, D-II

11. Choose the correct sequence of steps in Organising process:

A. Assignment of duties

B. Establishing reporting relationships

C. Identification of division of work

D. Departmentalisation

Choose the correct answer from the options given below:

(a) C, D, B, A

(b) D, C, A, B

(c) C, D, A, B

(d) D, C, B, A

12. Staffing process continues even after training and development of a candidate. Identify the step that are conducted after training and development:

A. Selection

B. Promotion and Career Planning

C. Recruitment

D. Performance Appraisal

E. Work load Analysis

Choose the correct answer from the options given below:

(a) B and D only

(b) A and B only

(c) C and D only

(d) B and C only

13. Ravi is manufacturing consumer goods. He needs to decide the organisation structure that he must follow to ensure that there is minimal duplication of efforts. This will help him to lower the cost or production. Identify the structure that Ravi should use:

(a) Functional structure

(b) Divisional structure

(c) Formal organisation

(d) Informal organisation

14. ABC Ltd. has placed a notice on the notice board of the enterprise specifying the details of the jobs available. Job seekers assemble outside the premises of the organisation on the specified date and selection is done on the spot. Identify the external source of recruitment being reflected here.

(a) Casual Callers

(b) Direct recruitment

(c) Advertisement

(d) Employment Exchange

15. Off the job training methods are those where employees are taken away from their place of work and then given training. Choose off the job training methods.

A. Apprenticeship Programme

B. Job Rotation

C. Vestibule Training

D. Internship Training

E. Conferences/Class Room Lectures

Choose the correct answer from the options given below:

(a) B and C only

(b) C and E only

(c) D and E only

(d) A and C only

16. Identify the function of management that is also termed as the generic function of management.

(a) Staffing

(b) Organising

(c) Planning

(d) Controlling

17. Arrange process of selection in sequential manner.

  A. Selection tests

  B. Preliminary screening

  C. Employment interview

  D. Medical examination

  E. Reference ad background

Choose the correct answer from the options given below:

  (a) B, A, C, E, D

  (b) A, B, C, D, E

  (c) C, A, E, D, B

  (d) D, A, C, E, B

18. Which of the following needs are referred to as belonging needs as per the Maslow's Need Hierarchy theory?

  A. Affection

  B. Acceptance

  C. Self respect

  D. Autonomy

  E. Friendship

Choose the correct answer from the options given below:

  (a) A and C only

  (b) A, B and E only

  (c) C and D only

  (d) E only

19. Match **List - I** with **List - II**.

List - I	List - II
A. Supervision	I. Process of influencing other
B. Motivation	II. Can be formal or informal
C. Leadership	III. Can be positive or negative
D. Communication	IV. Maintains group unity

Choose the correct answer from the options given below:

  (a) A-IV, B-II, C-I, D-III

  (b) A-I, B-III, C-II, D-IV

  (c) A-IV, B-I, C-III, D-II

  (d) A-IV, B-III, C-I, D-II

20. 'It is an activity of influencing people to strive willingly for group objectives'.

Which element of directing in highlighted here?

  (a) Supervision

  (b) Leadership

  (c) Motivation

  (d) Communication

21. In which network of formal communication a subordinate is allowed to communicate with his immediate superior as well as his superiors superior?

  (a) Circular (b) Wheel

  (c) Single chain (d) Inverted V

22. Match **List - I** with **List - II**.

List - I	List - II
A. Bonus	I. Provident fund, gratuity, pension
B. Retirement benefits	II. Offered over and above the wages/ salary
C. Perquisites	III. Offering shares at a set price lower than market price
D. Stock option	IV. Housing, medical aid and education to children

Choose the correct answer from the options given below:

  (a) A-I, B-II, C-III, D-IV

  (b) A-II, B-I, C-IV, D-III

  (c) A-II, B-I, C-III, D-IV

  (d) A-I, B-III, C-II, D-IV

23. Identify the method of analysing deviations in which managers can save time and efforts as they deal with only those deviations that arise in the key result area.

  (a) Management By Exception (MBE)

  (b) Critical Path Method

  (c) Supervision

  (d) Motivation

24. Identify the function of management without which planning is termed as meaningless?

  (a) Staffing

  (b) Directing

  (c) Organising

  (d) Controlling

25. One of the following is a qualitative standard. Identify

- (a) Labour turnover
- (b) Sales volume
- (c) Capital expenditure
- (d) Motivation level of employees

26. "A good control system ensures that employees know well in advance what they are expected to do and also the standards of performance on the basis of which they will be apprised." Identify the importance of controlling being referred here.

- (a) Accomplishing organisational goals
- (b) Facilitating coordination in action
- (c) Making efficient use of resources
- (d) Improving employee motivation

27. Identify the correct sequence of steps in the process of controlling.

- A. Analysing Deviations
- B. Measurement of actual performance
- C. Setting performance standards
- D. Comparing actual performance with standards
- E. Taking corrective action

Choose the correct answer from the options given below:

- (a) A, B, C, D, E
- (b) C, B, D, A, E
- (c) C, D, B, E, A
- (d) B, C, D, A, E

28. 'Young India' is a company into manufacturing of garments. The company now wishes to diversify into cosmetic for which they need to buy need machinery and adopt new technology. Which financial management decision is highlighted here?

- (a) Working capital decision
- (b) Capital Budgeting decision
- (c) Dividend decision
- (d) Financing Decision

29. What ratio takes care of deficiencies of the Interest Coverage Ratio?

- (a) Current Ratio
- (b) Return on Investment
- (c) Debt Service Coverage Ratio
- (d) Debt Equity Ratio

30. Primary aim of financial management is:

- (a) To maximise employee's wealth
- (b) To maximise employer's wealth
- (c) To maximise shareholder's wealth
- (d) To maximise owner's wealth

31. Which aspect of financial management helps in avoiding business shocks and surprises and also prepares the company for the future?

- (a) Financial resources
- (b) Financial risk
- (c) Financial planning
- (d) Business management

32. Varun is the owner of soft cell ltd. The total capital invested in business is 100 crore, which is obtained 70 crore from share @10 per share and 30 crore from a bank loan @20% per annum. Varun has earned an ROI of 40% this year. Calculate the EPS if tax rate is 50%.

- (a) 1.7
- (b) 2.5
- (c) 1.6
- (d) 0.7

33. The proportion of debt in the overall capital is also called ________.

- (a) Operating Leverage
- (b) Financial Leverage
- (c) Combined Leverage
- (d) Mixed Leverage

34. In which method is the allotment of securities by a company done to institutional investors and some selected individuals?

- (a) Private placement
- (b) Offer for sale
- (c) Rights issue
- (d) IPO

35. Identify the combination that is true about financial market.

- A. Money market is a market for short-term funds whose maturity period is upto 1 year
- B. Primary market is a market for sale & purchase of existing securities
- C. The price of securities are determined by the management of the company in case of new issue market
- D. Secondary markets deals in already issued securities.

Choose the correct answer from the options given below:

- (a) A, C, D only
- (b) B, C only
- (c) A, B only
- (d) B, D only

36. "Registration of collective investment schemes & mutual funds is the important function of SEBI. Identify the type of function given above."

(a) Development functions

(b) Protective functions

(c) Regulatory functions

(d) Management functions

37. XYZ company needs long-term finance to buy some machinery. In order to raise the long-term funds in the capital market the company will have to incur the floatation cost. Identify the instrument of primary market required to meet the floatation cost.

(a) Certificate of Deposits

(b) Commercial Bill

(c) Commercial Paper

(d) Call money

38. Identify the statements that are relevant to money market.

A. Shareholders can buy and sell shares

B. The involvement outlay is huge

C. Deals in short-term securities

D. Bonds and preference shares are instruments of the money market

E. Money market is considered less liquid than the capital market

Choose the correct answer from the options given below:

(a) B and C only   (b) A and D only

(c) A and C only   (d) B and D only

39. _______ is the document containing details of number of shares bought and sold, the price and brokerage charges issued within twenty four hours of execution of trade.

(a) Broker client agreement

(b) Trade confirmation slip

(c) Order confirmation slip

(d) Contract Note

40. Arrange the followings step of process of setting up a Business in proper sequences.

A. Preparation of business plan

B. Resource mobilisation

C. Development of product/service idea.

D. Scanning the environment for entrepreneurial opportunities

E. Appraisal by funding agencies

Choose the correct answer from the options given below:

(a) C, A, E, B, D   (b) A, B, C, D, E

(c) B, D, C, A, E   (d) E, B, D, C, A

Direction for Questions 41 to 45:

Read the following passage and answer the question based on it.

Sundari has started a company manufacturing washing machines which not only washes and dries clothes, but also has a system which removes the chemical from the used soap water making it fit to reuse for other domestic purposes. Sundari plans to come up with 2 variants of machine- top loading and front loading namely. Being a new entrant in a highly competitive market, Sundari wants to keep the prices low initially to survive in the market. The machines will be made available to the customers through a chain of wholesalers and retailers. Amongst the other services offered Sundari feels that after sale service, handling complaints and availability of original spare parts should be given importance. Her friend Kalpana, a graphic designer suggested her to use a design 'a drop of clean water' to convey the USP of her product to the target market.

41. Which function of marketing is referred to here?

(a) Branding

(b) Labelling

(c) Packaging

(d) Standardisation and grading

42. One of the factors affecting pricing decision has been highlighted in the case study? Identify

(a) Product Cost

(b) Demand and Utility

(c) Pricing Objectives

(d) Marketing Methods Used

43. Identify marketing philosophy that has been followed by Sundari in her business endeavour?

(a) Production concept

(b) Selling concept

(c) Product concept

(d) Societal Marketing Concept

44. Identify the elements of marketing mix that is not highlighted in the given case?

(a) Product   (b) Price

(c) Place   (d) Promotion

45. Identify the level of channels of distribution Sundari is planning to use to make her product available to the customers?

(a) Zero Level Channel

(b) One Level Channel

(c) Two Level Channel

(d) Three Level Channel

Direction for Questions 46 to 50:

Read the following passage and answer the question based on it.

Rajesh had purchased a jar of orange marmalade from a leading jam manufacturing company in the country. The packaging of the jam was quite attractive but does not have details of price, date of manufacturing & directions of use. On reaching home, while using marmalade he realised it had a foul smell, he rushed to the shopkeeper and put up his compliant. The shopkeeper refused to do anything and he said that marmalade was not sold by him and hence had no reason to attend to his complaint.

Sanjay his friend told him that he had the right to get relief in case the product falls short of his expectation but Rajesh could not do anything as he did not have a bill.

46. Which mark assures that the quality of marmalade jam is up to the standard or not?

(a) Eco mark
(b) Ag-mark
(c) BIS hallmark
(d) FPO

47. The marmalade jam did not have the information of price, date of manufacture, direction to use etc. Which right of consumer is violated here?

(a) Right of safety

(b) Right to choose

(c) Right to consumer calculation

(d) Right to be informed

48. Rajesh had realised a foul smell in jam, he rushed to the company to file the compliant. Which right of consumer is violated here?

(a) Right to be heard

(b) Right to seek redressal

(c) Right to safety

(d) Right to choose

49. Rajesh's friend Sanjay told him that he has a right to get relief in case the product falls short of his expectations. Identify the consumer right on which Sanjay is aware.

(a) Right to be heard

(b) Right to choose

(c) Right to be informed

(d) Right to seek redressal

50. Rajesh could not file compliant in the consumer forum because he had no proof for the purchase made. Which responsibility was ignored by Rajesh while purchasing the marmalade?

(a) File a compliant in an appropriate consumer forum

(b) Respect the environment

(c) Ask for cash memo on purchase of goods & services

(d) Read labels carefully so as to have information about price manufacturing dates etc.

Answer Keys

1. (a)	**2.** (d)	**3.** (b)	**4.** (c)	**5.** (d)	**6.** (c)	**7.** (d)	**8.** (b)	**9.** (c)	**10.** (b)
11. (c)	**12.** (a)	**13.** (a)	**14.** (b)	**15.** (b)	**16.** (a)	**17.** (a)	**18.** (b)	**19.** (d)	**20.** (b)
21. (d)	**22.** (b)	**23.** (b)	**24.** (d)	**25.** (d)	**26.** (d)	**27.** (b)	**28.** (b)	**29.** (c)	**30.** (c)
31. (c)	**32.** (a)	**33.** (b)	**34.** (a)	**35.** (a)	**36.** (c)	**37.** (c)	**38.** (a)	**39.** (d)	**40.** (c)
41. (a)	**42.** (c)	**43.** (d)	**44.** (d)	**45.** (c)	**46.** (d)	**47.** (d)	**48.** (c)	**49.** (d)	**50.** (c)

Explanations

1. (a) (i) Management of work It is concerned with performance of tasks in an organisation.

    (ii) Management of people It implies dealing with employees as individuals and dealing with individuals as a group.

    (iii) Management of operations It is interlinked with both management of work and management of people

2. (d) Survival

The basic objective of any organisation is survival. For this, an organisation must earn sufficient revenues to cover the cost.

3. (b) Management is a continuous or never ending function. All the functions of management are performed continuously.

Management is a group activity. Management is divided into people management where a leader shall manage his team, and the combined efforts only will yield fruitful results.

4. (c) Functional foremanship is the technique of scientific management that is the extension of the principle of division of work and specialisation.

5. (d) Full fledged profession - Management is not considered as a full-fledged profession

Restrict entry, Presence of professional associations, Existing of ethical code, etc.

6. (c) This henry fayol principle of management states that employees should be paid fair wages for the work that they carry out. Any organization that underpays its workers will struggle to motivate and keep quality workers. This remuneration should include both financial and non-financial incentives

7. (d) Specific forces such as investors, customers, competitors, suppliers, etc.

8. (b) (A)-(II), (B)-(I), (C)-(IV), (D)-(III)

9. (c) (C), (E), (A), (B), (D)

Setting objectives, Developing premises, Identifying alternative courses of action, Evaluating alternative courses are the steps followed in the planning process.

10. (b) (A)-(III), (B)-(I), (C)-(IV), (D)-(II)

11. (c) (i) Identifying (ii) Grouping (iii) Delegating (iv) Establishing relationship.

12. (a) (B) Promotion and Career Planning

(D) Performance Appraisal

13. (a) A functional structure is a type of business structure that organizes a company into different departments based on areas of expertise. These departments serve as functional units and are overseen by functional managers or department heads

14. (b) Under the direct recruitment, a notice is placed on the notice board of the enterprise specifying the details of the jobs available

15. (b) Job rotation is a process in which the trainee is systematically transferred from one job to another, so as to broaden his knowledge and attitudes in diversified fields.

16. (a) Since the structure & positions are decided, motivated to work in harmony with the goals of the organization, staffing is closely linked to organizing. Thus, staffing is seen as a generic function of management.

17. (a) (B), (A), (C), (E), (D)

18. (b) (A), (B) and (E) only

19. (d) (A)-(IV), (B)-(III), (C)-(I), (D)-(II)

20. (b) The action of leading a group of people or an organisation."

21. (d) in this network, the subordinate can communicate with his or her superior and also with the superior of the superior. This helps in the easy and fast transfer of information and reports.

22. (b) (A)-(II), (B)-(I), (C)-(IV), (D)-(III)

23. (b) The critical path method (CPM) is a technique where you identify tasks that are necessary for project completion and determine scheduling flexibilities.

24. (d) The function without which planning is meaningless is, "controlling". Controlling refers to an activity that ensures the proper working of the organizations as per the plans

25. (d) Employee motivation is the level of commitment, energy and innovation that a company's staff hold during the working day. It's as important as it is difficult to track; maintaining and improving motivation in the workplace can be a problem for many companies, as not every task will be interesting.

26. (d) Improving employees' motivation: Controlling helps employees in realising what they are expected to do and what are the standards of performance. This motivates them to perform better.

27. (b) (C), (B), (D), (A), (E)

28. (b) A capital budgeting decision is both a financial commitment and an investment. By taking on a project, the business is making a financial commitment, but it is also investing in its longer-term direction that will likely have an influence on future projects the company considers.

29. (c) The debt service coverage ratio (DSCR) is a key measure of a company's ability to repay its loans, take on new financing and make dividend payments.

30. (c) Wealth maximization (shareholders' value maximization) is also a main objective of financial management. Wealth maximization means to earn maximum wealth for the shareholders.

31. (c) Financial planning is the task of determining how a business will afford to achieve its strategic goals and objectives

32. (a) $40/100 \times 100 = 400000000$

   $(-)$ Int. $20/100 \times 300000000$

   $= \dfrac{60000000}{\text{EBT } 340000000}$

   $(-)$ Tax@50% = 17000000 = 17 crore.

   EPS $= \dfrac{17}{7} = 2.43.$

   * Error in the options given in the answer key actual answer is 2.43.

33. (b) The proportion of debt in the overall capital of a firm is called Financial Leverage or Capital Gearing. When overall debt in the firm increases, cost of funds declines as debt is a cheaper source of funds.

34. (a) Private placement: Under this method securities are allotted to institutional investors and some selected individuals.

35. (a) (A), (C), (D) only

36. (c) It regulates the operations of depositories, participants, custodians of securities, foreign portfolio investors, and credit rating agencies. It prohibits insider trading, i.e. fraudulent and unfair trade practices related to the securities market

37. (c) Commercial paper, also called CP, is a short-term debt instrument issued by companies to raise funds generally for a time period up to one year. It is an unsecured money market instrument issued in the form of a promissory note

38. (a) (B) and (C) only

39. (d) The contract note is the legal record of any trade made by a stockbroker on a stock exchange. It confirms the trade conducted on a specific day, on the client's behalf, performed on a stock exchange (BSE / NSE)

40. (c) (B), (D), (C), (A), (E)

41. (a) Branding is the process of creating and disseminating the brand name, its qualities and personality.

42. (c) Pricing objectives includes: Obtaining Market Share, Surviving in a Competetive Market and Attaining Product Quality.

43. (d) Societal marketing can be defined as a "marketing with a social dimension or marketing that includes non-economic criteria". Societal marketing "concerns for society's long term interests". It is about "the direct benefits for the organization and secondary benefit for the community".

44. (d) Promotion is a marketing tool, used as a strategy to communicate between the sellers and buyers. Through this, the seller tries to influence and convince the buyers to buy their products or services. It assists in spreading the word about the product or services or company to the people.

45. (c) A marketing channel in which there are two levels of intermediaries (for example, a wholesaler and a retailer) between the manufacturer and the end-user.

46. (d) Fruit products order. Certifying agency. Ministry of Food Processing Industries (India)

47. (d) The right to be informed: to be protected against fraudulent, deceitful, or grossly misleading information, advertising, labelling, or other practices, and to be given the facts needed to make informed choices. The right to choose: to have available a variety of products and services at competitive prices.

48. (c) Right to safety

49. (d) Consumers must make complaint for their genuine grievances. Many a times their complaint may be of small value but its impact on the society as a whole may be very large. They can also take the help of consumer organisations in seeking redressal of their grievances

50. (c) Ask for cash memo on purchase of goods & services.

1. Rajat is working in an organisation for the last one month and he is very happy with the way the work is done. He notices that all the employees in the organisation are satisfied by the working environment and despite having a total workforce of 10,000 employees there is no chaos.

   Identify the feature of management discussed above.

   (a) Management is an intangible force

   (b) Management is a dynamic function

   (c) Management is a group activity

   (d) Management is a continuous process

2. A good manager counsels through praise and criticism in such a way that it brings out the best the employee. Identify the function of Management

   (a) Planning   (b) Directing

   (c) Controlling   (d) Organising

3. Which function of management refers to monitoring organisational performance towards the attainment of organisational goals?

   (a) Planning   (b) Controlling

   (c) Directing   (d) Organising

4. Work must be divided into small tasks. A competent specialist is required to perform each job. Identify the principle of management.

   (a) Discipline   (b) Division of Work

   (c) Unity of Direction (d) Initiative

5. "The Interest of an organisation should take priority over the interest of any individual employee". Identify the Principle of Management referred to in the statement given above.

   (a) Esprit be Corps

   (b) Subordination of Individual Interest to General Interest

   (c) Stability of tenure of personnel

   (d) Remuneration of employees

6. Match the items of **List - I** with the correct items of **List - II**.

List - I	List - II
A. Science not rule of thumb	I. Managers served as a link between owners and workers
B. Harmony, not discord	II. Developed through study and analysis
C. Cooperation not individualism	III. One best way to doing the job
D. Method study	IV. Complete Cooperation between the Labour and Management

   Choose the correct answer from the options given below:

   (a) A-I, B-III, C-II, D-IV

   (b) A-IV, B-II, C-III, D-I

   (c) A-II, B-IV, C-I, D-III

   (d) A-II, B-I, C-IV, D-III

7. Attitudes towards product innovations, lifestyles, occupational distribution and consumer preferences constitute ______ dimension of business environment.

   (a) Technological environment

   (b) Social environment

   (c) Economic environment

   (d) Political environment

8. Business Environment doesn't help in:

   (a) Planning and policy formulation

   (b) Coping with rapid changes

   (c) Establishing standard for controlling

   (d) Tapping useful resources

9. Swarna Bhoomi is a resort in the outskirts of Delhi at Delhi-Gurgaon Express way. The unique feature of this resort was being a gadget free zone where families enjoy their time together. However, recently the visitors have been requesting for wifi, per care facilities and room pantry. The manager sensing the shift in consumer preference upgraded these facilities by providing:

   A. Fee Wi-fi zone

   B. A cretch for pets

   C. A cook-top with essentials for cooking in selected villas and rooms.

   The above case highlights that:

   (a) Business environment is complete in nature

   (b) Business environment is a relative concept

   (c) Business environment is dynamic in nature

   (d) Different elements of Business environment are closely interrelated

10. Arrange the process of planning in correct sequence.

   A. Setting objectives

   B. Identifying alternative course of actions

   C. Developing premises

   D. Selecting an alternative

   E. Evaluating alternative courses

Choose the most appropriate answer from the options given below:

(a) A, B, C, D, E

(b) A, C, D, B, E

(c) A, C, B, D, E

(d) A, C, B, E, D

11. Reena is working in a car manufacturing company. One day she approaches her supervisor to discuss a better procedure of manufacturing the car. But the superior informs her that he is helpless and cannot change the procedure as it is set by the higher level Management. Identify the limitation of planning highlighted here i.e., Planning:

(a) May not work in a dynamic environment

(b) Involves huge costs

(c) Is a time consuming process

(d) Leads to rigidity

12. The purpose of planning is to meet future events effectively to the best advantage of an organisation. Identify the feature of planning highlighted here:

(a) Planning is mental exercise

(b) Planning is futuristic

(c) Planning is continuous

(d) Planning involves decision making

13. Span of Management refers to __________.

(a) Number of members in middle level management

(b) Number of members in top level management

(c) Number of subordinates under a superior

(d) Length of term for which a manager is appointed

14. "Delegation does not mean abdication". This statement means:

(a) Authority granted to the subordinates cannot be taken back

(b) Responsibility depends on the extent of authority delegated to the subordinate

(c) The Manager shall be responsible for the performance of the assigned task and even accountable for the same

(d) Delegation is entrustment of responsibility and authority to the subordinate relieving the manager from accountability for performance

15. Staffing is putting people to jobs. It includes workforce planning and comprises the following process. State the correct sequence of the process.

   A. Estimating the Manpower Recruitment

   B. Placement and Orientation

   C. Training and Development

   D. Recruitment

   E. Selection

Choose the most appropriate answer from the options given below:

(a) A, B, E, D, C

(b) A, C, D, B, E

(c) A, D, E, D, C

(d) C, E, B, A, D

16. The objective of the step of Staffing Process is to create a pool of prospective candidates for the job. Identify the step of Staffing Process highlighted in the above statement.

(a) Casual Callers

(b) Recruitment

(c) Selection

(d) Placement and Orientation

17. The manager does not have confidence on his subordinates so he does not ask for any suggestions from them. Identify the type of Personal Barrier being highlighted in the above situation.

(a) Fear of challenge to authority

(b) Lack of confidence of superior on subordinates

(c) Unwillingness to communicate

(d) Lack of proper incentive

18. Match the items of **List - I** with the correct items of **List - II**.

List - I	List - II
A. Employee empowerment	I. Leadership style
B. Grapevine	II. Financial incentive
C. Laissez Faire	III. Non financial incentives
D. Co-Partnership	IV. Internal communications

Choose the correct answer from the options given below:

(a) A-I, B-II, C-III, D-IV

(b) A-III, B-IV, C-II, D-I

(c) A-III, B-IV, C-I, D-II

(d) A-III, B-I, C-IV, D-II

19. Arrange the elements of communication in a proper sequence.

A. Sender

B. Encoding

C. Receiver

D. Message

E. Decoding

Choose the most appropriate answer from the options given below:

(a) E, B, C, D, A

(b) A, B, C, D, E

(c) A, C, B, D, E

(d) A, D, B, E, C

20. Identify the function of management that helps in judging the accuracy of standards.

(a) Planning　　　　　(b) Staffing

(c) Directing　　　　　(d) Controlling

21. Maya, the owner of the firm, sets production target for each day and month, in consultation with the Production Manager and supervisors. They decided that deviation between standard production and actual production up to 5% is acceptable. Deviations beyond this, should be reported. Identify the concept mentioned above.

(a) Management by Exception

(b) Key Responsibility Areas

(c) ROI

(d) Budgetary Control

22. Arrange the following steps of controlling in proper order.

A. Analysing deviation

B. Comparing actual performance with standards

C. Setting performance standards

D. Taking corrective action

E. Measurement of actual performance

Choose the most appropriate answer from the options given below:

(a) C, E, B, D, A

(b) C, B, A, D, E

(c) C, E, B, A, D

(d) D, C, E, B, A

23. Match the items of **List - I** with the correct items of **List - II**.

List - I	List - II
A. Personal Observation	I. operations are planned in advance in the form of financial statement and actual results compared
B. Budgetary Control	II. Technique used to study relationship between cost, volume and profits
C. Break even Analysis	III. enables manager to collect first hand information
D. Statistical Reports	IV. information presented in the form of chart, graph, table etc.

Choose the correct answer from the options given below:

(a) A- III, B-I, C-II, D-IV

(b) A-III, B-I, C-IV, D-II

(c) A-II, B-III, C-I, D-IV

(d) A-III, B-II, C-I, D-IV

24. Which one of the following is NOT a limitation of controlling?

(a) Little control on external factor

(b) Ensuring order and discipline

(c) Resistance from Employees

(d) Costly affair

25. Which one of the following is NOT the function of Financial Market?

(a) Facilitating Price Discovery

(b) Composition of long term and short term funds

(c) Mobilisation of savings and channeling them into the most productive uses

(d) Providing the liquidity to Financial assets

26. Name the intermediary who is authorised to maintain the accounts of dematerialised shares:

(a) Depository

(b) Depository Participant (DP)

(c) BSE - Bombay Stock Exchange

(d) RBI - Reserve Bank of India

27. Name the money market instrument, used by large and credit worthy companies to raise the short terms funds at lower rates of interest than market rates.

(a) Call money

(b) Commercial Papers

(c) Certificate of Deposit

(d) Commercial Bill

28. In order to raise share capital, ABC Ltd., is issuing shares and giving privilege to the existing shareholders to subscribe to the new issue of shares according to the terms of conditions of the company. Identify the method of floatation used by the company.

(a) Private Placement

(b) Offer for sale

(c) Right issue

(d) e-ipo

29. "Financial Markets help to save time, efforts and money of both buyers and sellers of financial assets". Identify the function of financial markets being highlighted in the statement.

(a) Mobilisation of Savings and Channeling them into the most productive uses

(b) Reducing cost of transactions

(c) Facilitating price discovery

(d) Providing liquidity to financial assets

30. Dividend decision is affected by many factors. Identify the factors affecting dividend decisions.

A. State of Capital market

B. Control Consideration

C. Shareholder's Preference

D. Taxation Policy

E. Floatation Cost

Choose the most appropriate answer from the options given below:

(a) A, B and C only

(b) C and D only

(c) C, D and E only

(d) B, C and D only

31. Ravi has started his online business of selling Garments because of low cost of production. Identify the distributions channel used by Ravi.

(a) Zero Level

(b) One Level

(c) Two Level

(d) Three Level

32. Identify the function of marketing that is also given by F.W. Taylor as one of the Techniques of Scientific Management.

(a) Motion study

(b) Functional Foremanship

(c) Standardisation

(d) Fatigue study

33. Identify the correct sequence of factors affecting Price Determination from the following.

A. Product cost

B. Environmental factors

C. The Utility and Demand

D. Company Characteristics

E. The Extent of competition in the market

Choose the most appropriate answer from the options given below:

(a) A, B and C only

(b) A and C only

(c) A, D and C only

(d) A, C and E only

34. Richa purchased an ISI marked steam iron from a branded shop. When she switched the steam iron on, she got an electric shock. Due to the electric shock she got her fingers burnt. Identify the consumer right violated by the company.

(a) Right of Safety

(b) Right of Seek Redressal

(c) Right to be informed

(d) Right to consumer education

35. Many Business Organisation have set up their own consumer services and grievance cells so that the consumer can file a complaint in case of dissatisfaction with a good or service. Name the Consumer Right on which the Business Organisation are focussing:

(a) Right to be informed

(b) Right to be Heard

(c) Right to be Seek Redressal

(d) Right to Consumer Education

36. When DTH was launched in India all service providers were charging a flat rate in which all channels were provided. Consumers even had to pay for those channels which they did not want to see. Which consumer right is ignored by the DTH service providers?

(a) Right to be heard

(b) Right to be informed

(c) Right to be choose

(d) Right to be seek redressal

37. Match the items of **List - I** with the correct items of **List - II**.

List - I	List - II
(Marks)	**(Name)**
A. 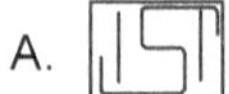	I. Food Process Order

B. 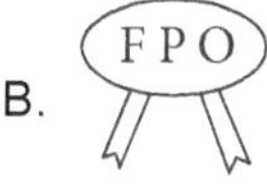 II. Electrical Goods

C. 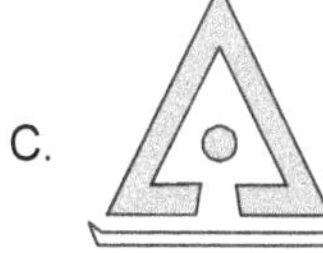 III. Eco-Mark

D. 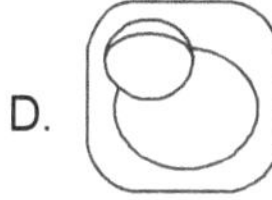 IV. BIS Hall mark

Choose the correct answer from the options given below:

(a) A-II, B-III, C-I, D-IV

(b) A-II, B-I, C-IV, D-III

(c) A-I, B-III, C-IV, D-II

(d) A-III, B-IV, C-II, D-I

38. Rohit died in a car accident as the air bags of the car did not open on impact. His family and friends are very angry about this defect in the car. They decided to file a case on the car company. Who can file a case on the car company under Consumer Protection Act?

(a) The Car Showroom owner

(b) The legal heir of Rohit

(c) The Consumer of another car company

(d) An Unregistered Consumer Association

39. Identify the Characteristics of entrepreneurship from the following.

(a) Behavioural

(b) Organisation of Production

(c) Fulfilling Social Responsibility

(d) Basis of Management Hierarchy

40. Which step in the process of organisation leeds to creation of management hierarchy?

(a) Identification and division of work

(b) Departmentalisation

(c) Assignment of duties

(d) Establishmenting reporting relationships

Direction for Questions 41 to 45:

Read the passage given below and answer the question.

Saksham, a newly appointed servicemen at M/s. Ghaziabad Petrol Station, G.T. Road, usually encounters problems while performing his job, 'like swiping the card when customer' pay; generally forgetting to bring down the meter to zero before filling the petrol tanks of various vehicles; considerable amount of petrol spills while filling the petrol tank and so on. Overall, he doesn't respond in the manner as expected. Hence, customers get irritated and often complain about him. Saksham feels sad that dispite his best efforts, he is not being able to perform his job properly. Saksham was appointed on the request of one of the close relatives of Petrol Pump Manager. Hence, the Petrol Pump Manager tries to improve Saksham's performance through maintaing good personal relations with him and thus to achieve goals of the organisation. Otherwise Petrol Pump Manager likes to give orders and expects his subordinates to obey them without any contradiction. He believes rewards and punishment both can be given depending upon the result.

41. The concept of staffing that may be used to improve Saksham's performance is:

(a) Recruitment

(b) Training

(c) Performance Appraisal

(d) Placement and Orientation

42. Identify the most suitable method that may be applied to make Saksham an efficient worker.

(a) Vestibule

(b) Internship

(c) Apprenticeship

(d) Induction

43. Identify the source of recruitment through which Saksham was appointed.

(a) Direct Recruitment

(b) Casual Caller

(c) Recommendation of Employee

(d) Management Consultants

44. Name the element of one of the functions of management being discussed in the above case:

(a) Leadership

(b) Motivation

(c) Communication

(d) Supervision

45. The leadership style usually followed by the Petrol Pump Manger is:

(a) Participative Leadership style

(b) Free-rein Leadership style

(c) Dogmatic Leadership style

(d) Free-Lancer Leadership style

Direction for Questions 46 to 50:

Answer the following questions based on case study.

Case Study

Mr. Rajesh Gulati is the Finance Manager of 'Health and Life Ltd.' a company dealing with health and organic food items. The company sells its products in smaller quantities in attractive containers. Moreover they have also decided to provide an additional layer of packaging for their products for the purpose of protections along with necessary storage, identification and even convenient transportation.

Keeping up with the latest packaging technology the company decided to upgrade its machinery. This, however, involved a major decision making as to how funds should be invested, so what the company is able to earn highest possible return.

Mr. Gulati estimated the amount of funds required for this purpose. He began with the preparation of sales forecast for the next four years.

He also collected the relevant data about the profit estimates in the coming years. By doing this he wanted to be sure about the availability of funds from internal sources. For the remaining funds he is trying to find out alternative sources.

46. Identify the concept of Financial Management being mentioned in the above case.
    (a) Wealth Maximisation
    (b) Financial Planning
    (c) Financial Transactions
    (d) Financial Decisions

47. The various objectives of financial planning concept identified in the case study are:
    A. To see for stock market reactions
    B. To ensure availability of funds whenever required
    C. To prepare financial budget
    D. To take care of purchasing raw material
    E. To see that the firm does not raise resources unnecessarily

Choose the most appropriate answer from the options given below:
    (a) A and B only
    (b) B and C only
    (c) D and B only
    (d) B and E only

48. Identify the financial decision taken by 'Health and Life Ltd.' that involves allocation of funds.
    (a) Investment decision
    (b) Dividend decision
    (c) Financing decision
    (d) Management decision

49. Identify the financial decision of Mr. Gulati about the requirement of finance to be raised for the company from various sources.
    (a) Investment decision
    (b) Management decision
    (c) Financing decision
    (d) Dividend decision

50. Name the various levels of packaging used by 'Health and Life Ltd.' as mentioned in the case study.
    A. Primary Package
    B. Secondary Package
    C. Tertiary Package
    D. Transportation Package
    E. Fancy Package

Choose the most appropriate answer from the options given below:
    (a) A, B and D only
    (b) A, B and C only
    (c) A, B and E only
    (d) B and D only

Answer Keys

1. (a)	**2.** (b)	**3.** (b)	**4.** (b)	**5.** (b)	**6.** (d)	**7.** (b)	**8.** (c)	**9.** (c)	**10.** (d)
11. (d)	**12.** (b)	**13.** (c)	**14.** (c)	**15.** (c)	**16.** (b)	**17.** (b)	**18.** (c)	**19.** (d)	**20.** (d)
21. (a)	**22.** (c)	**23.** (a)	**24.** (b)	**25.** (b)	**26.** (b)	**27.** (b)	**28.** (c)	**29.** (b)	**30.** (b)
31. (a)	**32.** (c)	**33.** (d)	**34.** (a)	**35.** (b)	**36.** (c)	**37.** (b)	**38.** (b)	**39.** (b)	**40.** (d)
41. (b)	**42.** (c)	**43.** (c)	**44.** (a)	**45.** (c)	**46.** (b)	**47.** (d)	**48.** (a)	**49.** (c)	**50.** (a)

Explanations

1. (a) Management is an intangible force, as it does not have any physical appearance. It can be felt, by the way an organisation functions.

2. (b) Directing refers to a process or technique of instructing, guiding, inspiring, counselling, overseeing and leading people towards the accomplishment of organizational goals.

3. (b) Controlling can be defined as that function of management which helps to seek planned results from the subordinates, managers and at all levels of an organization.

4. (b) Division of Work. The first henry fayol principle of management is based on the theory that if an employee is given a specific task to do, they will become more efficient and skilled in it. This is opposed to a multi-tasking culture where an employee is given so many tasks to do at once.

5. (b) Subordination of Individual Interests to General Interest is one of Fayol's fourteen administrative principles where any individual's interest that conflicts with an organizational interest must be subordinated to the interests of the organization.

6. (d) (A) (II), (B)-(I), (C)-(IV), (D)-(III)

7. (b) Social Environment consists of social forces like traditions, values, social trends, level of education, the standard of living etc. All these forces have a vast impact on business. Impact: More demand during festivals provides opportunities for various businesses.

8. (c) Establishing standard for controlling

9. (c) A dynamic environment is a business environment that is rapidly changing. In a dynamic market, businesses have to adapt quickly to changes and develop new ideas, products and services to keep up with technology and new trends.

10. (d) Setting objectives, Developing premises, Identifying alternative courses of action, Evaluating alternative courses are the steps followed in the planning process.

11. (d) Planning leads to rigidity: Once plans are made to decide the future course of action the manager may not be in a position to change them. Following predefined plan when circumstances are changed may not bring positive results for organisation. This kind of rigidity in plan may create difficulty

12. (b) Planning is futuristic: This means that business' goals and objectives need to be achieved at a particular time frame in the future and thus it is futuristic.

13. (c) Span of control (or span of management) is the number of subordinates who report directly to a manager or leader. The more employees assigned to a manager, the wider their span of control.

14. (c) The Manager shall be responsible for the performance of the assigned task and even accountable for the same

15. (c) (A), (D), (E), (D), (C)

16. (b) Recruitment is the process of finding, screening, hiring and eventually on boarding qualified job candidates.

17. (b) Lack of Confidence in Subordinates: Top-level superiors think that the lower-level employees are less capable and, therefore, they ignore the information or suggestions sent by them. They deliberately ignore the communication from their subordinates in order to increase their own importance.

18. (c) (A)-(III), (B)-(IV), (C)-(I), (D)-(II)

19. (d) The correct process in communication is Sender, Message, Encoding, Media, Decoding, Receiver, and Feedback.

20. (d) The purpose of the control function is to ensure that the organization makes progress towards the established goals.

21. (a) Management by Exception: This technique of management is based on the belief that 'an attempt to control everything results in controlling nothing'. According to this, only the essential and significant deviations that are beyond the acceptable limit should be controlled.

22. (c) (1) establish standards, (2) measure performance, (3) compare actual performance with standards and identify any deviations, (4) determine the reason for deviations, and (5) take corrective action if needed.

23. (a) (A)-(III), (B)-(I), (C)-(II), (D)-(IV)

24. (b) Ensuring Order and Discipline: Controlling ensures a close check on the activities of the employees. Hence, it helps in reducing the dishonest behaviour of the employees and in creating order and discipline in an organization.

25. (b) Composition of long term and short term funds

26. (b) The depository participant (DP) serves as an intermediary between the investor and the

Depository (NSDL or CSDL) who is authorised to maintain the accounts of dematerialised shares.

27. (b) Commercial Papers is issued by large and creditworthy companies to raise short-term funds at lower rates of interest than market rates. It usually has a maturity period of 15 days to one year

28. (c) Rights issue is a privilege given to existing shareholders to subscribe to a new issue of shares according to the terms and conditions of the company.

29. (b) Financial markets provide valuable information about securities being traded in the market. It helps to save time, effort and money that both buyers and sellers of a financial asset would have to otherwise spend to try and find each other

30. (b) (C) and (D) only

31. (a) Level Zero: A level zero distribution channel is the simplest. It involves a direct sale from manufacturers to consumers with no intermediary.

32. (c) Standardization refers to the process of setting standards for every business activity; it can be standardization of process, raw material, time, product, machinery, methods, or working conditions

33. (d) (A), (C) and (E) only

34. (a) Right of Safety

Means right to be protected against the marketing of goods and services, which are hazardous to life and property. The purchased goods and services availed of should not only meet their immediate needs, but also fulfil long term interests

35. (b) Right to be heard

Means that consumer's interests will receive due consideration at appropriate forums. It also includes right to be represented in various forums formed to consider the consumer's welfare.

36. (c) Means right to be protected against the marketing of goods and services, which are hazardous to life and property. The purchased goods and services availed of should not only meet their immediate needs, but also fulfil long term interests.

37. (b) (A)-(II), (B)-(I), (C)-(IV), (D)-(III)

38. (b) The legal heir of Rohit

39. (b) Entrepreneurship involves organizing all the factors of production under one roof to develop a new product and build a successful enterprise. It is the process of bringing all the factors together. The time, place, form utility, etc. needs to be considered while organizing the resources.

40. (d) Establishing responsibility relationships in an organisation structure implies the allocation of authority and responsibility among employees of the enterprise in such a way that each person should know who is responsible to whom and for what.

41. (b) It refers to improving a person's ability to do a particular job and to contribute to organisational goals.

42. (c) Apprenticeship is training for a profession under a mentor/professional. It is a way of acquiring new skills and getting hands-on industry experience before getting an educational degree or an entry-level job.

43. (c) Saksham was appointed on the request of one of the close relatives of Petrol Pump Manager.

44. (a) The action of leading a group of people or an organisation."

45. (c) Dogmatic and leads by the ability to withhold or give punishment or rewards, commands and expects compliance. Participative leader who usually consults with subordinates on proposed actions and decisions, and encourages participation from them.

46. (b) Financial planning involves looking at a client's entire financial picture and advising them on how to achieve their short- and long-term financial goals

47. (d) (B) and (E) only

48. (a) Investment decision refers to selecting and acquiring the long-term and short-term assets in which funds will be invested by the business.

49. (c) Financing decisions refer to the decisions that companies need to take regarding what proportion of equity and debt capital to have in their capital structure. This plays a very important role vis-a-vis financing its assets, investment-related decisions, and shareholder value creation.

50. (a) (A), (B) and (D) only

ECONOMICS

1. Match **List - I** with **List - II**.

   List - I :
   Foreign Exchange Rate

   List - II :
   Derived Meaning

   A. Fixed exchange rate
   I. Mixture of fixed and flexible exchange rate system.

   B. Floating exchange rate
   II. Determined by government.

   C. Managed floating
   III. Expectation of gain from appreciation of the currency

   D. Speculation
   IV. Determined by market forces of demand and supply of forex

   Choose the correct answer from the options given below:

   (a) A-IV, B-II, C-I, D-III
   (b) A-II, B-IV, C-I, D-III
   (c) A-I, B-IV, C-III, D-II
   (d) A-II, B-III, C-I, D-IV

2. Which of the following is not a component of current account:

   (a) Imports of machines
   (b) Trade in services
   (c) Grants received from a foreign government for rebuilding flood hit areas
   (d) Purchase of stock of a foreign company in London.

3. A change in the exchange rate of the Indian rupee and the British Pound from Rs.95 for a pound to Rs.100 for a pound will mean:

   (a) Indian exports of Britain will increase.
   (b) Indian imports from Britain will increase.
   (c) Indian exports to Britain will decrease.
   (d) There will be no change in exports and imports between the two countries

4. Which of the following will be included in national income, while using the income method to calculate the same:

   (Choose the correct option)

   (a) National debt interest.
   (b) Interest paid on a loan taken by a household from a bank to buy a car.
   (c) Interest received on debentures of a firm bought by a household
   (d) Interest paid on a loan taken by a employee from his employer.

5. What is the value of real GDP is nominal GDP is Rs. 3,300 crores and GDP deflator is 150?

   (a) Rs. 2,200 crores
   (b) Rs. 3,150 crores
   (c) Rs. 3,000 crores
   (d) Rs. 3,450 crores

6. Which of the following explains the concept of depreciation?

   A. An annual allowance for wear and tear of a capital good.
   B. The capital good gradually used up in each year's production process.
   C. Cost of replacement of a capital good due to an accident.
   D. Fall in the value of fixed asset due to unexpected change in technology.
   E. Cost of the good divided by number of years of its useful life.

   Choose the correct answer from the options given below:

   (a) A, B, C only
   (b) A, B, D only
   (c) A, B, E only
   (d) A, C, E only

7. If the value NVA_{FC} is Rs. 200 crores, intermediate consumption is Rs. 100 crores and depreciation is given as Rs. 40 crores, what will be the value of GVA_{FC}?

   (a) Rs. 140 crores
   (b) Rs. 340 crores
   (c) Rs. 60 crores
   (d) Rs. 240 crores

8. Identify the correct statements about the externalities as a limitation of GDP and welfare.

   A. GDP as measured does not include external production of goods.
   B. Inverse relationship between negative externality and welfare.
   C. No relation between GDP and welfare.
   D. Economic activities have both positive and negative externalities.
   E. Producers are rewarded with profit for positive externalities.

   Choose the correct answer from the options given below:

   (a) A and D only
   (b) B and E only
   (c) D and E only
   (d) B and D only

9. Coal used by a steel factory during the accounting year is a:

(a) Complementary good

(b) Intermediate good

(c) Substitute good

(d) Final good

10. Suppose a TV manufacturing unit wants to raise its inventories from 1000 units to 2000 units during the year. Expecting sale of 5000 units during the year, the firm produces 5000 + 1000 = 6000 TV sets. Actual sale for the firm are 5000 TV sets during the year.

This is an example of:

(a) Planned accumulation of inventories

(b) Unplanned accumulation of inventories

(c) Planned decumulation of inventories

(d) Unplanned decumulation of inventories

11. What will be the amount of initial reserves if Cash Reserve Ratio (CRR) is 20% and total credit creation is Rs. 500?

(a) Rs. 400   (b) Rs. 450

(c) Rs. 200   (d) Rs. 100

12. The currency issued by the Reserve Bank of India is called.

A. High powered money

B. Reserve money

C. Bank money

D. Monetary base

E. Fiscal base

Choose the correct answer from the options given below:

(a) A, B and D only

(b) B, C and E only

(c) C, D and E only

(d) A, C and E only

13. Identify which of the following measures taken by RBI will increase the money supply.

A. Increase in Cash Reserve Ratio

B. Decrease in Cash Reserve Ratio

C. Selling of a government bond

D. Buying of government bond

E. Decrease in Bank Rate

Choose the correct answer from the options given below:

(a) A and C only   (b) B and D only

(c) A, C and E only   (d) B, D and E only

14. Economic policies which have been adopted by both India and Pakistan are:

A. Mixed economy

B. Import-substitution

C. Green Revolution

D. Five Year Plans

E. Commerce system

Choose the correct answer from the options given below:

(a) B, C, D and E only

(b) C, D, E and A only

(c) A, B, C and D only

(d) D, C, B and E only

15. Arrange the events related to rural credit in the chronological order.

A. Setting up of NABARD as an apex body for rural financial system.

B. Kudumbashree programme implemented in Kerala

C. Green Revolution initiates diversification of rural credit portfolio

D. India adopts social banking and multiagency approach.

Choose the correct answer from the options given below:

(a) A, B, C, D

(b) C, D, A, B

(c) B, A, C, D

(d) D, C, B, A

16. The objective of Karve committee was rural development with a focus on

(a) Industrial Policy Resolution 1956

(b) Land reforms

(c) HYN seeds and their effectiveness

(d) Small Scale Industries.

17. Match **List - I** with **List - II**.

List - I	List - II
A. Solar Power	I. Earthworms
B. Gobar gas	II. Photovoltaic cells
C. Biopest Control	III. Neem
D. Biocomposting	IV. Rural areas

Choose the correct answer from the options given below:

(a) A-IV, B-I, C-II, D-III

(b) A-III, B-II, C-IV, D-I

(c) A-II, B-III, C-I, D-IV

(d) A-II, B-IV, C-III, D-I

18. Match **List - I** with **List - II**.

List - I	List - II
Economic issue	**Refers to**
A. Scarcity	I. Based on facts
B. Normative statement	II. Central problem of an economy
C. Positive statement	III. Problem of choice
D. What to produce	IV. Based on value judgement

Choose the correct answer from the options given below:

(a) A-III, B-II, C-I, D-IV

(b) A-III, B-IV, C-I, D-II

(c) A-III, B-IV, C-II, D-I

(d) A-IV, B-III, C-II, D-I

19. The downward movement along the demand curve of a commodity is due to:

Choose the correct option.

(a) Decrease in taxes.

(b) Decrease in the income of the consumer.

(c) Decrease in the price of its substitute.

(d) Decrease in the price of the commodity demanded.

20. Budget set of a consumer is defined as:

(a) The collection of all bundles that the consumer can be buy with the given income at the prevailing market price.

(b) The collection of all bundles that exactly cost the given income of the consumer at prevailing market price.

(c) The collection of all bundles that the consumer desires to purchase.

(d) The collection of all bundles that lies on budget line.

21. Liberation of trade and investment regime was initiated in the Indian Economy in 1991 to provide for:

A. International competitiveness of industrial production.

B. Promotion of competitiveness of local industries.

C. Collection of higher tariffs.

D. Adoption of modern technologies.

E. Control over imports.

Choose the correct answer from the options given below:

(a) A, B and C   (b) B, D and E

(c) A, B and D   (d) C, D and E

22. Identify the feature not found amongst the poor. (Choose the correct option)

(a) Malnutrition and hunger.

(b) Lack of basic literacy and skill.

(c) Gender equality in decision making within the family.

(d) Unable to negotiate their legal wages.

23. Which of the following is not a source of human capital?

(a) Expenditure on immigration.

(b) Expenditure on education.

(c) On-the-job training.

(d) Expenditure on health.

24. The organization which is responsible for providing estimates on poverty in India is:

(a) Central Statistical Organization

(b) NITI Aayog

(c) National Statistical Office

(d) Ministry of Human Resource Development

25. Match **List - I** with **List - II**.

List - I	List - II
Events	**Year**
A. Introduction of railways	I. Before 1921
B. First state of demographic transition	II. 1907
C. The Tata Iron and Steel Company (TISCO) incorporation	III. 1850
D. Suez Canal opening	IV. 1869

Choose the correct answer from the options given below:

(a) A-I, B-II, C-III, D-IV

(b) A-III, B-I, C-II, D-IV

(c) A-III, B-II, C-I, D-IV

(d) A-III, B-I, C-IV, D-II

26. On May 12,2020, our Prime Minister raised a clarion call to the nation giving a kick start to the Atmanirbhar Bharat Abhiyaan to fight COVID-19 pandemic in India. Which long term goal of India's five year plans does this campaign reflect? (Choose the correct alternative)

(a) Equity   (b) Self-reliance

(c) Growth   (d) Modernization

27. The contribution made by agriculture, industrial and services sector together contribute:

(a) Occupational structure

(b) Structural composition

(c) Demographic transition

(d) Regional disparity

28. Which of the following statements is/are correct?

A. Primary sector is still the major source of employment in India.

B. All the public sector establishment and those private sector establishment are called formal sector.

C. Majority of Indian work force is employed in the informal sector.

D. Majority of Indian work force is regular salaried.

E. Growth of employment has decelerated.

Choose the correct answer from the options given below:

(a) B and C only

(b) A and C only

(c) A and D only

(d) A and E only

29. Which organization collects the data related to unemployment in India?

(a) National Sample Survey Organization

(b) Central Statistical Organization

(c) Director General of Employment and Services.

(d) National Council of Education, Research and Training.

30. In an Economy, AD = Rs. 250 + cr + 0.6Y and at zero level of income consumption is Rs.150 crores. The value of autonomous investment will be:

(a) Rs. 100 cr.

(b) Rs. 150 cr.

(c) Rs. 50 cr.

(d) Rs. 200 cr.

31. Which of the following is true about the aggregate demand curve in the short run;

Choose the correct option:

(a) Aggregate Demand curve starts from the origin

(b) Aggregate Demand curve makes a positive intercept with the X-axis

(c) Aggregate Demand curve makes a positive intercept with the Y-axis.

(d) Aggregate Demand curve makes a negative intercept on the Y-axis.

32. The size of investment multiplier (k) depends on:-

(a) Average propensity to consume

(b) Average propensity to save

(c) Marginal propensity to consume

(d) Saving function

33. Identify the fiscal measures from the following that will help correct excess demand

A. Decrease in Repo rate.

B. Increase in taxes.

C. Decrease in government expenditure.

D. Increase in Repo rate

E. Decrease in taxes

Choose the correct answer from the options given below:

(a) A and E only

(b) B and C only

(c) C, D and E only

(d) A, D and E only

34. Assume that in an economy increased consumption is equal to increased saving, how many times will the national income increase in such an economy with an increase in investment?

(a) 2 times

(b) 3 times

(c) 4 times

(d) 1 times

35. If the equilibrium level of output is less than the full employment level, then it is a situation of:

(a) Balanced demand

(b) Deficient demand

(c) Excess demand

(d) Unemployment

36. A producer plans to add Rs.200 worth of goods to her stock by the end of the year. However due to an unexpected fall in the demand for her goods she adds Rs.250 worth of goods. Her ex-ante investment was ______ and ex post investment was ____.

(a) Rs. 150, Rs. 200

(b) Rs. 200, Rs. 150

(c) Rs. 200, Rs. 250

(d) Rs. 250, Rs. 200

37. Marginal propensity to save in zero when.

(a) Income is zero.

(b) Autonomous consumption is 1.

(c) The entire income is saved.

(d) The entire additional income is consumed.

38. Match **List - I** with **List - II**.

List - I	List - II
Programme	**Impact**
A. Creation of physical capital	I. Enhance labor productivity
B. On the job-training	II. Creates private and social benefit
C. Education	III. Create private benefit
D. Human capital	IV. Better social standing and pride.

Choose the correct answer from the options given below:

(a) A-II, B-I, C-III, D-IV

(b) A-III, B-I, C-IV, D-II

(c) A-I, B-III, C-IV, D-II

(d) A-III, B-IV, C-II, D-I

39. Increase in greenhouse gases since Industrial Revolution has caused the following environmental problem.

(a) Ozone depletion

(b) Global warming

(c) Land degradation

(d) Water contamination

40. Arrange the following events in the chronological order.

A. Establishment of People's Republic of China

B. Economic Reforms introduced in China.

C. Great Leap Forward.

D. Great Proletarian Culture Revolution.

E. Economic Reforms were initiated in Pakistan.

Choose the correct answer from the options given below:

(a) D, A, C, B, E

(b) A, C, D, B, E

(c) A, B, D, C, E

(d) A, D, C, B, E

Direction for Questions 41 to 45: Read the newspaper article given below and answer questions.

Accessible and affordable healthcare must: Mandaviya

'Centre aims to cut treatment cost, have more doctors'

The Union government will work holistically in the health sector with synergy between preventive health care and modern medical facilities. Union Health Minister Mansukh Mandaviya said on Monday.

Besides reducing the cost of treatment of the poor, efforts were on to rapidly increase the number of doctors, Mr. Mandaviya said while inaugurating a multispecialty outpatient and inpatient block (IPD) at Lady Hardinge Medical College (LHMC) and associated hospital here.

Holistic healthcare

The new IPD block will increase the bed strength of the LHMC from 877 to more than 1,000 beds. The IPD block houses an additional highly sophisticated facilities for holistic healthcare, including all medical and surgical specialties, Ayurveda, Yoga, Naturopathy and Homeopathy.

Mr. Mandaviya stated that the states played a vary crucial role in the implementation of any programme made by the Centre.

Nation comes first

"Making health accessible affordable and friendly is very important. Our effort need to be in the direction of advancement of the nation; the nation should always come first" be noted.

Bharati Pravin Pawar, Minister of state of health, said, it was important to not that better health facilities were not limited only to the treatment of diseases.

They also encouraged and promoted social justice. "When the poor get affordable and quality treatment, their faith in the system gets stronger", she said.

41. Multispecialty hospitals are included in the following tier of the health care system in India.

(a) Primary   (b) Secondary

(c) Tertiary   (d) Advanced

42. Identify which among the following constitute Indian system of medicine.

A. Naturopathy   B. Allopathy

C. Ayurveda   D. Yoga

E. Homeopathy

Choose the correct answer from the options given below:

(a) A, B, C, D and E only

(b) A, C, D and E only

(c) A, B, C and D only

(d) A, B, D and E only

43. The Union government is working towards the following to bring about holistic development of the health sector in India.

A. Accessibility.

B. Monopoly over healthcare provisions.

C. Import of medical services.

D. Affordability.

E. Modern medical facilities.

Choose the correct answer from the options given below:

(a) A, B and C only   (b) A, C and D only

(c) A, D and E only   (d) B, C and E only

44. Which of the following is not a part of health infrastructure.

(a) Nurses

(b) Doctors

(c) Hospital beds

(d) Senior secondary schools

45. Which of the following are used by the scholars to assess the health status of a nation.

(a) Paternal mortality, communicable and non-communicable diseases.

(b) Infant mortality, literacy rate and school enrollment ratio.

(c) Life expectancy, maternal mortality and nutrition levels.

(d) Nutrition levels, life expectancy and school dropout rates.

Direction for Questions 46 to 50:

BUDGET: 2022-23

Read some salient features of 'Budget 2022' and answer questions.

Finance Minister Nirmala Sitaraman presented the union Budget 2022.

There were a host of measures for a number of sectors, aimed at boosting growth amid high and rising inflation and continuing COVID uncertainties.

Few highlights

- Capex target expanded by 35.4%- from Rs. 5.54 lakh crore to Rs. 7.50 lakh crore. FY23 effective capex seen at Rs. 10.7 lakh crore.

- Top focus of the Budget this year are PM Gati Shakti.

- In 2022-33, states will be allowed fiscal deficit of upto 4% of GDP.

- Projected fiscal deficit of 6.4% of GDP in 2022-23.

- Receipt from disinvestment proceeds in next financial year pegged at Rs. 6,500 crore, lower than the current years mobilization of Rs. 78,000 crore.

- The government will tax income from digital asset transfers at 30%.

- Strategic transfer of ownership of Air India completed now.

- Rs. 4,800 crore allotted to PM Awas Yojana

- Rs. 6,000 crore allotted to provide tap water connections to 3.8 crore households in 2022-23.

46. PM Gati Shakti-National master plan for multi-modal connectivity is an example of:

(a) Capital expenditure

(b) Revenue expenditure

(c) Revenue receipt

(d) Capital receipt

47. Match **List - I** with **List - II**.

List - I : Description in Budget speech	**List - II : Figures in percent**
A. Projected Fiscal Deficit in 2022-23.	I. (−16.67%)
B. States Fiscal Deficit in 2022-23.	II. 6.4% of GDP
C. Change in disinvestment proceedings in FY 2022-23.	III. 35.4%
D. Change in Capex FY 2022-23.	IV. Upto 4% of GDP

Choose the correct answer from the options given below:

(a) A-IV, B-II, C-I, D-III

(b) A-II, B-IV, C-I, D-III

(c) A-II, B-IV, C-III, D-I

(d) A-IV, B-II, C-III, D-I

48. Rs. 60,000 crore allocated to provide tap water connection to 3.8 crore household. Provision of tap water by government is an example of

(a) Capital receipt.

(b) Revenue receipt.

(c) Private good.

(d) Public good.

49. Strategic transfer of ownership of Air India will lead to:

(a) Increase in capital expenditure

(b) Decreases in capital expenditure

(c) Increases in capital receipt.

(d) Decreases in capital receipt.

50. Identify the incorrect statement of the union budget of India 2022-23.

(a) Government has made provision to provide clean drinking water to households.

(b) Productivity Enhancement is one of the top focus of the budget 2022-23.

(c) Government has increased disinvestment to finance the deficit in FY 2022-23.

(d) Income from digital asset transfers will be taxable at 30%.

Answer Keys

1. (b)	**2.** (d)	**3.** (a)	**4.** (c)	**5.** (a)	**6.** (c)	**7.** (d)	**8.** (d)	**9.** (b)	**10.** (a)
11. (d)	**12.** (a)	**13.** (d)	**14.** (c)	**15.** (b)	**16.** (d)	**17.** (d)	**18.** (b)	**19.** (d)	**20.** (a)
21. (c)	**22.** (c)	**23.** (a)	**24.** (b)	**25.** (b)	**26.** (b)	**27.** (a)	**28.** (b)	**29.** (a)	**30.** (a)
31. (c)	**32.** (c)	**33.** (b)	**34.** (a)	**35.** (b)	**36.** (c)	**37.** (d)	**38.** (b)	**39.** (a)	**40.** (b)
41. (c)	**42.** (b)	**43.** (c)	**44.** (d)	**45.** (c)	**46.** (b)	**47.** (b)	**48.** (d)	**49.** (c)	**50.** (c)

Explanations

1. (b)

2. (d) Current account refers to an account which records all the transactions relating to export and import of goods and services and unilateral transfers during a given period of time.

3. (a)

4. (c) Loan taken by a firm for productive activities

5. (a) Real GDP = $\dfrac{3300}{150} \times 100 = 2200$

6. (c) Fall in the value of fixed asset due to normal wear and tear and foreseen obsolescence is called depreciation.

7. (d) (GVAfc = NVAfc + Dep.) (GVAfc = 200 + 40 = 240 Crore)

8. (d) Activities resulting in benefits to others are called positive externalities and increase welfare whereas those resulting in harm to others are called negative externalities and thus decrease welfare.

9. (b) Intermediate goods refer to those goods which are used either for resale or for further production.

10. (a) Planned Inventory: In case of an expected fall in sales, the firm will have unsold stock of goods which had not been anticipated.

11. (d) (Total Credit Creation = Initial Reserve × $\dfrac{1}{\text{LRR}}$)

(LRR = CRR + SLR) (Initial Reserve = 500 × 0.2 = 100)

12. (a)

13. (d) The supply of money means the total stock of all the forms of money (paper money, coins and demand deposits of banks) which are held by the public at any particular points of time.

14. (c)

15. (b) In 1969 when India adopted social banking and multi-agency approach to meet rural credit. Kudumbashree, the Kerala State Poverty Eradication Mission was launched on 17th May 1998. NABARD came into existence on 12 July 1982. The Green Revolution in India was initiated in the 1960.

16. (d)

17. (d)

18. (b)

19. (d) Downward Movement of Demand Curve - When the price of the commodity falls, the quantity demanded rises. It leads to the downward movement of the demand curve. It is also known as expansion of demand.

20. (a) Budget Set It refers to the set of all possible combinations of two goods which a consumer can afford at given income and prices in the market.

21. (c)

22. (c)

23. (a) Human capital refers to the stock of skill, ability, expertise, education, and knowledge in a nation at a point of time. Education investment is recognised as one of the main sources of human capital along with other sources like health, migration, on-job training, and information.

24. (b) Incidence of poverty is estimated by the Planning Commission (NITI Aayog).

25. (b)

26. (b) The first seven five years plans gave importance to self-reliance which means avoiding imports of those goods which could be produced in India itself.

27. (a)

28. (b)

29. (a)

30. (a) $(AD = C + I)$, Let $Y = 0$

So, $250 = (150 + 0.6Y + I)$

$(250 = 150 + I)$

$(I = 250 - 150 = 100 \text{ Cr})$.

31. (c) The curve intercepts on Y-axis because even at zero level of income, there is some consumption which is required for the very existence of life.

32. (c) Higher the MPC higher is value of K and vice-versa.

33. (b) Fiscal Measures employed by governments to stabilize the economy, specifically by manipulating the levels and allocations of taxes and government expenditures.

34. (a) $\left(K = \dfrac{1}{1} - MPC\right)$ $(MPC = 0.5)$ $(K = 2 \text{ Times})$

35. (b) A situation when the Aggregate Demand is less than the Aggregate Supply in an economy, corresponding to full employment in the economy, is termed as deficient demand.

36. (c)

37. (d) $(MPC + MPS = 1)$

38. (b)

39. (a) Ozone depletion is the gradual thinning of the earth's ozone layer in the upper atmosphere caused due to the release of chemical compounds containing gaseous bromine or chlorine from industries or other human activities.

40. (b) In 1988 Pakistan Economic Reforms, Great Proletarian Cultural Revolution was in 1966, The Great Leap Forward Campaign in 1958, China began to open up and reform its economy in 1978, On 1949, Creation of the People's Republic of China.

41. (c)

42. (b) The six systems of Indian Medicine are: Ayurveda, Yoga, Unani, Siddha, Naturopathy and Homoeopathy (AYUSH).

43. (c)

44. (d) Development of health infrastructure ensures a healthy manpower for production of goods and services to a country. Health infrastructure includes: hospitals, doctors, nurses and other paramedical professionals, beds, equipments required in hospitals and a well-developed pharmaceutical industry.

45. (c)

46. (b) Revenue expenditure is expenditure for the normal running of government departments and various services, interest charges on debt incurred by government, subsidies and so on.

47. (b)

48. (d) In economics, a public good refers to a commodity or service that is made available to all members of a society. Typically, these services are administered by governments.

49. (c) Capital Receipts are those receipts of the government which either create liability or cause any reduction in the assets of the government.

50. (c)

1. A person prefers to play badminton, read books and eating out. Taking this as the order of his performances what will be the opportunity cost of reading books?
   - (a) Playing badminton
   - (b) Listening to music
   - (c) Eating out
   - (d) Playing tennis

2. The consistent rise in petrol prices will lead to:
   - (a) A rise in the demand for petrol cars, as car and petrol are complementary goods.
   - (b) A fall in the demand for petrol cars, as car and petrol are complementary goods.
   - (c) A rise in the demand for petrol cars, as car and petrol are substitute goods.
   - (d) A fall in the demand for petrol cars, as car and petrol are substitute goods.

3. The price of a commodity has fallen by 40%. As a result, its quantity demanded has increased by 60%. The elasticity of demand for the commodity is:
   - (a) Perfectly elastic
   - (b) Unitary elastic
   - (c) Highly elastic
   - (d) Perfectly inelastic

4. Match **List - I** with **List - II**.

List - I **Nature of Goods**	**List - II** **Use**
A. Consumption goods	I. The things meant for final use and will not pass through any more stages of production
B. Goods that are durable character which are used in the production process	II. Raw material
C. Final goods	III. Food and clothing
D. Intermediate goods	IV. Capital goods

   Choose the correct answer from the options given below:
   - (a) A-I, B-II, C-III, D-IV
   - (b) A-IV, B-I, C-II, D-III
   - (c) A-III, B-I, C-II, D-IV
   - (d) A-III, B-IV, C-I, D-II

5. Which of the following are flow variables?
   - A. Population of India as on 31st March, 2022
   - B. Savings
   - C. National income of a country
   - D. Wealth
   - E. Capital

   Choose the correct answer from the options given below:
   - (a) A, B, C only
   - (b) A, B, E only
   - (c) B, C only
   - (d) B, C, E only

6. If the real GDP is Rs. 1000 and Price Index (with base = 100) is 120, calculate Nominal GDP.
   - (a) Rs. 1,200
   - (b) Rs. 1,120
   - (c) Rs. 1,220
   - (d) Rs. 920

7. Which of the following situation causes depreciation?
   - (a) Car damaged in an accident
   - (b) Closure of business firm due to lock down
   - (c) Loss of fixed assets due to floods
   - (d) Fall in value of fixed assets due to wear and tear with passage of time.

8. Which of the following is considered as a part of nominal flow in the circular flow of income?
   - (a) Flow of goods and services from firms to households
   - (b) Flow of factor payments from firms to households
   - (c) Flow of factor services from households to firms
   - (d) Flow of factors of production from households to firms

9. Which of the following is an example of normal resident of India?
   - (a) Foreign worker working in WHO located in India
   - (b) German citizen working as Direction in IMF located in India
   - (c) Ambassadors in India from the rest of the world
   - (d) Ambassadors of India in rest of the world

10. If national Income = Rs. 9,500 cr and Domestic Income = Rs. 9,800 cr, then which of the following options will be correct?
    - (a) Factor income from abroad = Rs. 1,200, factor income to abroad = Rs. 1,000.
    - (b) Factor income from abroad = Rs. 1,000, factor income to abroad = Rs. 1,200.
    - (c) Factor income from abroad = Rs. 500, factor income to abroad = Rs. 800.
    - (d) Factor income from abroad = Rs. 800, factor income to abroad = Rs. 500.

11. From the following data, calculate the GDP at MP

Items	Rs. in crores
i. Gross investment	90
ii. Net exports	10
iii. Net indirect taxes	5
iv. Depreciation	15
v. Net factor income from abroad	(–)15
vi. Private consumption expenditure	350
vii. Government purchases of goods and services	100

(a) Rs. 650cr   (b) Rs. 645cr

(c) Rs. 545cr   (d) Rs. 550cr

12. When C = 300 + 0.8Y and Y = 500 then saving at zero income level will be:

(a) –300   (b) 300

(c) 1100   (d) 800

13. If Marginal Propensity to Consume (MPC) = 1, the value of multiplier (k) will be:

(a) 1   (b) Zero

(c) 2   (d) Infinity

14. Match **List - I** with **List - II**.

List - I : Macroeconomic terms	List - II : Implication
A. Full employment equilibrium	I. Inflationary gap in the economy
B. Monetary policy	II. Underemployment equilibrium
C. Excess demand	III. No excess capacity
D. Deficient demand	IV. Pursued by the central bank of a country

Choose the correct answer from the options given below:

(a) A-IV, B-II, C-I, D-III

(b) A-III, B-I, C-IV, D-II

(c) A-III, B-IV, C-I, D-II

(d) A-II, B-IV, C-III, D-I

15. At point A in the give diagram which of the following holds true?

A. APC = 1   B. APC = 0

C. APS = 1   D. APS = 0

E. MPC = 1

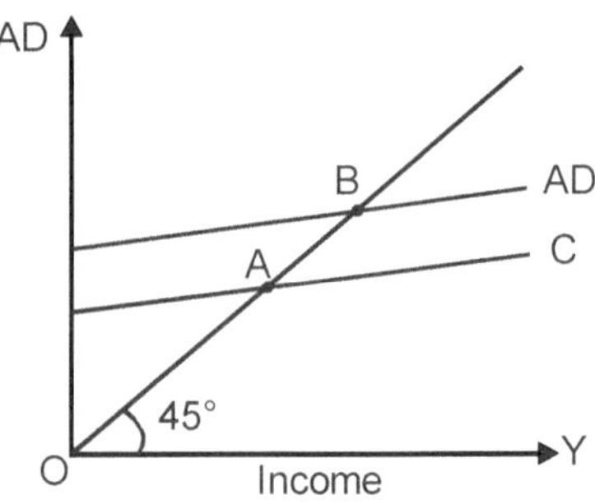

Choose the correct answer from the options given below:

(a) Both A and C only

(b) B only

(c) Both A and D only

(d) E only

16. In an ex-ante model,

When AD > AS, it will lead to,

(a) Planned inventory accumulation

(b) Fall in the planned inventory

(c) Unplanned inventory accumulation

(d) Fall in unplanned inventory

17. Fiscal measures to control deficient demand will be to:

(a) Increase public expenditure

(b) Decrease Repo rate

(c) Decrease public expenditure

(d) Increase taxes

18. Which of the following is NOT a feature of APC?

(a) APC rises with increase in income

(b) At breakeven level of income, APC is equal to 1

(c) APC can be greater than one

(d) APC can never be zero

19. Reserve Bank of India (RBI) was established in which year?

(a) 1930

(b) 1935

(c) 1945

(d) 1950

20. Calculate the value of the money multiplier and total deposit created if initial deposit is Rs.100 crores and Cash Reserve Ratio is 5%.

(a) 20, Rs.5000 crores

(b) 20, Rs.2000 crores

(c) 2, Rs.100 crores

(d) 2, Rs.200 crores

21. Which of the following represent the objective of the government budget?

   A. Creation of money

   B. Reallocation of resources

   C. Economic stability

   D. Reducing inequalities in income and wealth

   E. Open market operations

Choose the correct answer from the options given below:

   (a) A, B, C only

   (b) B, C, D only

   (c) C, D, E only

   (d) B, C, E only

22. Debt creating capital receipts of the Union budget include which of the following items?

   (a) PSU disinvestment

   (b) Recovery of loans

   (c) Market borrowing made by government

   (d) Loans advanced by Central government to Union territory government

23. When does zero primary deficit occur?

   (a) When revenue deficit is zero

   (b) When fiscal deficit is zero

   (c) When interest payment is nil

   (d) When borrowings and interest payment are equal

24. Which of the following items raise supply of foreign exchange in India.

   (a) Imports of goods from China

   (b) Indian students going to U.K for engineering

   (c) Purchase of land in U.S.A

   (d) Donations received from European countries

25. When the government decreases the exchanges rate, thereby making domestic currency costlier in a fixed exchange rate system, it is known as:

   (a) Appreciation

   (b) Revaluation

   (c) Depreciation

   (d) Devaluation

26. Arrange the following in the correct order of sequence in which RBI undertakes open market operation

   A. Increase in the money supply

   B. Increase in reserves in the economy

   C. Impending increase in deflation

   D. RBI buys government bonds in the open market

   E. Economy recovery

Choose the correct answer from the options given below:

   (a) C, D, B, A, E

   (b) A, E, D, C, B

   (c) D, A, C, B, E

   (d) C, E, B, D, A

27.

BOP terms		Relate to	
A.	Balance of payments	I.	Borrowings from abroad
B.	Accommodating transaction	II.	Export and import of invisible items
C.	Current account of balance of payments	III.	Below the line items
D.	Capital account of balance of payments	IV.	Flow concept

Choose the correct answer from the options given below:

   (a) A-I, B-II, C-III, D-IV

   (b) A-II, B-I, C-III, D-IV

   (c) A-III, B-IV, C-II, D-I

   (d) A-IV, B-III, C-II, D-I

28. Arrange the following events in the correct chronological order-

   A. First phase of the Green Revolution

   B. First Five Year Plan

   C. The Karve Committee noted the possibility of using small-scale industries for promoting rural development

   D. The Industrial Policy Resolution that formed the basis of the Second Five Year Plan

Choose the correct answer from the options given below:

   (a) D, B, A, C

   (b) A, D, C, B

   (c) B, C, D, A

   (d) C, D, B, A

29. NITI (National Institution for Transforming India) Aayog came into being as a successor of Planning Commission in

   (a) 2015

   (b) 2016

   (c) 2017

   (d) 2018

30. Globalization in India has produced the following positive results except:

  A. An opportunity in terms of greater access to global markets

  B. Increased economic disparities among nations and people

  C. Domestic companies face stiff competition from multinational companies

  D. Increased possibility for greater participation of large industries of developing countries

  E. Better and advanced technology

Choose the correct answer from the options given below:

  (a) A, B only

  (b) B, C only

  (c) C, D only

  (d) D, E only

31. The stagnation in the agriculture sector prior to 1947, in India, was caused mainly because of various systems of

  (a) Revenue settlement

  (b) Trade settlement

  (c) Land settlement

  (d) Agriculture settlement

32. Identify the correct statement.

  (a) Opportunity cost of environmental impacts need not be considered for sustainable development in India.

  (b) Opportunity cost of negative environmental impacts are high in India.

  (c) Opportunity cost of positive environment impacts are higher than the negative impacts in a growing economy like India.

  (d) Opportunity cost of negative environmental impacts is not a concern for development in India.

33. Which of the following types of farming is emerging as an environmentally sustainable production process:

  (a) Conventional farming

  (b) Organic farming

  (c) Water intensive cultivation

  (d) Shifting cultivation

34. People who are always poor and usually poor are categorized as:

  (a) Chronic poor

  (b) Transient poor

  (c) Churning poor

  (d) Occasionally poor

35. Identify the facility that can be categorized under social infrastructure.

  (a) Roads and highways

  (b) Ports

  (c) Gas pipelines

  (d) Sanitation

36. Indian System of Medicine (ISM) have huge potential and can solve a large part of our healthcare problems because they are:

  (a) Safe and ineffective

  (b) Expensive

  (c) Effective and expensive

  (d) Safe, effective and inexpensive

37. Match **List - I** with **List - II**.

List - I		List - II	
Human Development concept		**Meaning in Nature**	
A. Human capital formation		I.	Considers education and health as a means to increase labour productivity
B. Physical capital		II.	Flow concept
C. Human development		III.	Considers education and health integral to human well being
D. Human capital		IV.	Tangible

Choose the correct answer from the options given below:

  (a) A-IV, B-II, C-III, D-I

  (b) A-II, B-IV, C-III, D-I

  (c) A-II, B-IV, C-I, D-III

  (d) A-I, B-II, C-III, D-IV

38. Arrange the following events in chronological order.

  A. Announcement of first five year plan by China

  B. Great Leap Forward campaign

  C. Reforms in China

  D. People's Republic of China was established

  E. Great Proletarian Cultural Revolution

Choose the correct answer from the options given below:

  (a) D, A, C, B, E

  (b) A, C, D, B, E

  (c) C, D, A, E, B

  (d) D, A, B, E, C

39. Match **List - I** with **List - II**.

List - I : Indicators for India/China /Pakistan	List - II : Related to Countries/ Communes
A. Dual pricing	I. Commune
B. Very high fertility rate	II. China
C. Lowest sex ratio	III. India
D. Collective farming	IV. Pakistan

Choose the correct answer from the options given below:

(a) A-I, B-II, C-III, D-IV

(b) A-II, B-IV, C-III, D-I

(c) A-I, B-III, C-II, D-IV

(d) A-IV, B-II, C-I, D-III

40. Identify the incorrect statement:

While comparing Human Development in India, China and Pakistan, it is observed that

(a) India, China and Pakistan are able to provide improved drinking water source to the population.

(b) China and Pakistan are ahead of India in reducing population of people below poverty line.

(c) India and Pakistan have a very high maternal mortality rate.

(d) China has the largest share of infant mortality rate.

Direction for questions 41 to 45: Read the following case study and answer questions based on it.

Country and Product Identification Strategy for Enhancing India's Export Potential

As India revamps its trade policy strategy to re-engage with the rest of the world post COVID, an effective export promotion strategy identifies markets with high growth potential and augments comparative advantage of a larger set of products in the export basket. An empirical analysis to identify India's all weather partner using a measure of trade frequency i.e., the number of times country has registered as India's top 10 trade partners in the last decade may be useful. While countries such as the US, the UK, the UAE, Singapore, Hong Kong, Germany and China have consistently remained in the list of India's top 10 trade partners, trading partners such as Sri Lanka, South Korea, Indonesia, France and Brazil have made sporadic entries and exist.

The medium term growth potential of India's top trading partners is identified on the basis of IMF's latest growth projections in the post COVD-19 period i.e. 2023 yo 2026. The choice of the period ensures that a mechanical rebound on account of base effect does not overestimate the actual growth potential of a country. Next, revealed comparative advantage (RCA) is explored to gauge India's export potential.

Product differentiation is a short-run phenomenon between new trading partners and tis importance dissipates over time. From the medium term perspective, it is imperative that India captures a greater market share, based on differentiated products, especially during a time when global supply chain are going through a major transformation. Accordingly product classification in terms of organized exchange, referenced price and differentiated products is examined and mapped to sectoral RCA's and the medium term growth potential of India's trading partner.

41. Match **List - I** with **List - II**.

List - I : Description	List - II : Associated with
A. Trading partner	I. Germany
B. A top-10 trading partner	II. IMF growth projection post COVID-19
C. India's medium term growth potential	III. Indonesia
D. Product differentiation	IV. Short-run phenomenon

Choose the correct answer from the options given below:

(a) A-III, B-I, C-II, D-IV

(b) A-IV, B-I, C-II, D-III

(c) A-III, B-II, C-I, D-IV

(d) A-IV, B-III, C-II, D-I

42. India aims to capture a greater market share based on

(a) Special product

(b) Manufactured goods

(c) Product differentiation

(d) Global supply chains

43. Post COVID India's export promotion strategy aims at :

A. Removal of tariff and non-tariff barriers

B. Increase comparative advantage of larger export products

C. Arbitrary restriction on trade

D. Identifying markets with high growth potential

E. Rule base trading regime

Choose the correct answer from the options given below:

(a) A and C only

(b) B and D only

(c) A, B and E only

(d) C, D and E only

44. The countries that have consistently registered as India's top 10 trade partners in the last decade are referred to as:

(a) Unreliable partners

(b) Seasonal partners

(c) All-weather partners

(d) Occasional partners

45. Product differentiation will help India to

(a) More self-reliance

(b) Trade equity

(c) Decrease in imports

(d) Increase its exports

Direction for Questions 46 to 50: Read the following case study and answer question

The COVID-19 pandemic presented various socio-economic groups across countries with grave challenges. Migrant workers in India-mostly comprising daily wage labourers working in manufacturing and construction industries, and those engaged in agriculture, retail and services are one such group that was adversely affected. As the livelihoods of many of these workers were disrupted, several decided to return to their native towns and villages, leading to a situation where different state administrations had to manage their movements.

Consequently, Central and State Governments undertook various relief measures for migrant workers intended to provide them meals and arranging safe transportation to their native towns and villages. The Centre also started initiatives for creating jobs at the local level and supporting migrant workers through the Pradhan Mantri Garib Kalyan Yojana, Aatmanirbhar Bharat and Pradhan Mantri Garib Kalyan Rozgar Abhayan. The Ministry of Labour and Employment, Government of India, directed all states receiving migrant workers to undertake skill mapping of such labourers and provide them suitable livelihood opportunities. In this context, several states took commendable proactive steps for assisting stranded migrant workers and launching proactive steps for assisting stranded migrant workers and launching initiatives for livelihood generation for returned migrants and workers in the unorganized sector.

46. Identify the aspects that make migrant workers highly vulnerable in society

A. Social security benefits

B. No job security

C. Regular income

D. Limited skills

E. No surplus to sustain them

Choose the correct answer from the options given below:

(a) A and C only

(b) B and C only

(c) A, C and D only

(d) B, D and E only

47. Arrange the following statements in the correct sequence.

A. Migrant workers lose their livelihood

B. Central and State Government provide them meal and safe transportation to their native place

C. States undertake skill mapping and providing livelihood opportunity to migrant workers

D. COVID-19 Pandemic affects the country

E. They decide to return to their native towns and villages

Choose the correct answer from the options given below:

(a) A, B, C, D, E

(b) B, A, D, C, E

(c) D, A, E, B, C

(d) E, A, C, D, B

48. Which among the following programmes was not undertaken to create jobs for migrant workers?

(a) Pradhan Mantri Garib Kalyan Yojana.

(b) Aatmanirbhar Bharat

(c) Digital India Programme

(d) Pradhan Mantri Garib Kalyan Rozgar Abhayan.

49. Migrant workers work in the

(a) Organised sector

(b) Formal sector

(c) Public sector

(d) Unorganised sector

50. The prime reason for rural urban migration is

(a) Lack of facilities

(b) Lack of job opportunities

(c) Lack of social security

(d) Outdated technology

Answer Keys

1. (c)	**2.** (b)	**3.** (c)	**4.** (d)	**5.** (c)	**6.** (a)	**7.** (d)	**8.** (b)	**9.** (d)	**10.** (c)
11. (d)	**12.** (a)	**13.** (d)	**14.** (c)	**15.** (c)	**16.** (b)	**17.** (a)	**18.** (a)	**19.** (b)	**20.** (b)
21. (b)	**22.** (c)	**23.** (d)	**24.** (d)	**25.** (b)	**26.** (a)	**27.** (d)	**28.** (c)	**29.** (a)	**30.** (b)
31. (c)	**32.** (b)	**33.** (b)	**34.** (a)	**35.** (d)	**36.** (d)	**37.** (b)	**38.** (d)	**39.** (b)	**40.** (a)
41. (a)	**42.** (c)	**43.** (b)	**44.** (c)	**45.** (d)	**46.** (d)	**47.** (c)	**48.** (c)	**49.** (d)	**50.** (b)

Explanations

1. (c) Opportunity cost is commonly defined as the next best alternative. Also, known as the alternative cost, it is the loss of gain which could have been gained if another alternative was chosen.

2. (b) Complementary goods are goods that are typically used together, When the price of a certain good decreases, the demand for its complementary good will increase.

3. (c) (Ed = Percentage Change in Quantity Demanded / Percentage Change in Price)

$$\left(\frac{60}{40} = \frac{3}{2} = 1.5\right) (Ed > 1).$$

4. (d)

5. (c) Flow: These are defined as any quantity measured per unit at a particular period of time.

6. (a) $\left(\text{Price Index} = \dfrac{\text{Nominal GDP}}{\text{Real GDP}} \times 100\right)$

(Nominal GDP = 120 × 10 = 1200)

7. (d) Depreciation involves loss of value of assets due to the passage of time and obsolescence.

8. (b) Nominal flows refer to the flow of money in the form of money income and spending on goods and services.

9. (d) A normal resident of a country refers to an individual or an institution who ordinarily resides in the country and whose centre of economic interest also lies in that country. Normal residents include both, individuals and institutions.

10. (c) (NNPfc = NDPfc + NFIA)

(NFIA = –300)

(Net Factor Income From Abroad is 500 and Net Factor Income to Abroad is 800)

11. (d) (GDPmp = PFCE + GFCE + GDCF + Net Exports)

(GDPmp = 350 + 100 + 90 + 10)

(GDPmp = 550 Cr.)

12. (a) (S = Y – C) (Autonomous Consumption is 300 so Saving at Zero Income level is –300)

13. (d) $\left(K = \dfrac{1}{1} - MPC\right)$

14. (c)

15. (c) (APC + APS = 1) $\left(APC = \dfrac{C}{Y}\right)$

16. (b) Excess Demand: When the planned aggregate expenditure is greater than the available output at full employment level, the situation is termed as excess demand.

17. (a) Measures employed by governments to stabilize the economy, specifically by manipulating the levels and allocations of taxes and government expenditures.

18. (a) $APC = \dfrac{C}{Y}$

The ratio of APC falls with increase in disposable income because with increase in income the proportion of consumption expenditures is decreasing as it creates smaller part of income. Income also rises faster than consumption.

19. (b) The Reserve Bank of India Act, 1934 (II of 1934) provides the statutory basis of the functioning of the Bank, which commenced operations on April 1, 1935.

20. (b) $\left(\text{Money Multiplier} = \dfrac{1}{LRR}\right)$

(LRR = CRR + SLR)

$\left(\text{Total Money Creation} = \text{Initial Deposit} \times \dfrac{1}{LRR}\right)$

21. (b) Main objectives of the government budget is as follows: Reallocation of resources, Redistribution of activities, Stabilizing economic activities Management of public enterprises and Economic growth.

22. (c) The debt receipts are those which are to be repaid by the government.

23. (d) Primary deficit = Fiscal deficit − Interest payments. Therefore, the primary Deficit can be zero, if Fiscal Deficit = Interest Payments.

24. (d)

25. (b) A revaluation is an upward change in the currency's value.

26. (a)

27. (d)

28. (c) The first phase of the green revolution was started in the mid-1960, Karve committee was set up in the year 1955, Industrial Policy Resolution of 1956 (IPR 1956) is a resolution adopted by the Indian parliament in April 1956, 1 April 1951 with the launching of the First Five Year Plan (1951-56.

29. (a) NITI Aayog was formed via a resolution of the Union Cabinet on 1 January 2015.

30. (b)

31. (c) This stagnation in the agricultural sector was caused mainly because of the various systems of land settlement that were introduced by the colonial government.

32. (b) The country has to pay huge amount for damages done to human health. The health cost due to degraded environmental quality have resulted in diseases like asthma, cholera, etc. Huge expenditure is incurred in treating the diseases.

33. (b) Environmental sustainability is the responsibility to conserve natural resources and protect global ecosystems to support health and wellbeing, now and in the future.

34. (a) Chronic poor: People who are leading constant lives of poverty and who are normally poor but may have a small amount of money with them (for example, casual workers) are classified collectively as the chronic poor.

35. (d) Social infrastructure plays an important role in both the economic development of a nation and the development of society's quality of life. Few examples of social infrastructure are water supply, sanitation, health, housing, etc.

36. (d)

37. (b)

38. (d) Great Proletarian Cultural Revolution was launched by Mao Zedong in 1966, On October 1, 1949, Chinese Communist leader Mao Zedong declared the creation of the People's Republic of China (PRC), The reforms were launched by Chinese Communist Party (CCP) on December 18, 1978, The Great Leap Forward in 1958, In 1953, Mao launched China's First Five Year Plan.

39. (b) Under the Commune system, people collectively cultivated lands. In 1958, there were 26,000 communes covering almost all the farm population, The reform process also involved dual pricing in china, The fertility rate is also low in China and very high in Pakistan.

40. (a)

41. (a)

42. (c)

43. (b)

44. (c)

45. (d)

46. (d)

47. (c)

48. (c) Digital India is a flagship programme of the Government of India with a vision to transform India into a digitally empowered society and knowledge economy.

49. (d) The unorganised sector is characterised by small and scattered units, which are largely outside the control of the government.

50. (b) Lack of job opportunities is also called unemployment which is a state of joblessness. Joblessness results in the following consequences: poor health, illiteracy, frustration, and depression among youth, lack of peace in the families. Consequences also include discrimination, loss of skills, and loss of self-esteem.

1. What was the main motive of British rule in India?

   (a) To Prepare/Install industrial plants in India?

   (b) Making India as an importer of raw goods

   (c) To reduce the country to being a raw material supplier for Great Britain's expanding modern industrial base

   (d) Making India an exporter of materials to England.

2. Match **List - I** with **List - II**.

List - I Concept/Policy		List - II Meaning Objective
A. Promoted Excess	I.	Determining the largest amount of land a single person may own
B. Ceiling of land	II.	Policy of substituting native output for imports
C. Replacing the import	III.	Portion of agricultural products that the farmers sells in the trade
D. Granting of license	IV.	System of obtaining permission to start business

Choose the correct answer from the options given below:

   (a) A-IV, B-I, C-II, D-III

   (b) A-III, B-II, C-I, D-IV

   (c) A-III, B-I, C-II, D-IV

   (d) A-III, B-IV, C-II, D-I

3. Put the following chronologically:

   A. Installation of M/r. Tata Iron and Steel

   B. Starting Railways services during British Period

   C. Collection of Population details in British India

   D. Establishment of Planning commission

   E. Existence of Karve committee

Choose the correct answer from the options given below:

   (a) A, D, C, B, E

   (b) B, C, A, D, E

   (c) C, D, A, B, E

   (d) E, B, D, C, A

4. Identify the correct statements from the following:

   A. Currency is issued by the nation's Central Bank

   B. To address the budget deficit, Central Bank sends money to the government

   C. The economy's foreign exchange reserves are preserved by Central Bank

   D. Central Bank does not control money supply and credit through monetary policy

   E. Central Bank gives loans to the commercial Banks for short term

Choose the correct answer from the options given below:

   (a) B, C, D, E only

   (b) A, B, C, D only

   (c) B, C, D, A only

   (d) A, B, C, E only

5. Commercial banks have generated Rs. 12,000 crores and CRR is 25%. Initial payments will be in the amount of:

   (a) Rs. 48,000 crores

   (b) Rs. 6,000 crores

   (c) Rs. 3,000 crores

   (d) Rs. 30,000 crores

6. Match **List - I** with **List - II**.

List - I : Activity		List - II : Aim
A. Horticulture	I.	Switching from a single crop to a multiple-crop system
B. Diversification of crop production	II.	Premier bank for rural credit
C. NABARD	III.	It is a micro-finance scheme
D. Self-Help Groups	IV.	Growing tuber, fruit and vegetable crops

Choose the correct answer from the options given below:

   (a) A-I, B-II, C-IV, D-III

   (b) A-IV, B-I, C-III, D-II

   (c) A-IV, B-I, C-II, D-III

   (d) A-II, B-IV, C-I, D-III

7. Put the following schemes chronologically:

   A. Start of Jan Dhan Yojana

   B. Mahatma Gandhi National Rural Employment Guarantee Act

   C. Study group formed by the Planning Commission to estimate the number of poor in India.

   D. Task force on projection of minimum needs and effective consumption demand.

   E. Food for work programme was launched.

Choose the correct answer from the options given below:

   (a) A, B, C, E, D only

   (b) C, D, A, B, E only

   (c) C, E, D, B, A only

   (d) D, E, C, A, B only

8. Identify the correct statements from the following:

A. Revenue expenditure is any lay out that result in a decrease in financial assets or an increase in financial liabilities

B. Capital expenditure is expenditure which results in creation of financial assets or reduction in financial liabilities

C. Capital receipts are receipts which leads to reduction in financial assets or creation of liability

D. Revenue receipts are receipts which lead to decrease in financial assets or increase of financial liability

E. Revenue receipts are receipts which neither lead to reduction in financial assets nor creation of financial liability

Choose the correct answer from the options given below:

(a) A, C, D only   (b) C, D, E only

(c) B, C, E only   (d) A, D, E only

9. If NNPMP = Rs. 5,330, indirect tax = Rs. 1,770 and consumption of fixed capital = Rs. 1,550 then GNPFC will be x. The value of x is.

(a) 4,110   (b) 5,000

(c) 5,110   (d) 6,000

10. Which of the following is a factor income?

(a) Interest

(b) Money received from sale of land

(c) National debt interest

(d) Subsidy received from government

11. Identify the stock variable from the following:

(a) Wealth

(b) Income

(c) Savings

(d) Capital Formation

12. GDPMP will be equal of GDPFC if

(a) Gross domestic capital formation = Net domestic capital formation

(b) Indirect taxes = subsidy

(c) Factor income from abroad = Factor income to abroad

(d) Opening stock = Closing stock

13. Match **List - I** with **List - II**.

List - I	List - II
National income terminology	**Known as**
A. Income generated by own account workers	I. Nominal national income
B. National income at current prices	II. Corporate tax
C. Component of profit	III. Change in stock
D. Closing stock-opening stock	IV. Mixed income of self employed

Choose the correct answer from the options given below:

(a) A-IV, B-II, C-I, D-III

(b) A-I, B-III, C-II, D-IV

(c) A-IV, B-I, C-II, D-III

(d) A-II, B-III, C-I, D-IV

14. Identify the correct statements from the following:

A. Fees to a mechanic paid by a firm is not included in the estimation of national income

B. Income tax paid by an individual is not included in national income

C. Interest paid by a garment manufacture on a loan taken from bank is included in national income

D. Payment of old age pension will not be included in national income as it is a transfer payment

E. Insurance premium paid by household to an insurance company is not included in the estimation of national income

Choose the correct answer from the options given below:

(a) A, D, E only   (b) A, B, C, D only

(c) A, B, E only   (d) B, D, E only

15. Identify the correct statement from the following:

A. The Household's investing is not considered to be the cost of building a residence

B. Net factor revenue from overseas includes money from Exports

C. The sum of factor incomes equals the net value added

D. The assessment of national income takes into account the market value of both final and intermediate items

E. Profit earned by non-resident company in India is a part of domestic income of India

Choose the correct answer from the options given below:

(a) A, D only   (b) B, E only

(c) D, E only   (d) C, E only

16. Which of the following correctly represents value at market price?

(a) Factor cost + net indirect taxes

(b) Factor cost – net indirect taxes

(c) Factor cost + indirect taxes

(d) Factor cost – indirect taxes

17. When all of an economy's output is sold during a single accounting year, the value of output is represented by:

(a) Sales + change in stock

(b) Sales only

(c) Sales – change in stock

(d) Change in stock

18. If a farmer sells wheat to miller for Rs. 500 and miller sells flour to baker for Rs. 700 and baker sells bread to the consumer for Rs. 1,000, then total value added by miller and baker is:

(a) 500   (b) 550

(c) 800   (d) 1,200

19. Match **List - I** with **List - II**.

List - I	**List - II**
Concept under Theory of Income determination	**Meaning**
A. Saving < Investment	I. When AD < AS
B. $\dfrac{1}{1-mpc}$	II. Under employment equilibrium
C. National income will fall	III. Planned inventory would fall below the desired level
D. AD = AS at a point less than full employment	IV. Multiplier

Choose the correct answer from the options given below:

(a) A-II, B-III, C-IV, D-I

(b) A-III, B-IV, C-I, D-II

(c) A-IV, B-II, C-III, D-I

(d) A-III, B-IV, C-II, D-I

20. Identify the correct statement from the following:

A. Consumption curve starts from the origin

B. The sum of APC and APS is equal to 1

C. Aggregate demand and market demand mean the same

D. The value of MPC and MPS varies between 0 and 1

E. At breakeven point saving is zero

Choose the correct answer from the options given below:

(a) A, D, E only   (b) B, C, D only

(c) B, D, E only   (d) A, C, E only

21. In a time of deflation, the Central Bank should:

(a) Lower the Bank rate and purchase securities

(b) Increase the Bank rate and purchase securities

(c) Lower the Bank rate and sell securities

(d) Increase the Bank rate and sell securities in the open market

22. Identify the monetary invention that can Close the inflationary group:

(a) Lowering of the bank rate

(b) Reduction in availability of credit

(c) Cut back on government spending

(d) An increase in taxes

23. Actual aggregate demand's gap from that needed to achieve full employment equilibrium is referred to as:

(a) Surplus supply

(b) Deflationary gap

(c) Inflationary gap

(d) Excess supply

24. At equilibrium level of income in an economy:

(a) Consumption = Investment

(b) Aggregate demand = Consumption

(c) Saving = Investment

(d) Consumption = Saving

25. If the ratio between MPC and MPS is 4 : 1, the value of investment multiplier will be:

(a) 4   (b) 8

(c) 5   (d) 2

26. In an economy if equilibrium level of national is Rs. 2,000 crores. Autonomous consumption = Rs. 400 crores and Investment expenditure = Rs. 200 crores, then MPC will be:

(a) 1.2   (b) 0.2

(c) 0.9   (d) 0.7

27. In an economy MPS = 0.20 and investment is increased by Rs. 400 crores, than total increase in income is ________ Crores.

(a) Rs. 2,100

(b) Rs. 2,500

(c) Rs. 2,700

(d) Rs. 3,200

28. ______ is included in the government budget as a capital receipt.

(a) Current transfers received from foreign countries

(b) Borrowing from IMF

(c) Profits and dividends of public sector enterprises

(d) GST collection of Central government

29. Arrange the following in correct chronological order:

A. Goods and Service Tax came into effect

B. WTO was founded

C. GATT was established

D. Demonetization in India

E. Privatization of Air India

Choose the correct answer from the options given below:

(a) C, D, B, A, E   (b) C, A, E, D, B

(c) C, B, D, A, E   (d) C, B, A, D, E

30. The cause for the demand curve's movement is:

(a) Change in income of the Consumer

(b) Change in price of the given good

(c) Change in population

(d) Change in price of raw material

31. The demand for normal good _______ with an increase in income of the consumer.

(a) Moves upward on Demand Curve

(b) Remains unchanged

(c) Decreases

(d) Increases

32. The main issues of an economy are:

(a) What to produce? How to produce? For whom to produce?

(b) What to employ? How to employ? How much to employ?

(c) What to save? How to save? How much to save?

(d) What to invest? How to invest? Where to invest?

33. A consumer is consuming two goods X and Y.

If Muy = 20, Mux = 60 price of good Y = Rs. 4, then what will be the price of good X if consumer it at equilibrium.

(a) Rs. 15   (b) Rs. 12

(c) Rs. 3   (d) Rs. 5

34. Arrange the following in correct chronological order:

A. Great Leap Forward campaign

B. Economic reforms in China

C. Great Proletarian Cultural Revolution

D. People's Republic of China was established

E. Announcement of First Five Year Plan by China

Choose the correct answer from the options given below:

(a) A, E, D, C, B

(b) D, E, A, C, B

(c) D, C, A, B, E

(d) D, E, C, A, B

35. Which of the following is correct about Human Development Index:

(a) It does not include health indicators

(b) It does not include income indicators

(c) It does not include literacy indicators

(d) It does not include democratic indicators

36. _______ best defines the social infrastructure:

(a) Economy   (b) Geo-Communication

(c) Environment   (d) Housing

37. Arrange the following in correct chronological order:

A. Adoption of one child policy in China

B. Economic reforms in Pakistan

C. New Economic Policy in India

D. Announcement of First Five Year Plan by India

E. Announcement of First Five Year plan by Pakistan

Choose the correct answer from the options given below:

(a) C, B, A, E, D   (b) D, C, A, B, E

(c) D, E, A, B, C   (d) E, D, B, C, A

38. Global Burden of Disease (GBD) as an indicator is used to assess:

(a) The quality of life lived by the people

(b) Deaths caused by non-communicable diseases

(c) People dying prematurely due to a particular disease and number of years spent by them in state of disability

(d) Death caused by communicable diseases

39. Match **List - I** with **List - II**.

List - I : Employment Condition		List - II : Reference
A.	People can work at going rate of pay, Yet they are unable to find employment in economy.	I. Informalisation of workforce
B.	More people are engaged in work than are really needed	II. Open unemployment
C.	Increase in proportion of workforce in informal sector to total workforce	III. Unemployed people
D.	Labour force-work force	IV. Disguised unemployment

Choose the correct answer from the options given below:

(a) A-II, B-IV, C-III, D-I

(b) A-II, B-IV, C-I, D-III

(c) A-IV, B-II, C-III, D-I

(d) A-II, B-III, C-IV, D-I

40. Moving from self employment and regular employment to temporary work is referred to as:

(a) Casualization of workforce

(b) Frictional unemployment

(c) Structural unemployment

(d) Informalisation of workfare

Direction for questions 41 to 45: Based on the case study given below answer the questions that follow:

Case Study

GST Council way may replace 5% rate with 3%, 8% slabs.

With states on board to raise revenue so that they do not have to depend on centre for compensation, the GST council at its meeting next month is likely to consider a proposal to do away with the 5% slab by moving some goods of mass consumption to 3% and the remaining to 8% categories, sources said.

Currently GST is a four tier structure of 5,12,18 and 28%. Besides gold and gold jewellery attract 3% tax.

In addition there is an exempt list of items like unbranded and unpacked food items, which do not attract the levy. Sources said in order to augment revenue the council may decide to prune the list of exempt items by moving some of the non-food items to 3% slab.

Sources said that discussions are on to raise the 5% slab to either 7 or 8% or 9%, a final call will be taken by the GST council which comprises Finance Ministers of both Centre and States.

Every 1 percentage point increase in the 5% slab, which mainly includes packaged food items, would roughly yield an additional revenue of Rs 50,000 crore annually. Although various options are under consideration, the Council is likely to settle for an 8% GST for most items that currently attract 5% levy.

Under GST, essential items are either exempted or taxed at the lowest rate while luxury and demerit items attract the highest tax. Luxury and sin goods also attract cess on top of the highest 28% slab. This cess collection is used to compensate States for the revenue loss due to GST rollout. With the GST compensation regime coming to an end in June, it is imperative that States become self-sufficient and not depend on the centre for budging the revenue gap in GST collection.

41. Which of the following is an example of Goods and service tax (GST)?

(a) Direct tax

(b) Indirect tax

(c) VAT

(d) GST

32. Percent is excluded from GST four tier formation

(a) 5%   (b) 12%

(c) 25%   (d) 28%

43. Pick out the incorrect one:

(a) The least expensive rate of tax or exemption is applied to essential item

(b) One percent increase in 5% GST slab will yield Rs 50,000 crores annually

(c) Gold and jewellery attract 5% tax

(d) GST council decides the charges in tax slabs of GST

44. Items under 5% tax slab includes

(a) Fuel

(b) Gold ornaments

(c) Packaged food items

(d) Luxury and sin goods

45. Cess on the luxury and sin goods benefitted.

(a) Centre Government

(b) States

(c) Ministry of Finance

(d) RBI

Direction for questions 46 to 50: Read the following case study carefully and answer questions based on it.

Case Study

Employment has remained one of the top challenges of Indian policy makers, and over the years this has only become more complex. One there is considerable improvement in literacy, schooling and attainment of higher education and skills and vocational education in the country. The educated and trained manpower looks not for jobs alone but for decent jobs with better work environments, regular employment and better remuneration. However, job creation for this kind of employment has not kept pace with the increase in the number of job seekers. Two the aspirations of the labour class have been rising with the overall development of the country. Three the growth of industry and service sectors has been very uneven across different regions and states. This has resulted in a mismatch in employment opportunities and the supply o labour at local levels. Fourth there is a strong divergence between structural changes in the composition of output and employment. The industry and services sectors, which constitutes more than 80 percent of the gross value added in the country, provides employment to 54.4 percent of the workforce, and agriculture which accounted for 18.29 percent of GVA in 2019-20, retains 45.6 percent workforce. This divergence in sectoral in sectoral share in income and employment is manifested in the rising gap in per worker income in the agriculture and non-agriculture sectors, lastly, due to job security assured salary and other pay and prestige associate with it, preference towards government jobs has increased tremendously.

India has experienced more or less consistent and steady changes in the structure of the output of the economy, especially after the economic reforms of 1990-91. The growth rate of the economy, measured by the gross value added, at constant prices, accelerated from 4.27 percent twenty years before the economic reforms to 6.34 percent twenty years after the reforms. The growth rate in GVA showed further acceleration to reach 6.58 percent during 2010-11 to 2019-20 at 2011-12 prices. This growth trajectory was accompanied by a steady decline in the share of agriculture and a steady increase in the share of non-agriculture sector in total economy. The change in sectoral shares accelerated over time.

46. If the share of agriculture in the economy deceases and the share of non-agricultural sectors rises, then it may be called as:

(a) Industrial classification

(b) Structural change

(c) Structural composition

(d) Sectoral classification

47. The complexity of the job challenge has been increased because of

A. Improvement in health infrastructure

B. Improvement in skills

C. Diversification of productive activities

D. Attainment of higher education

Choose the correct answer from the options given below:

(a) A and C only

(b) B and D only

(c) B, D and E only

(d) A, C and D only

48. The difference in the growth rate of GVA at constant prices for 1970-71 and 2010-11 is approximately ______ percent.

(a) 2.9

(b) 1.37

(c) 2.09

(d) 3.9

49. Find out the correct statement pertaining to the formal sector employment:

(a) Insecurity of employment

(b) Prestige

(c) Fixed wages

(d) Do not get regular income

50. Match **List - I** with **List - II**.

List - I	List - II
Reference in case study	**Fact given**
A. Post economic reforms	I. Employment with an improved workplace.
B. Industry and service sector	II. Employ's 45.6% workforce
C. Trained man-power want	III. Acceleration in GVA growth rate
D. Agriculture	IV. 80% of GVA in 2019-2020

Choose the correct answer from the options given below:

(a) A-III, B-II, C-I, D-IV

(b) A-II, B-I, C-III, D-IV

(c) A-I, B-IV, C-III, D-II

(d) A-III, B-IV, C-I, D-II

Answer Keys

1. (c)	**2.** (c)	**3.** (b)	**4.** (d)	**5.** (c)	**6.** (c)	**7.** (c)	**8.** (c)	**9.** (c)	**10.** (a)
11. (a)	**12.** (b)	**13.** (c)	**14.** (b)	**15.** (b)	**16.** (a)	**17.** (b)	**18.** (a)	**19.** (b)	**20.** (c)
21. (a)	**22.** (b)	**23.** (b)	**24.** (c)	**25.** (c)	**26.** (c)	**27.** (*)	**28.** (b)	**29.** (c)	**30.** (b)
31. (d)	**32.** (a)	**33.** (b)	**34.** (b)	**35.** (d)	**36.** (d)	**37.** (c)	**38.** (c)	**39.** (b)	**40.** (a)
41. (b)	**42.** (c)	**43.** (c)	**44.** (c)	**45.** (b)	**46.** (d)	**47.** (b)	**48.** (*)	**49.** (c)	**50.** (d)

Explanations

1. (c) The following is the motive -

Making India a supplier of raw materials - The main motive of the British Government was to make India a mere supplier of cheap raw materials to feed its own rapidly expanding industries.

2. (c)

3. (b) It was established in the year 1907 in Jamshedpur, British rulers introduced railways in India in 1850, The details of the Demographic condition regarding the population of British India, were primarily obtained through a census in 1881, The Planning Commission is a government agency in India that was established in 1950 to oversee the country's economic and social development, primarily through the development of five-year plans, Small scale industrial committee was set up in the year 1955. It was also called a Karve committee.

4. (d)

5. (c) Total Money Creation = Initial Deposit $\times \dfrac{1}{LRR}$

12000 = Initial Deposit $\times \dfrac{1}{0.25}$

Initial Deposit = $0.25 \times 12000 = 3000$

6. (c)

7. (c) Pradhan Mantri Jan Dhan Yojana was announced by the Hon'ble Prime Minister Shri Narendra Modi on 15th August 2014 from the ramparts of the Red Fort and launched by him on 28th August 2014 across the country.

MGNREGA was enacted in September 2005.

In post-independent India, there have been several attempts. The Planning Commission formed a Study Group in 1962.

The 'Task force on projections of minimum needs and effective consumption demand' was formed in 1979.

Food For Work Programme was launched in 1977-78

8. (c) Revenue expenditure are the expenditure incurred for the basis other than the creation of physical or financial assets of the central government.

Capital Expenditure are the expenditure of the government that result in the creation of physical or financial assets, or depletion in financial liabilities.

Revenue Receipt are those receipt of the government which neither creates any liability nor it creates any reduction in the assets of the government.

Receipts that either create liabilities or reduce assets of the government are called capital receipts.

9. (c) NNPfc = NNPmp – NIT

NNPfc = 5330 – (1770 – 0)

NNPfc = 3560

GNPfc = NNPfc + Depreciation

GNPfc = 3560 + 1550 = 5110

10. (a) The owner of capital gets interest. The entrepreneur gets profit. Factor income is the income accruing to the owner of the factor of production in return for the services rendered to the production units. There are four types of factor incomes in the form of wages, interest, rent and profits.

11. (a) Wealth is a stock as it is measured at a particular point of time.

12. (b) Net Indirect Tax (NIT) refers to the difference between indirect taxes and subsidies. Net indirect taxes are equal to zero in case indirect taxes are equal to subsidies.

13. (c)

14. (b)

15. (b)

16. (a) Factor cost is the 'Price' of the commodity from the producer's side. Market price is derived after adding the indirect taxes to the factor cost of the product.

The formula to calculate is Market Price = Factor Cost – Subsidies – Indirect Taxes.

17. (b) Sales revenue is calculated by multiplying the number of products or services sold by the price per unit.

Value of Output = Sales + Change in Stock + Production for Self Consumption

18. (a) Farmer to Miller – 500

Miller to Baker – 700

Baker to Consumer – 1000

(Value Added is 200 + 300 = 500)

19. (b)

20. (c)

21. (a) Deflation is termed as the decrease in price levels of goods and services in an economy. Impact on demand. Demand for products and services increase in inflation. Demand for products and services decrease in deflation.

22. (b) Monetary policy concerns the decisions taken by central banks to influence the cost and availability of money in an economy.

23. (b) Deflationary Gap is the amount by which the aggregate demand falls short of aggregate supply at the full employment level. It is called deflationary because it leads to a fall in the price level.

24. (c) In the saving and investment approach, the equilibrium is attained at the point where saving and investment will intersect each other, i.e. leakages are equal to injections.

25. (c) As MPC = $\dfrac{4}{5}$ = 0.8 and MPS = $\dfrac{1}{5}$ = 0.2, then

Multiplier (K) = $\dfrac{1}{MPS}$ = $\dfrac{1}{0.2}$ = 5

26. (c) Y = C + I

2000 = (400 + b × 2000) + 200

2200 = 400 + 2000 × b

b = $\dfrac{1800}{2000}$

b = 0.9

27. K = $\dfrac{1}{MPS}$

K = $\dfrac{1}{0.20}$

K = 5 Then, K = Change in Income/Change in Investment

5 = Change in Income/400

Change in Income = 2000 Crores

28. (b) Borrowings from the International Monetary Fund (IMF) is a capital receipt. This is because borrowings creates liability for the government.

29. (c) In 2016, the Indian Parliament passed a law, Goods and Services Tax Act 2016, to simplify and introduce a unified indirect tax system in India. This law came into effect from July 2017.

WTO- World Trade Organisation, was established in 1995 as the heir organisation to the GATT (General Agreement on Trade and Tariff). GATT was founded in 1948 with 23 nations as the global (international) trade organisation to serve all multilateral trade agreements by giving fair chances to all nations in the international exchange for trading prospects.

On 8 November 2016, the Government of India announced the demonetisation of all Rs.500 and Rs.1,000 banknotes of the Mahatma Gandhi Series. It also announced the issuance of new Rs.500 and Rs.2,000 banknotes in exchange for the demonetised banknotes.

Tata Group formally took over Air India in January 2022 after the government's long-awaited privatisation of the debt-laden and loss-making airline in a 180 billion rupee deal ($2.2bn) for 100 per cent ownership.

30. (b) Keeping all other factors the same, when there is a change in demand of a commodity due to change in price, it is referred to as the change in quantity demanded. It is shown as a movement along the demand curve when expressed graphically.

31. (d) Normal goods refer to those goods whose demand increases with an increase in income.

32. (a) The three Central Problems of an Economy are? What to Produce and in What Quantity? How to Produce? For Whom to Produce?

33. (b) $\dfrac{Mu_x}{P_x} = \dfrac{MU_y}{P_y}$

$\dfrac{60}{P_x} = \dfrac{20}{4}$

240 = 20 P_x

$P_x = \dfrac{240}{20}$

P_x = 12

34. (b) Great Proletarian Cultural Revolution was launched by Mao Zedong in 1966, On October 1, 1949, Chinese Communist leader Mao Zedong declared the creation of the People's Republic of China (PRC), The reforms were launched by Chinese Communist Party (CCP) on December 18, 1978, The Great Leap Forward in 1958, In 1953, Mao launched China's First Five Year Plan.

35. (d) The HDI is a summary composite measure of a country's average achievements in three basic aspects of human development: health, knowledge and standard of living.

36. (d) Few examples of social infrastructure are water supply, sanitation, health, housing, etc.

37. (c) The one-child policy was a program in China that limited most Chinese families to one child each. It was implemented nationwide by the Chinese government in 1980, and it ended in 2016.

In 1988, Pakistan adopted policies geared towards economic stabilization and structural reforms.

Though economic liberalization in India can be traced back to the late 1970s, economic reforms began in earnest only in July 1991.

While India announced its first Five Year Plan for 1951-56, Pakistan announced its first five year plan, now called the Medium Term Development Plan, in 1956.

38. (c) Global Burden of Disease (GBD) is an indicator used by experts to know the number of people dying prematurely due to a particular disease as well as the number of years spent by them in a state of 'disability' owing to the disease.

39. (b)

40. (a) The process of moving from self-employment and regular salaried employment to casual wage work is known as casualisation of workforce.

41. (b) The full form of GST is Goods and Service Tax. GST is a single, indirect tax levied by the Indian Government.

42. (c) The GST council has fitted over 1300 goods and 500 services under four tax slabs of 5%, 12%, 18% and 28% under GST.

43. (c) The GST rate for gold, gold jewellery, precious stones and precious metals is 3%. While purchasing gold jewellery or other gold items, the end consumer will have to pay 3% of the taxable value mentioned on the invoice.

44. (c) The Central Board of Indirect Taxes and Customs (CBIC) clarified that all pre-packaged items with up to 25 kg quantity will attract 5% GST.

45. (b)

46. (d)

47. (b)

48. (*) GVA at constant price for 1970-71 is 4.27%
GVA at constant price for 2010-11 is 6.34 %

49. (c)

50. (d)

1. Every society must decide whether to have more agricultural goods or to have industrial products. This statement represents the central problem of:
   (a) Why to produce?
   (b) What to produce?
   (c) How to produce?
   (d) For whom to produce?

2. Identify the reason behind the rightward shift in the demand curve of a normal good from amongst the following alternatives:
   (a) Fall in the price of the substitute good
   (b) Fall in the own price of the good
   (c) Fall in the price of the complementary good
   (d) Fall in the income of the consumer consuming normal good

3. Suppose there was a 4% decrease in the price of a good and as a result, the quantity demanded increased by 2%. What will be the price elasticity of demand?
   (a) (–) 1.5
   (b) (–) 0.5
   (c) (–) 2
   (d) (–) 4

4. Match **List- I** with **List- II**.

List - I :		List - II :	
Item		**Nature/Estimate**	
A.	Factor payment	I.	Unilateral
B.	Net factor income from Abroad	II.	Profit of a small enterprise
C.	Transfer payments	III.	Indirect tax - subsidies
D.	Net indirect taxes	IV.	Difference between national and domestic income

   Choose the correct answer from the options given below:
   (a) A-II, B-IV, C-III, D-I
   (b) A-II, B-IV, C-I, D-III
   (c) A-II, B-III, C-I, D-IV
   (d) A-IV, B-III, C-II, D-I

5. Depreciation of a capital good refers to:
   (a) sudden destruction, capital loss
   (b) disuse of capital, investment
   (c) wear and tear, unexpected obsolescence
   (d) wear and tear, expected obsolescence

6. Given national income as Rs. 5,500 crores, operating surplus as Rs. 1,500 Cr, compensation of employees as Rs. 2,800 crores and net factor income to abroad as Rs. 50 crores, the mixed income of the self employed will be equal to:
   (a) Rs. 1,250 crores
   (b) Rs. 1,150 crores
   (c) Rs. 2,650 crores
   (d) Rs. 1,200 crores

7. Identify the expenditure to be included while calculating national income using the expenditure method.
   A. Metro fare paid by a household.
   B. Expenditure on shares by a household.
   C. Expenditure on financial relief given by the government to flood victims.
   D. Expenditure on subsidies given to farmers by the government.
   E. Expenditure on ovens by a baker.
   Choose the correct answer from the options given below:
   (a) A, E only
   (b) A, B only
   (c) A, C, E only
   (d) A, D, B only

8. Identify the flow variable amongst the following alternatives.
   (a) Cash at bank in the saving account of a household
   (b) Interest received by a household on his deposits in the bank
   (c) Capital stock of a firm
   (d) Wealth of an industrialist

9. _________ refers to the harmful effects of an economic activity carried out by a firm or an individual in a society, for which they are not penalised directly.
   (a) Positive externalities
   (b) Negative externalities
   (c) Monetary exchanges
   (d) Non-monetary exchanges

10. The value of the nominal GNP of an economy was Rs.5,000 crores in the year 2019. The value of GNP of that country during the same year, evaluated at the prices of the year 2018 was Rs.6,000. What will be the value of the GNP deflator for the year 2019:
    (a) 120.00
    (b) 20.00
    (c) 63.33
    (d) 83.33

11. Given that the autonomous consumption being Rs. 100, marginal propensity to save being 0.25 and investment being Rs. 1,100, the equilibrium level of income is:
    (a) Rs. 900
    (b) Rs. 4,800
    (c) Rs. 4,400
    (d) Rs. 2,500

12. If ex-ante demand is less than ex ante supply. Then arrange the following in a chronological order.

    A. Producer reacts by reducing output and employment

    B. The process goes on till ex-ante demand becomes equal to ex ante supply

    C. It will lead to unintended accumulation of inventories

    D. When output reduces income also reduces

Choose the correct answer from the options given below:

(a) B, D, A, C   (b) C, A, D, B

(c) A, C, D, B   (d) C, B, A, D

13. Match **List - I** with **List- II**.

List - I	List - II
Concepts	**Implications**
A. Marginal propensity to consume	I. Positive constant
B. Average propensity to save	II. Consumption per unit of income
C. Average propensity to consume	III. Can take a negative value
D. Autonomous investment	IV. Addition to consumption per unit of additional income

Choose the correct answer from the options given below:

(a) A-IV, B-II, C-III, D-I   (b) A-II, B-IV, C-I, D-III

(c) A-IV, B-III, C-II, D-I   (d) A-IV, B-III, C-I, D-II

14. Calculate the value of investment multiplier when half of the additional income is added to saving:

(a) 2   (b) 0.5

(c) 4   (d) 5

15. The size of the investment multiplier depends upon the value of:

(a) marginal propensity of consume

(b) marginal propensity to save

(c) average propensity to consume

(d) average propensity to save

16. The level of consumption which is independent of income is called:

(a) autonomous consumption

(b) induced consumption

(c) ex ante consumption

(d) ex post consumption

17. Which of the following statement is correct?

    A. At break-even level of income (Y), $C = Y$

    B. At break-even level of income (Y), $C > Y$

    C. At break-even level of income (Y), $S = I$

    D. At break-even level of income (Y), $S = 0$

    E. At break-even level of income (Y), $C = 0$

Note: C = Consumption

        Y = Income

        S = Saving

        I = Investment

Choose the correct answer from the options given below:

(a) B and C only   (b) A and E only

(c) A and D only   (d) A and B only

18. In a situation when RBI decides to increase the money supply in the economy, which of the following measures will be adopted?

    A. Increase in the Bank rate

    B. Decrease in the Bank rate

    C. Increase in the Cash Reserve Ratio

    D. Decrease in the Cash Reserve Ratio

    E. Buying of government securities in open market

Choose the correct answer from the options given below:

(a) A and C, E only   (b) B and D, E only

(c) A and B, D only   (d) B and C, E only

19. Suppose in an economy the Cash Reserve Ratio announced by its central bank is 25 percent with initial deposits being Rs. 2000 crore. The total deposits created by the commercial banks will be:

(a) Rs. 500 crores   (b) Rs. 5,000 crores

(c) Rs. 6,000 crores   (d) Rs. 8,000 crores

20. Which of the following is a part of digital transaction in an economy?

    A. Coins

    B. National Financial Switch

    C. E-wallet

    D. Aadhar enabled payment systems

    E. Physical bank notes

Choose the correct answer from the options given below:

(a) A, B and C only

(b) B, C and D only

(c) C, B and E only

(d) A, D and E only

21. Match **List - I** with **List - II**.

List - I : Financial Terms	List - II : Linked to
A. Money Supply	I. Guarantee by the issuing authority
B. Legal tender	II. Formal financial system
C. Fiat money	III. Stock variable
D. Banks	IV. Cannot be refused by any citizen of the country for settlement of a transaction

Choose the correct answer from the options given below:

(a) A-I, B-II, C-III, D-IV (b) A-III, B-IV, C-I, D-II

(c) A-III, B-I, C-IV, D-II (d) A-IV, B-III, C-II, D-I

22. Match **List - I** with **List - II**.

List - I : Exchange Rate System	List - II : Conceptual meaning
A. Fixed exchange rate	I. Determination of exchange rate by its worth in terms of gold
B. Managed floating	II. Forex rate is determined by market forces
C. Gold standard	III. Dirty floating
D. Flexible exchange rate	IV. A country pegs the level of its exchange rate

Choose the correct answer from the options given below:

(a) A-I, B-III, C-II, D-IV (b) A-II, B-III, C-I, D-IV

(c) A-IV, B-III, C-I, D-II (d) A-IV, B-I, C-III, D-II

23. Which of the following items will increase the supply of foreign exchange?

(a) Purchase of land in England

(b) Donation of US $ 50 million received from Microsoft

(c) Indian students going to USA for MBA

(d) Import of goods from China

24. Current account surplus indicates that:

A. Receipts on current account are equal to the payments on current account.

B. The nation is a borrower from other countries.

C. Exports of goods and services are more than imports of goods and services, transfer payments being zero.

D. Receipts on current account are greater than payments on current account.

E. Receipts on current account are less than payments on current account.

Choose the correct answer from the options given below:

(a) A and B only (b) B and C only

(c) C and D only (d) D and E only

25. The commune system adopted in China encouraged the people to.

(a) Collectively cultivate land

(b) Start industries in their backyard

(c) Migrate to the country side

(d) Partner with government for production purpose

26. Identify the global economic grouping from the following options.

(a) SAARC (b) G - 8

(c) ASEAN (d) European Union

27. Arrange the following events in chronological order and choose the correct alternative.

A. Establishment of Republic of China

B. Announcement of First Five Year Plan in India

C. Announcement of First Five Year Plan in Pakistan

D. India and Pakistan become independent nations

Choose the correct answer from the options given below:

(a) E, A, C, B, D (b) E, B, A, C, D

(c) E, A, D, B, C (d) E, B, A, D, C

28. Which of the following would be included in economic infrastructure?

(a) Schools

(b) Pharmaceutical Industry

(c) Power Stations

(d) Drinking Water Facilities

29. Match **List - I** with **List - II**.

List - I : Institution/ Programme	List - II : Objectives
A. Khadi and Village Industries Commission	I. Collects data on consumption expenditure
B. Antyodaya Scheme	II. Published data on poverty
C. National Sample Survey Organisation	III. Upliftment of the poorest of the poor
D. Niti Aayog	IV. Prime Minister's Rozgar Yojna

Choose the correct answer from the options given below:

(a) A-II, B-III, C-IV, D-I (b) A-IV, B-III, C-I, D-II

(c) A-IV, B-I, C-II, D-III (d) A-III, B-IV, C-II, D-I

30. Policy instruments which help in the improvement of agricultural marketing are:

 A. Distribution of food grains and sugar through Public Distribution System.

 B. Cooperative Marketing.

 C. Minimum support price for agricultural produce

 D. Periodic Market

 E. Buffer Stock

 Choose the correct answer from the options given below:

 (a) A, B and C only (b) A, C and D only

 (c) A, C and E only (d) B, C and E only

31. The indicator used by experts to gauge the number of people dying prematurely due to a particular disease:

 (a) Global Burden of Disease (GBD)

 (b) Indian Burden of Disease (IBD)

 (c) Foreign Burden of Disease (FBD)

 (d) Local Burden of Disease (LBD)

32. Which of the following is not a source of Human Capital Formation?

 (a) Investment in education

 (b) Investment in health

 (c) On th job training

 (d) Investment in immigration

33. Match **List - I** with **List - II**.

List - I : Nature of Expenditure	List - II : Impact
A. Expenditure on on-the-job training	I. Enhanced earnings
B. Expenditure on migration	II. Proportion of income committed to the development of education in the country
C. Education expenditure as a percentage of total government expenditure	III. Enhanced labour productivity
D. Education expenditure as a percentage of GDP	IV. Importance of education in the scheme of things before the government

Choose the correct answer from the options given below:

(a) A-I, B-III, C-IV, D-II (b) A-II, B-IV, C-I, D-III

(c) A-III, B-I, C-IV, D-II (d) A-IV, B-II, C-III, D-I

34. Which of the following is an example of self employed worker?

 A. Construction labourer

 B. A doctor working in his private clinic

 C. Cement shop owner

 D. A handloom weaver employed by Khadi Gramodyog

 E. Vegetable Vendor

 Choose the correct answer from the options given below:

 (a) A, B and C only (b) B, C and D only

 (c) B, C and E only (d) C, D and E only

35. Match **List - I** with **List - II**.

List - I : Concepts	List - II : Meaning
A. Carrying capacity	I. Gradual increase in the average temperature of the earth's lower atmosphere
B. Absorptive capacity	II. Reduction in the amount of ozone in the stratosphere
C. Global warming	III. The resource extraction is not above the rate of regeneration of the resource
D. Ozone depletion	IV. Ability of the environment to absorb degradation

Choose the correct answer from the options given below:

(a) A-III, B-I, C-II, D-IV (b) A-IV, B-I, C-III, D-II

(c) A-III, B-IV, C-I, D-II (d) A-III, B-I, C-IV, D-II

36. The concept of Sustainable Development was emphasised by:

 (a) Brunt land Commission

 (b) Ministry of Environment

 (c) Central Pollution Control Board

 (d) United Nations Conference on Environment and Development

37. AICTE stands for:

 (a) All India Council of Technical Education

 (b) All India Committee of Training and Education

 (c) All India Commission of Teacher Education

 (d) All India Commission of Technical Education

38. In a country, the status with which a worker is placed in an enterprise tells us about:

(a) quality of employment

(b) quantity of employment

(c) gender equality

(d) gender inequality

39. Arrange policies and programmes towards poverty alleviation in the proper chronological sequence:

A. Programmes launched to provide minimum basic amenities to the people.

B. Pradhan Mantri Jan Dhan Yojana scheme launched in the country.

C. Poverty alleviation programmes initiated in the country.

D. Parliament passes Mahatama Gandhi National Rural Employment Guarantee Act.

Choose the correct answer from the options given below:

(a) B, A, C, D   (b) C, A, D, B

(c) A, C, B, D   (d) D, B, A, C

40. Identify the non-conventional sources of energy:

A. Coal   B. Solar rays

C. Petroleum   D. Wind power

E. Firewood

Choose the correct answer from the options given below:

(a) B and D only   (b) A and C only

(c) C and E only   (d) B, C and E only

Direction for Questions 41 to 45: Based on the case study given below answer the questions that follow.

GST : On Nation, One Tax, One Market

The Goods and Services Tax (GST), the biggest tax reform in the country since independence was rolled out on the mid-night of 30 June/1 July, 2017 during a special midnight session of the Parliament, is the single comprehensive indirect tax, operational from 1 July 2017, on supply of goods and services, right from the manufacturer/services provider to the consumer. It is applicable throughout the country with one rate for one type of goods/service. It has amalgamated a large number of Central and State taxes and cesses. It has replaced large number of taxes on goods and services levied on production/sale of goods or provision of service. As there have been a number of intermediate goods/services, which were manufactured/provided in the economy, the pre GST tax regime imposed taxes not on the value added at each stage but on the total value of the commodity/service. The total value included taxes paid on intermediate goods/services. This amounted to cascading of tax. Under GST, the tax is discharged at every stage of supply and the credit of tax paid at the previous stage is available for set off at the next stage of supply. In view of our large and fast growing economy, it extends principles of 'value-added taxation' to all goods and services and addresses to establish parity in taxation across the country. It has replaced various types of taxes/cesses, levied by Central and State/ UT Governments. Some of the major taxes that were levied by Centre were Central Excise Duty, Service Tax, Central Sales Tax, cesses like KKC and SBC. The major State taxes were VAT/Sales Tax, Entry Tax, Luxury Tax, Octroi, Entertainment Tax, cesses like KKC and SBC. The major State taxes were VAT/Sales Tax, Entry Tax, Luxury Tax, Octroi, Entertainment Tax, cesses like KKC and SBC. Taxes on Advertisements, Taxes on Lottery/ Betting/Gambling, State cesses on goods etc. These have been subsumed in GST.

Five petroleum products have been kept out of GST for the time being but with passage of time, they will get subsumed in GST. State Governments will continue to levy VAT on alcoholic liquor for human consumption. Tobacco and tobacco products will attract both GST and Central Excise Duty. Under GST, there are 6 (six) standard rates applied i.e., 0%, 3%, 5%, 12%, 18% and 28% on supply of all goods and/or services across the country.

GST has simplified the multiplicity of taxes on goods and services. The laws, procedure and rates of taxes across the country are standardised and thus created a common market in the country. It is aimed at reducing the cost of business operations and cascading effect of various taxes on consumers. It has also reduced the overall cost of production, which will make Indian products/services more competitive in the domestic and international markets. It will also result into higher economic growth as GDP is expected to rise by about 2%. Compliance will also be easier as all tax payment related services like registration, returns, payments are available online through a common portal www.gst.gov.in. It has expanded the tax base, introduced higher transparency in the taxation system, reduced human interface between Taxpayer and Government and is furthering ease of doing business.

41. Which of the following taxes/duties have not been subsumed in the GST initially

(a) Tax on petroleum products

(b) Entertainment Tax

(c) Octroi

(d) Luxury Tax

42. The introduction of GST has resulted in:

(a) One tax rate for one type of good/service across the country

(b) Cascading effect of tax on consumers

(c) Contraction of tax base

(d) Increased human interface between the taxpayer and the government

43. Cascading effect of taxes results due to:

(a) Different tax rates on one type of goods/services in different states and UTs

(b) Very high rates of taxes

(c) Imposition of taxes on value added at each stage of production

(d) Imposition of taxes on total value of goods at each stage of production with minimal facility of utilisation of Input Tax Credit

44. The six standard rates of taxes applied under GST are:

(a) 0%, 5%, 12%, 20%, 24% and 28%

(b) 3%, 5%, 12%, 18%, 21% and 24%

(c) 0%, 3%, 5%, 12%, 18% and 28%

(d) 0%, 5%, 10%, 15%, 20% and 25%

45. Identify the direct tax among the following:

(a) Service tax   (b) Corporate tax

(c) Central sales tax   (d) Octroi

Direction for Questions 46 to 50: Based on the case study given below answer the questions that follow.

One natural question is what Covid-19 will mean for globalisation. Globalisation is the accelerated flow of goods, people, capital, information, and energy across borders, often enabled by technological developments. Over the past three decades, globalising trends were assumed to be the new normal. Trade without tariffs, international travel with easy or no visas, capital flows with few impediments, cross-border pipelines and energy grids, and seamless global communication in real-time appeared to be the natural endpoints towards which the world was moving, if at different rates for different places. How could Covid-19 impact these trends? There will almost certainly be calls for the re-nationalisation of manufacturing, particularly for what are considered critical or essential goods. The recent bickering over personal protective equipment (PPE) and pharmaceuticals have brought this to the fore. This will further complicate trade agreements, both those in force and those under negotiation.

The globalisation of people, including short-term tourist or business traffic, may face new kinds of restrictions. National governments will have to weigh the risks of contagious diseases against the benefits of ease of travel or may have to consider stronger safeguards. In turn, the globalisation of finance will be indirectly affected: Less migration and business travel coupled with incentives to invest at home will hinder transactional capital flows.

46. Which of the following is most likely not true about the process of globalisation?

(a) It is the accelerated flow of goods, people, capital and information across borders.

(b) It aims at transforming the world towards greater interdependence and integration

(c) It promotes social justice and welfare and removes disparities

(d) It involves creation of networks and activities transcending economic, social and geographical boundaries

47. Identify the structural reform undertaken under the New Economic Policy 1991 which was expected to increase the inflow of foreign capital into country:

(a) Removal of trade barriers

(b) Removal of import licensing

(c) Reduction of tariff rates

(d) Removal of barriers on foreign direct investment

48. Keeping in view, the recent crisis over Pharmaceuticals, Covid 19 is most likely to disrupt the process of globalisation in terms of flow of goods between nations by:

(a) Extensive privatisation and disinvestment

(b) Encouragement of private sector to produce critical goods and services

(c) Public sector taking over the production of critical goods and services

(d) Simplification of trade agreement

49. Identify the reason most unlikely responsible for globalisation:

(a) Growth of Information Technology

(b) Foreign institutional investors free to invest in Indian financial market

(c) Abolition of import licensing except for a few industries

(d) Passing of Goods and Services Tax Act in 2017

50. Covid-19 can threaten the process of globalization by:

(a) Free flow of technology between counties

(b) Lesser migration and business travel

(c) Free flow of goods amongst nations

(d) Free flow of capital amongst nations

Answer Keys

1. (b)	**2.** (c)	**3.** (b)	**4.** (b)	**5.** (d)	**6.** (b)	**7.** (a)	**8.** (b)	**9.** (b)	**10.** (d)
11. (b)	**12.** (b)	**13.** (c)	**14.** (a)	**15.** (a)	**16.** (a)	**17.** (c)	**18.** (b)	**19.** (d)	**20.** (b)
21. (c)	**22.** (c)	**23.** (b)	**24.** (c)	**25.** (b)	**26.** (b)	**27.** (a)	**28.** (c)	**29.** (b)	**30.** (c)
31. (a)	**32.** (d)	**33.** (c)	**34.** (c)	**35.** (c)	**36.** (d)	**37.** (a)	**38.** (a)	**39.** (b)	**40.** (a)
41. (a)	**42.** (a)	**43.** (d)	**44.** (c)	**45.** (b)	**46.** (c)	**47.** (c)	**48.** (c)	**49.** (d)	**50.** (b)

Explanations

1. (b) This problem involves selection of goods and services to be produced and the quantity to be produced of agricultural and industrial products.

2. (c) Example – Shuttlecock is a Normal Good and in the sport of Badminton, Racket and shuttlecock are complementary Goods. If Price of Racket i.e. complementary good will fall then demand for shuttlecock i.e. normal good will increase and thereby the demand curve of normal good (here, shuttlecock) will shift rightward.

3. (b) Price Elasticity of demand = % change in quantity demanded/% change in price = $(-)\dfrac{2}{4}$

$= (-)0.5$

4. (b)

5. (d) Capital depreciation refers to the decline in value of a capital asset. It is expected wear and tear

6. (b) Income Method – NDPfc = COE + OS + MI and NNPfc(National Income) = NDPfc + NFIA (5500 − 50 = 2800 + 1500 + MI i.e. MI = 1150)

7. (a) Metro Fare by household is Private final consumption expenditure whereas purchase of oven by a baker is Investment Expenditure

8. (b) Interest

9. (b) Activities resulting in benefits to others are called positive externalities and increase welfare whereas those resulting in harm to others are called negative externalities and thus decrease welfare

10. (d) GNP Deflator = (Nominal GNP/Real GNP)*100 = (5000/6000)*100 = 83.33

11. (b) (AS)Y = C + I (AD)

(Y = 100 + 0.75Y + 1100 i.e. 0.25Y = 1200 and Y = 4800)

12. (b)

13. (c)

14. (a) If Half of the income is saved, then MPS = 0.5 and investment multiplier $k = \dfrac{1}{MPS}$ i.e.

$K = \dfrac{1}{0.5} = 2$

15. (a) The size of investment multiplier directly depends on Marginal Propensity to consume as $K = \dfrac{1}{1 - c}$

i.e. if MPC increases then size of investment multiplier also increases.

16. (a) Autonomous consumption is that level of consumption which does not depend on the level of income

17. (c)

18. (b) Bank Rate- Bank rate is the rate of interest at which central bank lends to commercial banks without any collateral (security for purpose of loan)

CRR – It refers to the minimum percentage of a bank's total deposits, which it is required to keep with the central bank.

Decrease in these rates makes commercial bank to decrease their lending rates, which encourages borrowers from taking loans, which encourages investment and increase Money Supply

Central bank purchases of government securities and bonds from commercial bank increases the power of commercial bank of giving loans increases, which will increase money supply

19. (d) Total Deposits = Initial Deposits × $\dfrac{1}{CRR}$

$= \dfrac{2000}{0.25} = 8000$

20. (b) National Financial Switch is the largest network of shared automated teller machines in India

A digital wallet, also known as an e-wallet, is an electronic device, online service, or software program that allows one party to make electronic transactions with another party bartering digital currency units for goods and services

Aadhaar Enabled Payment System (AEPS) is a payment service that allows a bank customer to use Aadhaar as his/her identity to access his/her Aadhaar enabled bank account and perform basic banking transactions like balance enquiry, cash withdrawal, remittances through a Business Correspondent.

21. (c)

22. (c)

23. (b)

24. (c) Current account surpluses refer to positive current account balances, meaning that a country has more exports than imports of goods and services

25. (b) The Great Leap Forward (GLF) was a campaign initiated in 1958 in China by Mao's, which was aimed to modernise the China's economy. The campaign was imitated towards the large-scale industrialisation in the country not concentrated only in the urban areas. The people were motivated to set up industries in their backyards.

26. (b) Global Economic Groups – Countries who share similar economic status – G8 (Group of Developed Countries)

27. (a) India and Pakistan got Independence in 1947

People's Republic of China established in 1949

Announcement of First Five Year Plan by India in 1951

Announcement of First Five Year Plan by China in 1953

Announcement of First Five Year Plan by Pakistan in 1956

28. (c) Economic infrastructure directly supports economic growth.

29. (b)

30. (c) Policy Instruments-

Guarantee of Minimum Support Prices (MSP) for agricultural products

Storage of surplus stocks (buffer) of wheat and rice by Food Corporation of India (FCI)

Distribution of food staples and sugar through PDS

31. (a) Global Burden of Disease (GBD) is an indicator used by experts to know the number of people dying prematurely due to a particular disease as well as the number of years spent by them in a state of 'disability' owing to the disease

32. (d)

33. (c)

34. (c) Self-employed means engaging in one's own business or profession. Construction labour is casual wage labour whereas a handloom weaver employed by KhadiGramodyog is a regular salaried worker

35. (c)

36. (d) The concept of sustainable development was emphasised by the United Nations Conference on Environment and Development (UNCED), which defined it as: 'Development that meets the need of the present generation without compromising the ability of the future generation to meet their own needs'.

37. (a) All India Council for Technical Education (AICTE), is an Apex body and a Regulator of Technical Education in the Country. It is responsible for planning and coordinated development of the Technical Education system throughout the Country.

38. (a)

39. (b)

40. (a) Non-conventional sources are also known as renewable sources of energy. Examples of non-conventional sources of energy include solar energy, bioenergy, tidal energy and wind energy

41. (a) Five Petroleum products have been kept out of GST

42. (a)

43. (d) The pre-GST Tax Regime imposed tax on the total value of good/service which included tax paid on intermediate good/service and this resulted in cascading effect of tax

44. (c)

45. (b) A direct tax is a tax that a person or organization pays directly to the entity that imposed it.

46. (c)

47. (c) Reduction in tariffs to make Indian Economy attractive to global investors

48. (c)

49. (d)

50. (b) Lesser migration and business travel will hinder transactional capital flows and thereby threaten process of globalisation.

1. A hypothetical economy has a piece of land which, in order of priority, can be used for building a school, a hospital, a factory and a residential complex. What is the opportunity cost of choosing the best alternative?
   (a) A school
   (b) A hospital
   (c) A factory
   (d) A residential complex

2. The price and quantity at a point on the demand curve of a good are given as 10 and 50 respectively. If the price is changed to 6 and as a result quantity changes to 65, how do you explain the change.
   (a) Increases in demand for the good
   (b) Decrease in quantity demanded
   (c) Decrease in demand for the good
   (d) Increase in quantity demanded

3. Find the value of price elasticity of demand of a good whose demand decreases by 20% for an increase in its price of 10%.
   (a) 1   (b) 2
   (c) 0.2   (d) 0.5

4. Identify normal residents of India from amongst the following.
   (a) Seasonal workers coming to India from Bangladesh.
   (b) Medical patients going from India to the U.S.A. for treatment.
   (c) A Japanese woman working in the office of W.H.O located in India for less than one year.
   (d) Australian ambassador posted in New Delhi.

5. If a Country's real GDP is Rs. 400 crores and its nominal GDP is Rs. 1,000 crores, its GDP deflator is: (Choose the correct alternative).
   (a) 250
   (b) 40
   (c) 2.5
   (d) 4000

6. Identify the items which will be classified as stock items.
   A. Production
   B. Money supply
   C. Interest on deposits
   D. Savings

E. Capital stock in a Country

Choose the correct answer from the options given below:
   (a) B and E only
   (b) D and E only
   (c) A and E only
   (d) E only

7. Which out of the following are intermediate goods?
   A. Milk purchased by a household
   B. Sugar purchased by a restaurant
   C. Furniture purchased by school
   D. Chalk and duster purchased by school
   E. Printer purchased by a lawyer

Choose the correct answer from the options given below:
   (a) B, D, E only
   (b) B, D only
   (c) A, B, D only
   (d) A, B, C, D, E

8. Identify the situation when value of Domestic Income is equal to the value of National Income.
   (a) When there are no exports in the economy
   (b) When net factor income from abroad is zero
   (c) When net investment in the economy is zero
   (d) When there are no imports in the economy

9. If Gross Domestic Product at Market Price (GDPmp) = 2995 crore. Private final consumption expenditure = 1100 crore. Gross domestic fixed capital formation = 1000 crore. Government final consumption expenditure = 900 crore. Net imports = 75 crore.

The change of stock will be:
   (a) (–) 80 crore
   (b) 80 crore
   (c) 70 crore
   (d) 75 crore

10. ______ can never be negative while ______ can have value as 1.
   (a) APS, APC
   (b) MPC, APS
   (c) APC, APS
   (d) MPS, APC

11. Economics all across the globe are facing the problem of deficient demand post covid 19. Such a situation in India can be corrected by: (Choose the correct alternative).

(a) Selling government securities to the Commercial Bank by the Reserve Bank of India.

(b) Raising of the margin requirements by the Reserve Bank of India.

(c) Reducing the reverse repo rate by the Reserve Bank of India.

(d) Raising of the bank rate by the Reserve Bank of India.

12. If the autonomous consumption is given as 100 and the tendency of the people to increase consumption for an increase in income is only 20%, then derive the savings function.

(a) $S = -100 + 0.8\,Y$

(b) $S = 100 + 0.8\,Y$

(c) $S = 100 + 0.2\,Y$

(d) $S = -100 + 0.2\,Y$

13.

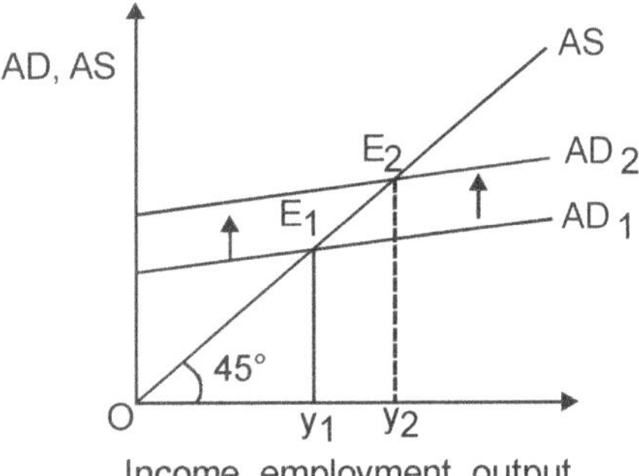

Assume a two sector economy in the above diagram, the initial demand curve AD_1 shifts upward to AD_2 due to:

(a) Increase in average propensity to save

(b) Increase in aggugate supply

(c) Increase in marginal propensity to consume

(d) Increase in autonomous investment

14. In an economy, every time the National Income rises 20% of the rises in income is saved by households. Now suppose there is a rise in investment by Rs. 100 crores, then the National Income in this economy will rise by:

(a) Rs. 125 crores

(b) Rs. 500 crores

(c) Rs. 2,000 crores

(d) Rs. 20 crores

15. If the level of effective demand is much below the level of full employment equilibrium then which situation will appear in the economy?

(a) Full employment equilibrium

(b) Under employment equilibrium

(c) Beyond full employment equilibrium

(d) Excess demand

16. Identify the incorrect statement.

A. Money is what money does

B. There are many assets which carry functions of money

C. In modern sense, money creates instability

D. The first and foremost role of money is that it acts as medium of exchange

E. Money acts only as convenient unit of account

Choose the correct answer from the options given below:

(a) A and B only   (b) C and E only

(c) C and D only   (d) D and E only

17. Buying and selling of government securities by the Reserve Bank of India to the public is called:

(a) Margin Requirement

(b) Bank Rate

(c) Open Market Operations

(d) Repo Rate

18. Match **List-I** with **List-II**.

List - I : Banking	List - II : Function
A. Commercial Bank	I. Long term lending rate by RBI
B. Reserve Bank of India	II. Short term lending rate by RBI
C. Bank Rate	III. Credit creation
D. Repo Rate	IV. Lender of last resort

Choose the correct answer from the options given below:

(a) A-IV, B-III, C-I, D-II

(b) A-III, B-IV, C-I, D-II

(c) A-III, B-IV, C-II, D-I

(d) A-IV, B-III, C-II, D-I

19. Suppose in an economy, the legal required ratio fixed by the Central Bank is 20% and the value of initial deposits is Rs. 1,000 crores. What is the value of loans extended by the Commercial Banks?

(a) Rs. 5,000 crores

(b) Rs. 4,000 crores

(c) Rs. 2,000 crores

(d) Rs. 20,000 crores

20. High powered money comprises of:

(a) Notes and coins in circulation with Public and Vault cash of Commercial Banks and deposits held by Government and Commercial Banks with RBI.

(b) Notes and coins in circulation with Public and deposits held by Government.

(c) Currency and deposits held by bank with RBI.

(d) Notes and Vault cash of Commercial Banks.

21. Identify Indirect Tax among the following:

(a) Gift Tax

(b) Income Tax

(c) Capital Gains Tax

(d) Goods and Services Tax (GST)

22. Public Goods are always:

(a) Rivalrous but non excludable

(b) Non-rivalrous and non excludable

(c) Non-rivalrous but excludable

(d) Rivalrous and excludable

23. The government in its budget has announced the construction of seven textile parks under the scheme of mega-investment textile parks. Which objective of the government budget is most likely being reflected here? (Choose the correct alternative).

(a) Reallocation of resources

(b) Redistribution of income

(c) Bringing economic stability

(d) Reducing fluctuations in the general price level

24. Which of the following deficit shows excess of government expenditure over receipts other than burden of interest payments?

(a) Revenue Deficit   (b) Fiscal Deficit

(c) Primary Deficit   (d) Budgetary Deficit

25. Match **List - I** with **List - II.**

List - I : Transactions	**List - II : Heads**
A. Loans extended by the Indian Government to the Sri Lanka Government	I. Revenue Receipts
B. Expenditure by the Government on Covid Vaccines	II. Capital Receipts
C. Dividend received by the Government on shares bought by it	III. Capital Expenditure
D. Public Provident Fund held by Public	IV. Revenue Expenditure

Choose the correct answer from the options given below:

(a) A-IV, B-III, C-II, D-I

(b) A-II, B-I, C-IV, D-III

(c) A-III, B-IV, C-I, D-II

(d) A-I, B-II, C-III, D-IV

26. Devaluation of domestic currency will make:

(a) Imports and Exports both become expensive

(b) Imports become expensive and Exports become cheaper

(c) Imports become cheaper and Exports become expensive

(d) Imports and Exports both become cheaper

27. Indian Real Estate Company receives rent from Microsoft from London. This transaction will be recorded in _______ Account.

(a) Credit side of current

(b) Debit side of current

(c) Credit side of capital

(d) Debit side of capital

28. Consider the statements:

A. Almost 60% of population lived in villages on the eve of Independence.

B. India was self sufficient in food grains, during Pre-British India.

C. Britishers encouraged capital goods industry in India.

D. India was major exporter of finished goods on the eve of Independence.

E. TISCO was established in the year 1907.

Choose the correct answer from the options given below:

(a) B and E only   (b) B and A only

(c) D and E only   (d) C and D only

29. Choose the incorrect statement about subsidies given below:

A. Subsidies are economic benefits granted by Government.

B. Subsidies help in increasing production.

C. Subsidies are burden on Government budget.

D. Subsidies are Capital expenditure.

E. Subsidies were needed to encourage formers to test the new technology.

Choose the correct answer from the options given below:

(a) B and C   (b) C and D only

(c) B and C only   (d) A and E only

30. Which of the following is not a characteristic of Industrial Policy Resolution (IPR), 1956, was used for?

(a) Promoting only small scale industries

(b) Promoting public sector enterprises

(c) Promoting industries in the backward region

(d) Private sector was kept under control through licensing.

31. Match **List-I** with **List-II**.

List - I : Economic Policy		List - II : Objective
A. Outsourcing	I.	Integration of the economy of the country with the world economy
B. Liberalisation	II.	Company having regular services from external sources
C. Globalisation	III.	Shedding of ownership/ management of a government owned enterprise
D. Privatisation	IV.	Put an end to restrictions that regulate economic activities

Choose the correct answer from the options given below:

(a) A-II, B-III, C-IV, D-I

(b) A-IV, B-II, C-I, D-III

(c) A-II, B-IV, C-III, D-I

(d) A-II, B-IV, C-I, D-III

32. To determine poverty line in India, minimum calorie intake in rural areas has been fixed at:

(a) 2100 Calories   (b) 2400 Calories

(c) 2800 Calories   (d) 2600 Calories

33. The period between 1991 and 2003 is referred to as the 'Golden Revolution' in India. It is related to the increased production of:

(a) Wheat and Rice   (b) Honey and Horticulture

(c) Milk   (d) Millets

34. Which of the following factors are contributing to Global Warming?

A. Burning of coal

B. Deforestation

C. Methane gas released in animal waste

D. Use of fossil fuel

E. Use of Hydropower

Choose the correct answer from the options given below:

(a) A and B only   (b) A, B, C and D only

(c) A, B and C only   (d) A, B and D only

35. Match **List-I** with **List-II**.

List - I		List - II
A. Increase in proportion of workforce in informal sector	I.	More people are engaged to work, then required
B. Open unemployment	II.	Informalisation of work force
C. Disguised unemployment	III.	Worker uses his own resources to make a living
D. self-employment	IV.	People are willing to work, but fail to get work

Choose the correct answer from the options given below:

(a) A-III, B-I, C-IV, D-II

(b) A-II, B-IV, C-I, D-III

(c) A-I, B-III, C-II, D-IV

(d) A-IV, B-II, C-III, D-I

36. Consider the table:

Worker population ratio in India [2017-18]

Sex	Worker Population Ratio		
	Total	Rural	Urban
Men	52.1	51.7	53.0
Women	16.5	17.5	14.2
Total	34.7	35.0	33.9

Identify the incorrect statement.

(a) In India, compared to females, more male found to be working.

(b) The difference in participation rate between men and women is larger in rural areas.

(c) In India, compared to rural men, more non urban men are found to be working.

(d) In India, compared to urban women, more non rural women are found to be working.

37. Government has announced the scheme of 'Jan Dhan Yojana' to encourage adults to open bank accounts. Which of the following is incorrect about the scheme?

A. The account holders get an accidental insurance coverage.

B. Wages, social security payments and old age pension directly get transferred to bank accounts.

C. There is a need to keep a minimum bank balance.

D. The account does not allow overdraft facilities.

E. This scheme promotes thrift habit.

Choose the correct answer from the options given below:

(a) B and C only　　　　(b) A and E only

(c) C and D only　　　　(d) A and D only

38. Match **List-I** with **List-II**.

List - I : Health Infrastructure	List - II : Deal With
A. Primary Health Centre	I. Advanced equipments dealing with complicated health problems
B. Secondary Health Centre	II. Manned by single doctor, a nurse and limited quantity of medicine
C. Tertiary Health Centre	III. Better facility for surgery, x-ray, ECG etc.
D. AYUSH	IV. Indian system of medicine

Choose the correct answer from the options given below:

(a) A-I, B-II, C-III, D-IV

(b) A-II, B-III, C-IV, D-I

(c) A-III, B-II, C-I, D-IV

(d) A-II, B-III, C-I, D-IV

39. Match **List-I** with **List-II**.

List - I : Country	List - II : Feature
A. India	I. Global regional grouping
B. China	II. Largest democracy in the World
C. SAARC	III. Deceleration in all three sectors of economy
D. Pakistan	IV. Followed classical development pattern

Choose the correct answer from the options given below:

(a) A-IV, B-II, C-I, D-III

(b) A-I, B-IV, C-III, D-III

(c) A-II, B-IV, C-I, D-III

(d) A-II, B-III, C-IV, D-I

40. Arrange the following events in chronological order and choose the correct alternative.

A. First Five year plan of China.

B. The great proletarian cultural revolution.

C. Establishment of people's Republic of China.

D. The great leap forward programme.

E. Reformes introduced in China.

Choose the correct answer from the options given below:

(a) C, A, B, D, E　　　　(b) C, A, D, B, E

(c) C, B, A, D, E　　　　(d) C, D, A, B, E

Direction for Questions 41 to 45: Read the passage carefully and answer the questions.

The causes of the Asian Financial Crisis are complicated and disputable. A major cause is considered to be the collapse of the hot money bubble. During the late 1980s and early 1990s, many Southeast Asian Countries, including Thailand, Singapore, Malaysia, Indonesia, and South Korea, achieved massive economic growth of an 8% to 12% increase in their Gross Domestic Product (GDP). The achievement was known as the "Asian Economic Miracle". However, a significant risk was embedded in the achievement.

The economic development in the Countries mentioned above were mainly boosted by export growth and foreign investment. Therefore, high-interest rates and fixed currency exchange rates (pegged to the U.S. dollar) were implemented to attract hot money. Also, the exchange rate was pegged at a rate favorable to exporters. However, both the capital market and corporates were left exposed to foreign exchange risk due to the fixed currency exchange rate policy.

In the mid-1900s, following the recovery of the U.S. from a recession, the Federal Reserve raised the interest rate against inflation. The higher interest rate attracted hot money to flow into the U.S. market leading to an appreciation of the U.S. dollar.

The currencies pegged to the U.S. dollar also appreciated, and thus hurt export growth with a shock in both export and foreign investment, asset prices, which were leveraged by large amounts of credits, began to collapse. The panicked foreign investors began to withdraw. This translated into increased demand for US dollars. Further, there was no perceptible increase in the supply of dollars as wary investors shied away from investing in these economies. With demand being greater than supply, the US dollar appreciated with the domestic currency depreciating. The depreciation of the local currencies fuelled more investments being pulled out of these economies thus resulting in a crisis.

Thus Thai Government first ran out of foreign currency to supports its exchange rate, forcing it to float the baht. The value of the baht thus collapsed immediately afterward. The same also happened to the rest of the Asian Countries soon after.

41. The likely impact of a depreciation of the domestic currencies of the South East Asian Countries on exports to the US would be:

(a) The exports will rise

(b) The exports will fall

(c) The exports will remain unchanged

(d) The imports will rise

42. Identify the most unlikely reason or appreciation of the US dollar.

(a) The Federal Reserve raising the interest rate against inflation.

(b) The rising demand for the US dollar with the investors withdrawing their investments.

(c) High rates of economic growth experienced by the South East Asian Countries during late 1980's and early 1990's.

(d) Fall in prices of assets of the Southeast Asian Countries.

43. The likely impact of an appreciation of the US dollar, on imports of the South East Asian Countries from the U.S. would be:

(a) The imports will rise

(b) The imports will fall

(c) The imports will remain unchanged

(d) The imports may rise or fall

44. The likely impact on the Balance of payment position of Countries facing a financial crisis would be:

(a) There is a deficit on the Balance of Payment account

(b) There is surplus on the Balance of Payment account

(c) There is no impact on the Balance of Payment account

(d) There is a balance on the Balance of Payment account

45. The likely reason for investors from Western Countries pulling out their investments from these nations was:

(a) The returns on their investments were falling as their domestic currency was depreciating.

(b) The returns on their investments were falling as their domestic currency was appreciating.

(c) The returns on their investments was expected to rise in the near future.

(d) They wanted to take their investments back to their own respective nations.

Direction for Questions 46 to 50: Read the passage carefully and answer the questions.

PPPs will help in bridging treatment gap, enhance care delivery in India.

Dr. Shravan Subramanyam

05 Apr 2022,

The Government's focus on digitization over the past few years has enabled enhanced delivery of healthcare in India, increasing capacity and efficiency in the sector. There has been an 85% surge in teleconsultation, and digital platforms have eased accessibility to crucial healthcare solutions, supported by the National Digital Health Mission. This has evolved the way we look at healthcare challenges, and has presented Inida with an opportunity to address issues at the grassroots level. The Production-Linked Incentive (PLI) Scheme and the draft paper on Medical Devices Manufacturing Policy 2022 will further promote domestic manufacturing of medical devices that will help deepen access to quality and affordable healthcare solutions.

The Government has extended support for local manufacturing of medical equipment with an aim to increase healthcare expenditure to 2.5% of gross domestic product by 2025. The Atmanirbhar Bharat initiative provides further impetus to the industry to develop and enhance healthcare infrastructure with continued technological upgradation. Public-Private Partnerships (PPPs) will help increase access to healthcare and improve patient outcomes. PPPs bring together the expertise and finances of the private sector with the access and subsidies of the public sector. It can bring in resources the Government needs for its healthcare goals, as well as create a sustainable long-term model. The need for PPPs is further underlined considering the layout of medical infrastructure in India. According to a report by Niti Aayog, 60% of medical infrastructure is densely populated across metropolitan cities. Addressing this, private hospital chains are increasingly expanding beyond the metros to tier-2 and -3 cities. Private players are also seeking accreditation and developing new healthcare models at an increasing rate. PPPs will also help address the shortage of skilled workers by establishing programmes to up skill the health workforce with the ability to adapt to technological advancements......

46. According to the report by NITI AAYOG, the current medical infrastructure in density populated across.

(a) Village only

(b) A few states only

(c) Metropolitan cities only

(d) Urban areas only

47. Which of the following is incorrect about Public Private Partnerships (PPP) in health infrastructure in India?

    (a) It will improve accessibility in healthcare system.

    (b) It will help Government to achieve the long-term sustainable health goals.

    (c) It will increase the member of skilled workforce in health infrastructure.

    (d) It will increase the rich-poor divide in accessing good healthcare infrastructure in India.

48. Match **List - I** with **List - II**.

List - I : Programme		List - II : Objective
A.	Public-Private Partnership(PPP)	I. Helps in enhancing Health care infrastructure with continued technological upgradation
B.	PLI Scheme	II. Supports digitalisation of Indian Health infrastructure
C.	Aatmanirbhar Bharat	III. Integrates the expertise and the finances of the private sectors with the access and subsidies of the public sectors
D.	National Digital Health Mission	IV. Promotes domestic manufacturing of medical devices

Choose the correct answer from the options given below:

    (a) A-III, B-II, C-I, D-IV

    (b) A-IV, B-III, C-I, D-II

    (c) A-III, B-IV, C-I, D-II

    (d) A-I, B-II, C-III, D-IV

49. A few challenge in the healthcare sector in India are:

    A. Adequate investment by both public and private sector in health infrastructure in India.

    B. Lack of proper medical facilities in semi-urban and rural areas.

    C. Lack of skilled workers in health workforce.

    D. Proper awareness of health and hygiene.

    E. Lack of access to healthcare facilities.

Choose the correct answer from the options given below:

    (a) B, C, E only

    (b) B, C, D only

    (c) A, B, C only

    (d) A, B, C, D only

50. Teleconsultations has shown a surge of ______% in the last few years in India and it is therefore an upcoming field in health infrastructure.

    (a) 100%

    (b) 85%

    (c) 50%

    (d) Inadequate information

Answer Keys

1. (a)	**2.** (d)	**3.** (b)	**4.** (b)	**5.** (a)	**6.** (a)	**7.** (b)	**8.** (b)	**9.** (c)	**10.** (d)
11. (c)	**12.** (a)	**13.** (d)	**14.** (b)	**15.** (b)	**16.** (b)	**17.** (c)	**18.** (b)	**19.** (a)	**20.** (a)
21. (d)	**22.** (b)	**23.** (a)	**24.** (c)	**25.** (c)	**26.** (b)	**27.** (a)	**28.** (a)	**29.** (b)	**30.** (a)
31. (d)	**32.** (b)	**33.** (b)	**34.** (b)	**35.** (b)	**36.** (b)	**37.** (c)	**38.** (d)	**39.** (c)	**40.** (b)
41. (a)	**42.** (d)	**43.** (b)	**44.** (a)	**45.** (a)	**46.** (c)	**47.** (d)	**48.** (c)	**49.** (a)	**50.** (b)

Explanations

1. (a) For an Economy, following is the decreasing order of priority – A Hospital > A School > A Factory > A Residential Complex. Therefore, The Economy will choose to make Hospital on a piece of land and the opportunity cost (Cost of next best alternative forgone) will be a School.

2. (d) When the change in quantity of a good is due to its price, it is known as change in quantity demanded. Here, because of reduction in price from 10 to 6, the quantity increased from 50 to 65. Therefore, it is increase in quantity demanded

3. (b) Price Elasticity of demand = % change in quantity demanded/% change in price

$$= \frac{(-)20}{10} = (-)2$$

4. (b) A resident is said to be a person (or an institution) who ordinarily resides in a country and whose centre of economic interest lies in that country. He is called a normal resident since he normally lives in the country of his economic interest. The centre of economic interest of medical patients going from India to U.S.A. for treatment lies in India.

5. (a) GNP Deflator = (Nominal GNP/Real GNP) × 100

$$= \left(\frac{1000}{400} \right) \times 100 = 250$$

6. (a) Stock refers to any quantity that is measured at a particular point in time. Money Supply and Capital Stock in a country are measured at a particular point in time

7. (b) Intermediate goods are products that are used in the production process to make other goods. The intermediate goods are sold industry-to-industry for resale or to produce other products. Sugar purchased by a restaurant and chalk; duster purchased by school are intermediate goods.

8. (b) National Income = Domestic Income + Net Factor Income from Abroad (NFIA). When NFIA = 0, National Income = Domestic Income

9. (c) GDP(MP) = PFCE + GFCE + GDFCF + Change in stock + Net Exports (Expenditure Method to calculate National Income) > 2995 = 1100 + 900 + Change in stock – 75 > 2995 – 2925 = 70 = Change in stock

10. (d) MPS can never be negative because change in consumption (C) can never be more than change in Y while APC is 1 when C = Y at break-even point.

11. (c) Reverse repo rate is the rate of interest at which the Reserve Bank of India or RBI borrows money from commercial banks for a short period. This helps the RBI have a ready source of liquidity in case of any situation. The Reserve Bank of India offers the commercial banks great interest rates in return for the amount borrowed by it. In case of deficient demand, RBI will increase money supply by reducing the rates Less funds are kept with the RBI to generate interest income.

12. (a) C = 100 + 0.2Y and S = Y – C = Y – 100 – 0.2Y i.e. S = –100 + 0.8Y

13. (d) In two sector economy, AD=C+I and since the diagram shows parallel shift in AD from AD   to AD, so it is due to increase in autonomous Investment

14. (b) If 20% of the income is saved, then MPS = 0.2 and investment multiplier $k = \dfrac{1}{MPS}$ i.e.

$K = \dfrac{1}{0.2} = 5$ = Change in Y/Change in I i.e.

Change in Y = 5 × 100 = Rs. 500 crores

15. (b) Effective demand is much below level of full employment equilibrium which means demand is not enough to employ all factors of production.

16. (b) Note – You have to identify incorrect statement and if you cannot come to exact answer so use elimination technique where you eliminate options that consists of correct statement. Also, in (E) "only" is a strong word that makes the statement wrong

17. (c) Buying and selling of government securities by the RBI to the public is called Open Market Operations.

18. (b) Commercial Bank- Credit CreationReserve Bank of India – Lender of last resort Bank Rate- Long Term lending rate by RBI Repo Rate – Short term lending rate by RBI.

19. (a) Total Deposits = Initial Deposits $\times \dfrac{1}{LRR} = \dfrac{1000}{0.20}$

= 5000

20. (a) The total liability of the monetary authority of the country, RBI, is called high powered money. It consists of currency in circulation with public, vault cash of commercial banks and deposits held by the government and commercial banks with RBI

21. (d) An indirect tax is collected by one entity in the supply chain, such as a manufacturer or retailer, and paid to the government, GST is an indirect tax levied on the supply of goods and services.

22. (b) The two main criteria that distinguish a public good are that it must be non-rivalrous and non-excludable. Non-rivalrous means that the goods do not dwindle in supply as more people consume them; non-excludability means that the good is available to all citizens.

23. (a) The Union Cabinet approved the setting up of seven Mega Integrated Textile Region and Apparel (PM MITRA) Parks at an outlay of Rs. 4,445 crore. The MITRA park aims to integrate the entire textile value chain from spinning, weaving, processing/dyeing, printing to garment manufacturing at one location. Reallocation of resources helps to distribute resources, keeping in view the social and economic advantages of the country.

24. (c) Primary Deficit = Fiscal Deficit – Interest Payment

25. (c) Capital expenditures are one-time large purchases of fixed assets that will be used for revenue generation over a longer period. Revenue expenditures are the ongoing operating expenses, which are short-term expenses used to run the daily business operations. Capital Receipts are the income generated from investment and financing activities of the business. Revenue Receipts are the income generated from the operating activities of the business.

26. (b) Devaluation happens when a government makes monetary policy to reduce a currency's value. A key effect of devaluation is that it makes the domestic currency cheaper relative to other currencies because of which Exports will become cheaper and imports become expensive

27. (a) The Current account refers to the account which records the transactions of the domestic country with the rest of the world. The rent received by the company will increase the revenue of the company that is why it is recorded on the credit side of the current account.

28. (a)

29. (b) Subsidies are a type of benefit that is offered by the government to the people, it results in reduction in the value of the subsidised product. It can be offered to individuals or public and private institutions. Subsidies are a part of non-plan expenditure.

30. (a) The IPR 1956, stressed the importance of cottage and small-scale industries for expand-ing employment opportunities and for wider decentralization of economic power and activity. The 1956 Policy emphasized the need to expand the public sector, to build up a large and growing coop-erative sector and to encourage the separation of ownership and management in private in-dustries and, above all, prevent the rise of pri-vate monopolies.

31. (d)

32. (b) Indian Council of Medical Research (ICMR) recommends per-person per-day calorie norms of 2400 kcal for rural areas

33. (b) The period between 1991 to 2003 is known as the period of Golden Revolution in India. The Golden revolution is related to the production of honey and horticulture

34. (b) Burning of coal, Deforestation, Methane gas released in animal waste and use of fossil fuel are the causes of global warming

35. (b)

36. (b) Note – In Option C, it should be urban men and not "non-urban men".

37. (c) One of the pillars of Jan Dhan Yojana is - Basic savings bank accounts with overdraft facility (OD) of Rs. 10,000/- to every household which makes statement D incorrect and There is no requirement to maintain any minimum balance in PMJDY accounts which makes statement C incorrect.

38. (d)

39. (c)

40. (b) People's Republic of China established in 1949 Announcement of First Five Year Plan by China in 1953The Great Leap forward programme in 1958 The Great proletarian cultural revolution in 1965 Reforms introduced in China in 1978

41. (a) In the event of depreciation of the country's currency, its exports tend to increase while imports tend to decrease.

42. (d) Appreciation of US dollar led to appreciation of currencies pegged to US Dollar thus giving a shock to both exports and foreign investment because of which asset prices began to collapse

43. (b) Appreciation of US Dollar implies that it became expensive in comparison to domestic local currencies of South East Asian Countries which makes overall imports of the South East Asian countries from US costly that further leads in fall of imports

44. (a) A BoP crisis, also called a currency crisis, occurs when a nation is unable to pay for essential imports or service its external debt repayments. Typically, this is accompanied by a rapid decline in the value of the affected nation's currency.

45. (a) The depreciation of the local currencies fuelled more investments being pulled out resulting in a crisis

46. (c)

47. (d)

48. (c)

49. (a)

50. (b)